Routledge Revivals

The Industrial Worker in India

First published in 1939, *The Industrial Worker in India* examines the problems of industrial labour and industrial legislation at the time. It addresses the labour movement as it emerged against the backdrop of colonial rule and industrialization, providing insights into the social conditions that shaped working-class consciousness.

The author traces the origins and evolution of labour organization, analyzing the attitudes of government authorities, capitalist employers, and workers themselves. Through an account of labour leadership and the struggles for representation, the book explores the challenges faced by industrial workers in pre-independence India. It reviews the legislative framework governing industrial relations and offers a portrait of the daily realities—both in the workplace and beyond—that defined labourer existence.

This book will be a valuable resource for students and researchers of colonial and economic history.

The Industrial Worker in India

B. Shiva Rao

ROUTLEDGE REVIVALS
Routledge
Taylor & Francis Group

First published in 1939
by George Allen & Unwin Ltd

This edition first published in 2026 by Routledge
4 Park Square, Milton Park, Abingdon, Oxon, OX14 4RN

and by Routledge
605 Third Avenue, New York, NY 10158

Routledge is an imprint of the Taylor & Francis Group, an informa business

Publisher's Note
The publisher has gone to great lengths to ensure the quality of this reprint but points out that some imperfections in the original copies may be apparent.

Disclaimer
The publisher has made every effort to trace copyright holders and welcomes correspondence from those they have been unable to contact.

For Product Safety Concerns and Information please contact our EU representative GPSR@taylorandfrancis.com. Taylor & Francis Verlag GmbH, Kaufingerstraße 24, 80331 München, Germany

A Library of Congress record exists under LCCN: 40002101

ISBN: 978-1-041-37252-3 (hbk)
ISBN: 978-1-042-00693-9 (ebk)
ISBN: 978-1-041-37255-4 (pbk)

Book DOI 10.4324/9781042006939

THE INDUSTRIAL WORKER IN INDIA

by
B. SHIVA RAO

London

George Allen and Unwin Ltd

FIRST PUBLISHED IN 1939

PREFACE

By an accident I was brought into intimate association with the first organized trade union in India, the Madras Textile Workers' Union, towards the end of 1918. For at least fifteen years thereafter I gave the greater part of my time to the movement, concerning myself almost entirely with the task of organizing the workers in some of the large-scale industries in South India and guiding the unions in my charge through difficulties which, particularly during periods of stress and excitement, proved almost overwhelming. The factual portions of this volume are drawn mostly from official reports and the source has been indicated in every instance. For the conclusions, which are based on personal observations and experience, I take the responsibility.

Some of the material has already appeared in articles both in India and abroad, and I am indebted particularly to the editors of the *Manchester Guardian* and of *Foreign Affairs* of New York for permission generously accorded to utilize my contributions in the preparation of this volume. *New India* of Madras, on whose staff I learnt my first lessons in journalism, is defunct, having gone down after a gallant fight for the enlargement of India's liberty; and its distinguished editor, Dr. Annie Besant, who was a never-failing source of encouragement, is dead. But their memory and inspiration continue, fresh and living. Above all, to thousands of men and women workers scattered all over South India, whose splendid human qualities and comradeship were ample compensation for an arduous life, I owe far more than is revealed in this volume.

B. SHIVA RAO

SIMLA, INDIA

October 1, 1938

CONTENTS

CONTENTS

PART 5
Industrial Disputes

PART 6
Legal Protection for the Worker

PART 7
The Future

LIST OF ILLUSTRATIONS

PART 1

THE BACKGROUND

CHAPTER I

EARLY BEGINNINGS

UNTIL the end of the Great War in 1918 there was no real organization among the industrial workers of India. Strikes there were occasionally, but they roused no great interest among the middle-class politicians who led the political movement of those days; and industrial disputes, when they occurred, were regarded with almost complete apathy by those not immediately concerned in them.

And then, in April of that year, occurred a small incident in Madras which seemed to be the signal for the industrial workers in all the main industrial centres of India to organize themselves to obtain better economic conditions. Two young men,* who had interested themselves for some time in social and religious work among the textile workers of Madras, visited the office of *New India*, the late Dr. Annie Besant's now defunct daily paper, to seek the advice and co-operation of Mr. B. P. Wadia, her assistant editor. Mr. Wadia was a politician with somewhat radical leanings, and the Madras Government had conferred on him in the previous year the distinction of interning him with Dr. Besant and another colleague for their ardent advocacy of home rule for India.

The political movement in India was at this time showing signs of a reaction after the hectic propaganda in favour of home rule in the latter half of the period of the war. For Mr. Wadia and his associates this appeal for help from the industrial workers seemed to come at a psychological hour and proved irresistible. The taunt of the European-edited papers had always been that the Indian politician knew little and cared less about the interests of the masses. Mr.

* They are still connected with the Madras Textile Workers' Union as its General Secretaries: Mr. G. Ramanujulu Naidu and Mr. G. Chelvapathi Chetti. The latter went as an adviser to the Indian workers' delegate to the International Labour Conference at Geneva in 1937, and is now a member of the Madras Municipal Corporation and of the Provincial Legislative Assembly.

Wadia grasped the opportunity without much hesitation, when it came unsought, for establishing contacts with the textile workers of Madras. He listened to the descriptions of the two men who had approached him to enlist his support for a workers' organization in the city—"the few minutes for food" at the midday interval, "swallowing a few morsels and running back lest they be shut out."

Mr. Wadia went with his new acquaintances to the mill gates and watched the scene. At that time, the Factories Act in India permitted a twelve hours' working day with half an hour's interval for food and rest. A decision was quickly taken, and that evening Mr. Wadia addressed a meeting of a few hundred workers from the mills.

Another meeting followed attended by a very much larger number, and a third. By the end of April, definite steps had been taken to start a union with a monthly subscription of an anna (about a penny). Membership was at first not confined to the textile workers alone: tramway-men, rickshaw-pullers, in fact, workers without any distinction of industry or calling enrolled themselves as members of the union, though the vast majority were from the textile mills. And curiously enough, what attracted the attention of these early builders of the Indian trade union movement was not so much the economic condition of the workers as the treatment meted out to them by the European assistants in the mills. A number of prosecutions were instituted for criminal assaults, some of which ended in the courts in apologies or small fines. It was evident, even in the first few days of the work, that there were immense possibilities in the workers' movement. Their enthusiasm was unmistakable; to sit in the open air after dark (factory hours were so long, twelve a day, that the workers were not free earlier) and to address huge audiences of several thousands of eager men anxious to assert their rights was an exhilarating experience. There was a magic in numbers which no words could explain. Here was humanity in the mass, ready to respond to a new gospel and willing to make sacrifices for the cause.

The inspiration for all this work was, perhaps, in one sense political. Mr. Wadia wrote at the time: "Without the masses, there can be no true democracy. . . . We want to bring the masses into line with the educated classes. Much lecturing work has been done already, and what seems now necessary is to combine them. . . . Let common interests in each *taluk* (subdivision of a district) and village combine to remedy the evils from which they are suffering. The masses do possess a political outlook; but they have lost the art of making themselves heard, and our task should be to persuade them into speed and action. . . ."

"It is very necessary to recognize the labour movement as an integral part of the national movement. The latter will not succeed in the right direction of democracy if the Indian working classes are not enabled to organize their forces and come into their own. Unless this is done for all classes of labourers—peasants, plantation workers, factory hands, and miners—even the Montagu Reforms* will only succeed in transferring the power of the bureaucracy from foreign to native hands; that is not democracy."

Success was unexpectedly quick after the establishment of the union; the midday statutory interval of half an hour for food was lengthened by the employers to forty minutes. It had an extraordinary effect on the workers. No one had spoken to them so far, until Mr. Wadia appeared on the scene, of their rights; and encouraged by this small concession, they joined the union in their thousands. Mr. Wadia spoke strongly at their meetings against the cruel injustice of the factory system in India. Looking back, after an interval of nearly twenty years, it seems somewhat strange (though it was inevitable at the time) that in the absence of precise knowledge of the general conditions of industrial labour in India, his lashing criticisms should have been directed against two mills which, on standards commonly accepted in India, could show a good deal of which they had reason to be legitimately proud.

And circumstantially, judging by the conditions then

* The scheme associated with the late Mr. E. S. Montagu was then under discussion; it became law in 1919 and came into force early in 1921. It was replaced by the Government of India Act of 1935, one part of which, relating to provincial autonomy, was inaugurated in April 1937.

existing, it may be admitted that there was some room from the official standpoint for suspicion as to Mr. Wadia's motives in first organizing the workers in what were, comparatively, two of the most efficiently run mills in India. To add to his difficulties, these mills were under British management and engaged actively in war work. Moreover, Mr. Wadia was a politician whose activities had brought on him the sharp disapproval of the Government. *New India*, the paper with which he was connected and in which he wrote, had forfeited its security, and incurred the wrath of the officials more than once for the vigour with which during the war it had pressed India's claims to dominion home rule.* If Mr. Wadia's concern was only the economic well-being of the worker (so the official mind argued) why did he concentrate his attention on these European concerns, and leave in comparative peace some of the Indian-owned mills where wages were appreciably lower and conditions beyond question less satisfactory?

And yet the plain truth was that this first contact between the political leaders and the industrial workers was, I have already said, almost an accident. It was unfortunate that the beginnings of the Indian workers' movement were thus wrapped up in suspicion of a sinister design being at work underneath. If the British official had approached the problem with an open mind, he would have found ample justification for the criticisms of India's industrial system in an authoritative document, far more weighty, if less vehement, than the utterances of Mr. Wadia and his colleagues.

Dealing with the alleged inefficiency of Indian labour, the Indian Industrial Commission appointed by the Government of India wrote almost at the same time as these efforts at organizing the workers were being made in Madras: "If the children of workers are provided with education under

* The fact is worth noting, as proof of the rapidity with which political aspirations have grown in India, that Dr. Annie Besant's paper, *New India*, was penalized, as was the editor, for advocating during the war Home Rule for India within the British Commonwealth. Independence, in the sense of severance of the tie with Britain, was not accepted by the Indian National Congress as its creed until 1927.

tolerable conditions of life, a new generation of workers will grow up who will learn to regard mill work as their fixed occupation. Better housing is a most urgent necessity, especially in the large congested industrial cities. Facilities for health, amusement, shorter hours of work (though reduction may for a time decrease output), and other measures for economic betterment, such as cheap shops for the sale of articles required by the mill hands and co-operative societies, are almost equally important. . . . The problem, not only on moral grounds, but also for economic reasons, must be solved with the least avoidable delay, if the existing and future industries of India are to hold their own against the ever-growing competition which will be fiercer after the war. No industrial edifice can be permanent which is built on such unsound foundations as those afforded by Indian labour under its present conditions." (*Indian Industrial Commission's Report*, para. 236.)

Such were the early beginnings of the trade union movement in India. The rest of the story of this particular union need not be told here. But it may be said that the war marked a definite and sharp break with the past, in almost every sphere of India's life—in politics, in the social and economic conditions of the country, in the attitude of the Government, and in the aspirations of the people. The work in Madras, although the forerunner of similar activities in other industrial centres during the two years following the termination of the war, was not the first of its kind in India. Actually, as early as 1884, a social worker in Bombay (Mr. N. M. Lokhande) had met with a certain amount of success in improving the conditions of the women and children in the textile mills of that city. A memorial embodying their demands was presented in that year to a commission set up to enquire into the conditions of textile labour. In 1889, under the same leadership, the Governor-General was requested to introduce some amendments to the Factories Act; and in the following year Mr. Lokhande became the President of the "Bombay Mill-hands' Association," which obtained a weekly holiday for the workers.

But these and other efforts made in subsequent years to improve the conditions of the working classes were spasmodic outbursts which subsided as soon as some definite end was achieved. There was no general consciousness to work upon, and the conditions for a permanent organization were lacking, until the war swept all the old landmarks out of existence and created new forces and circumstances which, alike for the Government and the people, compelled action radically different from the traditional policy of the past.

It is difficult, perhaps, at this distance of time to realize how profoundly the war had stirred the imagination of the people. A home rule movement (to which reference has already been made) was inaugurated in its early stages, and brought into play a technique which was both new and extremely effective in its results. Never before, in Indian politics, had there been a movement so widespread and carrying on such intensive propaganda by all the methods known in the West—pamphleteering, meetings, posters, and demonstrations. Everywhere there was hope and expectation that the end of the war would mark the dawn for India, not merely of a political advance, but of a new status.

This ferment had not left the masses unaffected; and particularly in the urban areas forces were released which might otherwise have slumbered for years. Before the war the superiority of the white man was unquestioned and seemed unquestionable. But the war almost completely destroyed that notion; a sense of equality came almost fiercely into prominence. There was the thrill of a new experience for the humble worker in a factory, accustomed to be docile and bear harsh treatment and kicks without a protest, to register a complaint against his European superior in a law court for assault. It was not just the vindication of a human right: it was even more—the assertion of racial equality.

That was really the biggest change brought about by the war; and this psychological factor made itself felt in every detail of life. And to this must be added the economic factor, due to an unprecedented rise in prices in the later stages of the hostilities. In fact, prices rose so sharply and so high that there was fear of riots in some of the urban areas. One of the earliest steps taken by the young labour union in Madras was to establish a cheap food stores and to request the Government to establish control over the export of foodstuffs. Wages had markedly failed to keep pace with prices, as was proved by the numerous strikes which occurred in the industrial areas in almost all the provinces, and the large measure of success that attended them.

Moreover, the end of the war synchronized with the oubreak of an epidemic of influenza for which there is no parallel in modern India. Millions, it is true, had died during periods of famine in the eighteenth and nineteenth centuries; but the ravages of influenza were unique because of the comparatively brief period in which they occurred, and the estimate of a death-roll of twelve millions through influenza in less than a year was regarded by the official authorities themselves as "conservative." How devastating it was is borne out by the Census Report for the decade ending with 1921. While the increase in India's population in the previous decade was 7·1 per cent, that between 1911 and 1921 was only 1·2 per cent; and in certain parts of the country there was actually a decrease recorded. There was also this difference between famine and influenza: that whereas famine killed the very young and the extremely old, influenza, on the other hand, marked down the able-bodied, especially among women.* The result of the two successive waves of influenza within a year was to create, for a time at least, a shortage of labour in some of the industrial centres.

The commencement of the post-war period in India thus witnessed a combination of several factors, all of which were peculiarly favourable to the growth of organization among the workers: a radical political movement, the enunciation of the doctrine of racial equality, rising prices and consequent economic distress, and, finally, the reactions of the influenza epidemic, resulting in a shortage of labour.

* In fact, the birth-rate in India was reduced to below normal for some years following the outbreaks.

CHAPTER II

CAPITALIST ATTITUDE TOWARDS LABOUR

BEFORE proceeding to study some of the problems of the worker in greater detail, it is necessary to understand the attitude of the capitalists in India towards measures intended to improve the conditions of labour. If the organization of the workers was deeply suspect in the eyes of the Government, as inspired in part at least by political motives, so was any official effort to introduce labour legislation regarded by the capitalists as a subtle design to check the growth of industries in India.

Indian opinion, as expressed by the educated classes, had been demanding for more than a generation a more active policy of State assistance to Indian industries than the Government was willing to adopt. Keen resentment was felt for many years that free trade doctrines were forced upon India—even to the extent of sacrificing revenue considerations during years of financial stringency—because of pressure from British manufacturers. The contrast was too sharp to escape the vigilant notice of the Indian politicians and the industrialists (and these two classes always worked together) that while Britain had not hesitated to impose heavy duties on Indian manufactures so long as they were imported within her borders, the same policy was not allowed to be adopted by India, when in the later years of the nineteenth century the position was more or less reversed and she became an importer of manufactured articles. When India entered definitely in the second half of the last century upon the first stages of industrial development in the Western sense of the term, there was a deep-rooted conviction among her educated classes that Britain's economic policy in India was directed by the selfish interests of her own industrialists.*

* There was little concealment of the fact that in 1876, with a terrible famine raging in South India in which millions perished, the Earl of Lytton, who was then Viceroy of India, disregarded the opposition of a majority of his European Councillors and agreed to the repeal of import duties on certain classes of cotton goods—thus sacrificing in the interest of Lancashire a source

The feelings of Indian industrialists need to be appreciated, because, unfortunately for Indian labour, the attitude and motives of the Government in regard to labour legislation did not appear to them disinterested. They had powerful support for their claims to State aid in the report of the Indian Famine Commission of 1880 which had declared, "at the root of much of the poverty of the people of India and the risks to which they are exposed in seasons of scarcity lies the unfortunate circumstance that agriculture forms almost the sole occupation of most of the people."

When, in spite of handicaps, the Bombay textile industry showed signs of progress and expansion, enquiries into labour conditions were held, but practically always on the initiative of Lancashire. It is worthy of note, for instance, that in November 1888, the Manchester Chamber of Commerce passed a resolution that in view of the excessive hours of work in the cotton mills of British India, the provisions of the British Factory Act, in so far as they related to the employment of women and young persons and children, should be extended to include the textile factories in India. On that occasion even the European Chairman of the Madras Chamber of Commerce—a British organization—was moved to write to the Government of India expressing his Chamber's disapproval of the interference of Manchester and its claims to have Indian labour conditions regulated by British standards. The proposal to extend British factory regulations to India, he caustically observed, was not prompted by disinterested concern for the Indian operatives. Indeed, the Madras Chamber of Commerce went so far as to attribute

of revenue when it was badly wanted. One of his colleagues, Mr. W. Stokes, warned the Viceroy that this action was bound to be interpreted in India as having been dictated by Manchester, and added with delicate sarcasm: "Of course the people of India are wrong: they always must be wrong when they impute selfish motives to the ruling race." When the financial situation in India in 1895 compelled a return to customs duties for revenue purposes, an excise duty was imposed on all Indian cotton manufactures, of 3½ per cent, in response again to agitation in Lancashire. For nearly thirty years it remained on the statute book, a source of constant bitterness and friction. Even during the war, when normal considerations were in the background, the Government of India was not allowed by the British Cabinet to apply the enhanced customs duties to Lancashire goods.

Manchester's action to jealousy, to the dictates of self-interest and to the discovery that competition in India was becoming too severe for Lancashire.

If such language could be used by European capitalists in India towards Lancashire, the attitude of Indian capitalists may easily be understood. They had even less hesitation in dismissing, as an excuse, the plea of humanitarian interest in the well-being of the workers of India. And it was not the capitalist alone who resented this interference from Britain. There was formidable opposition from several Provincial Governments to any new advance in statutory protection for the workers.* In fact, on every occasion that a step forward was taken in India to safeguard the rights of the worker, there was no difficulty in raising the cry of interested interference and thus obscuring the vital needs of the human factor in industry.

One has only to read some of the evidence placed before the Bombay Factories Commission of 1906 to realize how utterly blind employers in India could be to every human consideration in their anxiety to build up industry in the country. In the Khandesh ginning and pressing works (in the Central Provinces), the usual working hours for the workers, including women, were from 4 or 5 a.m. to 8 or 9 p.m. Sometimes, said the manager of a factory before the Commission in evidence, they would work consecutively day and night for eight days without a break. Another employer

* For instance, in 1891 Lord Cross practically compelled the Government of India to adopt immediate legislation (in accordance with the recommendations of the Berlin Conference of the previous year) for the limitation of children's hours of work to six per day, with half an hour's interval for rest, the extension of the rest interval for women from an hour to an hour and a half, the prohibition of the employment of women and children at night, and the raising of the minimum age for the employment of children from nine to ten. The Government of India, in agreeing to the immediate passage of the Bill, pointed out certain difficulties and ultimately secured one or two compromises in favour of Indian capitalists before the measure became law. Lord Cross, in further correspondence with the Viceroy, in taking cognizance of the opposition of Provincial Governments and commercial organizations to restrictions in regard to the employment of labour, forwarded to him the correspondence between the Blackburn Chamber of Commerce and the India Office, in which anxiety had been expressed by the former in regard to the discrepancy between the British and the Indian Factories Acts.

(Mr. R. F. Wadia) admitted that in the months of March and April the same workers worked night and day, with half an hour's interval, at a daily wage of three or four annas. "When they were tired out," he said, "we tried to get more workers from Bombay." A third witness (Mr. Thomas Drewett) declared that gins and presses never stopped for meals. "As a rule," he said, "the hands take their meals at the gins," and he had seen a large number of cases in which they supplied the gins and ate their food at the same time; often, also, a woman, with a child in one arm, had the other arm busy at the gin. Is it any wonder that in conditions such as these, workers found it impossible to stand the strain of factory conditions for long, and there was a complete change of personnel within eighteen months?

From the standpoint of labour, Dr. T. M. Nair's minute of dissent appended to the report of the Factories' Commission* of 1908 was a masterly document. It needed great courage to write such a note at a time when political feeling was running high and nationalist sentiment was strong. He refused to shut his eyes to obvious facts, and gave credit to Lancashire for having in the past sought and obtained (whatever the motive) improvement in the conditions of Indian labour. He drew attention to the report, then recently submitted, of a special officer, Mr. S. H. (now Sir Selwyn) Fremantle, who had been deputed by the Government of India to enquire into the causes of the shortage of labour in some of the industrial centres in the United Provinces, Behar, and Bengal. The report was clear on one point: the shortage was due to the fact that the workers found the strain of the incredibly long hours too great, and preferred to return to the villages after a brief period of factory work.

The principle on which textile mills worked in India at that time was "sunrise to sunset"—which meant working 15¼ hours a day in the summer at Agra (in a shade temperature which often exceeded 115°) and 13¼ hours in the winter; 14½ hours at Delhi in the summer and 14 in the winter. There was an overwhelming mass of evidence before the Commission that tuberculosis, pthisis, and other forms of lung trouble

* This was an all-India Commission.

were extremely common among factory workers, especially in the textile mills. A comparison between the bodily weights of the prisoners and mill workers in every province disclosed, almost without exception, a higher standard of physique in the former. Conditions in factories which were outside the scope of the Factories Act were even more ghastly; there were ginning factories working for 17 to 18 hours a day, flour mills 20 to 22 hours a day, and printing presses for 22 hours a day for seven consecutive days.

It is, no doubt, a terrible indictment to make against the employers in this country—but the ruthless exploitation of industrial labour stands out in sinister relief through the history of the last seventy-five years. They could understand British policy only on one assumption: namely, that the Government was determined not to allow Indian industries to flourish. The enforcement by His Majesty's Government for many years of a free trade policy on the Government of India; the imposition, when a small customs duty became inevitable for revenue purposes, of a countervailing excise duty (in 1895) on Indian cotton manufactures; the appointment of factory commissions and the gradual advancement in labour legislation—in marked contrast to the comparative neglect of workers in the mines and plantations—all these, the Indian Nationalists and capitalists alike were convinced, formed integral phases of the same policy. To be fair, they were probably right in their interpretation, as the official records of their time show. But in their desperate struggle for existence and advance, the industrialists overlooked the needs of the workers. Strikes were very few and far between. Often, and perhaps with a semblance of truth, the employers could point to the unwillingness of the workers themselves to accept shorter hours or improvements in working conditions. As long as labour was available—"plentiful and cheap"—the employers had no need to worry themselves about the effects of factory work on the health and the physique of the workers.

In fact, the only safeguard for the workers in the pre-war era seems to have been the definite shortage of labour caused by epidemics. In certain industrial areas, on account of a devastating outbreak of bubonic plague which, commencing in Bombay in the closing years of the last century, spread rapidly all over India and was responsible for very heavy mortality, such was the panic among the workers that there was a general exodus, with the consequence that the problem of labour shortage became somewhat acute.

The workers were unwilling, in view of the altered circumstances, to accept the old conditions of work and learnt the value of strikes almost for the first time in India for forcing better terms out of the employers. One somewhat unexpected development was that employers felt compelled to increase the amenities for workers and induce them to accept industrial life as a permanent occupation. There is no doubt that it was the advent of the plague which led some of them, at any rate, to undertake house-building for the workers, as in Bombay, Cawnpore, and the suburbs of Calcutta. Another factor which enabled the workers to bargain for better terms with the employers was that industrial development in the last decade of the nineteenth century was somewhat rapid. In 1892 there were 656 factories under the Factories Act, employing 317,000 persons; in 1902 there were 1,533 factories with a factory population of 524,000. There was also a similar expansion in mines and railways. But the increasing demand for labour and the consequent rise in the rates of wages demanded by adults had one curious result: there was a keener demand for child labour. Evasions of the Act attained the proportions of a scandal, and the factory staff, it was evident, was inadequate to cope with the imposition of work on children beyond the statutory hours and the employment of under-aged children.

There was also an interesting change in the general attitude of the workers. It was pointed out by Mr. Walsh (the special factory inspector in Bengal) in connection with several strikes which had occurred in the jute mills at this time that in the workshops, where hours were shorter than in the textile factoies, there was not the same difficulty in obtaining labour. In the nineties of the last century it may have been true that industrial labour, being essentially migratory, did not object seriously to longer hours; but in the following decade, when there was a permanent increase in the hours of labour (one of the results of the introduction of electricity), and many workers had begun to make industry their life-work, the demand for some reduction in the hours of work became general and insistent.

This was a period when political forces were assisting industrial development. Lord Curzon's provocative utterances and measures as Viceroy of India had created in the country in the early years of this century, and in Bengal in particular (because of its partition as an administrative measure), acute political discontent. For the first time in India, the weapon of boycott of British goods was used, and a vigorous *Swadeshi* (literally meaning indigenous) movement was inaugurated for persuading the people to buy Indian goods in preference to British. These factors had an immediately stimulating effect on the Indian textile industry.

Unfortunately for labour legislation (in view of its previous history) Lord Morley, who was Secretary of State for India at this time, decided upon the appointment of a Textile Factory Labour Committee with instructions to report whether the hours of work in factories were excessive, and whether any abuses existed in connection with the employment of children and young persons. The scope of the enquiry was confined to Bombay; but it was added, that should the results establish a *prima facie* case, a comprehensive enquiry on an all-India basis would follow.

It was unfortunate, because at this time an industrial conference was organized in connection with sessions of the Indian National Congress to afford a common platform to industrial magnates from all over the country. One of the first demands of the industrial conference was active encouragement by the State of industrial development; instead of which Lord Morley decided, in an atmosphere of considerable distrust of his motives, upon a labour commission to amend the existing Act in the light of experience and the tightening up of its administration.

This was the genesis of the enquiry into labour conditions in 1907. The commission found that the provisions relating to children were being almost completely ignored. In Calcutta, for instance, the headquarters of a factory inspector, from 30 to 40 per cent of the children employed half-time in jute factories were under nine years, and 25 per cent of the full-timers were under fourteen. The commission also found that hours for adults in textile mills were very long, ranging from 13½ hours to 15 per day. Nevertheless, the majority argued, it would be impracticable to enforce any limitation of hours, partly because most of the employers would be opposed to it! Dr. Nair, an Indian medical member of the commission, alone stood out and in a scathing note of dissent advocated (with much success) the limitation of hours for adult workers.

It was discovered that the abuses in the employment of children were of a most serious character. The law had practically ceased to be operative, a large number of children under fourteen were treated as adults, and many more under nine were allowed to work on the excuse they were over that age. Parents and guardians were not liable to punishment (that did not become a provision in the law until 1926), and the factory staff obligingly allowed employers to reduce the law to a farce.

The commission's proposals were extremely modest, and in some respects (such as the statutory age limit for children and the hours of work for women) almost retrograde. The Government of India, however, in formulating proposals for legislation, favoured a more liberal advance in accordance with Dr. Nair's views, in spite of the opposition of the majority of the employers' organizations even to the commission's recommendations.

It is significant that Mr. Montagu, who had just then commenced his parliamentary career, was so struck with the extremely unsatisfactory conditions of Indian labour as revealed by the report of the commission, that he made a fervent appeal to Indian politicians at the time of the inauguration of the scheme of political reforms associated with the name of Lord Morley to make special efforts for their improvement. His words were:

"The leaders of Indian opinion must set their faces against

the degradation of labour, and they need to be specially vigilant because India's working classes, besides being themselves unorganized, are not represented on the legislative councils whose Indian members come almost exclusively from the landlord and capitalistic classes."

This appeal is worth remembering, particularly because, through a striking combination of circumstances, Mr. Montagu became responsible, eight years later, as Secretary of State for India during a critical period of the war, for a new scheme of reforms which, so far as the industrial workers were concerned, almost entirely ignored their rights and interests.

CHAPTER III

POST-WAR DEVELOPMENTS IN INDIA

WITH the outbreak of the war in 1914, the situation underwent a rapid and extraordinary change. As hostilities continued year after year, the Government of India (and the military authorities in particular) found themselves compelled to take action and to resort to measures which in normal times they would have, and indeed had, refused to adopt. The war revealed, especially in its later stages, how utterly dependent India was on manufactured goods from England and the rest of Europe, even for her most essential needs—electrical and agricultural plant, accessories for her growing industries and even such simple things as screws and bolts and nails. Everything seemed to be lacking in India—capital, skilled labour, and expert management and industrial experience—everything, except an unrivalled opportunity for development. The absence of imports of manufactured articles created conditions similar to those which would have developed under a policy of high tariffs, while the demands of the Government alone were sufficient as an incentive to industrial growth. And as the war dragged its course, revenue considerations compelled the Government to increase its customs duties to an enormous extent. The policy of an active encouragement by the State, which Lord Morley had opposed so resolutely in the previous decade, was almost completely abandoned in favour of the one advocated by Indian Nationalists because of the overwhelmingly pressing necessities created by the war.

It seemed at the time an astonishing thing—though looking back, one can now see nothing surprising or illogical in the step taken by the Government—that when war was at its height in 1916, an industrial commission was appointed by the Government of India with Sir Thomas Holland as chairman, and a number of distinguished men (both British and Indian) as members, some of whom had practical and varied experience of Indian industries. The commission was asked to report upon the possibilities of furthering industrial development in India and to take into special consideration such matters as the profitable employment of Indian capital in commerce and industry, State encouragement through technical advice and demonstration of the practical possibility on a commercial scale of particular industries, and financial assistance, directly or otherwise, to industrial enterprise. One question was not within the purview of the commission: the problem of tariffs was specifically ruled out, but reserved for consideration after the war. Also, no reference was made to the conditions of labour in its terms of reference, though the commission dealt with the subject with extraordinary lucidity and foresight.

Indeed, so anxious was the situation created by the war that the Government of India could not wait for the report of the industrial commission. While the enquiry was still in its early stages, the Commander-in-Chief suggested—and the Government agreed to—the creation of an Indian Munitions Board with its functions clearly defined: "to control and develop Indian resources with special reference to the needs created by the war, to regulate contracts, to limit and co-ordinate demands for articles not manufactured in India, and to apply the manufacturing resources of India to war purposes, with the special object of reducing demands on shipping." The board, it is significant to note, had for its president the chairman of the Industrial Commission—Sir Thomas Holland—and anticipated in its working many of its recommendations.

Into the detailed recommendations of the Industrial Commission it is not necessary to enter. It is sufficient to note, as indicating the extent of the departure from the old and established policy of the Government, that the commission, in making its numerous recommendations, was guided in the main by two principles of a fundamental character: (*a*) in the future the Government should play an active part in the industrial development of the country; and (*b*) secondly, the Government could not undertake this work unless it was provided with adequate administrative equipment and forearmed with reliable scientific and technical advice. The recommendations covered a wide field and included research, industrial and technical education, commerical and industrial intelligence, direct assistance to industry, both technical and financial, and the purchase of stores.

The commission devoted a brief but luminous chapter in its report to the problems of labour. Contentment with a very low standard of comfort and inferiority of physique—the result largely of preventible disease—it declared to be at the root of the trouble, the obvious remedies being, as the witnesses who gave evidence were agreed, a rise in the standard of living and an improvement in public health, attained by education, adequate housing, and a general policy of betterment, with particular reference to public health.

One of the best-informed witnesses before the commission was Major Norman White (then Sanitary Commissioner with the Government of India), whose admirable note on industrial development and public health was found to be of such practical value that it was reproduced in full as an appendix to the report.

Major White commented on the fact that the subject of industrial hygiene had received remarkably little attention in India and its importance was not realized, though the neglect of public health brought "an immediate and striking punishment." He attributed this neglect primarily to the fact that "labour in India has been in the past both plentiful and cheap." The farmer, living an out-door life, and engaged in agricultural pursuits, could resist a considerable degree of parasitic infection, though malaria and hookworm were most common and widespread; but transference to industrial centres and lack of out-door life, he held, tended to upset the compromise between the body and parasitic infection built up in the rural areas.

The note also gave expression to the conviction that an improvement in general health conditions was absolutely necessary for industrial development. Three diseases were mentioned as being the most potent causes of inefficiency—malaria, hookworm, and tuberculosis. Of the first two,

Major White wrote: "Both are almost universally prevalent in India; both exercise their malign influence from earliest childhood and seriously interfere with bodily and mental growth and development; both, by undermining the constitution, render the body more prone to infection with other diseases. Directly or indirectly, they are responsible for an enormous mortality bill." Tuberculosis, he also included, "because of the special risks, with regard to the spread of infection entailed by large aggregations of labour in any but the best hygienic conditions. . . . The three diseases together can, in fact, be used as a reliable gauge of the sanitary and health conditions of any community."*

To pursue the development of forces and the sequence of events in the region of politics would be outside the scope of this volume; but it would be almost impossible to deal with India's economic problems (including those of labour) without a reference to their political background. After the report of the Indian Industrial Commission and the establishment of an Indian Munitions Board during the war, it was not practical politics to revert to the pre-war *laisser faire* policy of Lord Morley. State encouragement to industry could no longer be denied; moreover, the circumstances created by the war made it inevitable that industrial development through tariffs should be considered on a definite and permanent basis. There was also, implicit in the terms of reference of the industrial commission, a promise to consider India's fiscal position after the termination of the war.

This question was, in fact, brought to the fore by the Joint Select Committee of Parliament which considered the

* India did not have to wait for long for a tragic illustration of Major White's penetrating analysis. Before his note was barely a year old, two successive waves of influenza swept over the country, killing in less than a year about twelve million people. The natural sequence to this should have been the immediate appointment of a Public Health Commission, with the conditions of industrial labour as one of the subjects for enquiry. But certain political factors could not, obviously, be overlooked. The plain fact is that at this time Indian Nationalism was rapidly becoming a formidable force. Political discontent, was growing in India and across her frontier Afghanistan was in no friendly mood. The Government of India decided consequently upon the appointment of a Fiscal Commission.

Indian Reforms Bill in 1919. Dealing with the subject of fiscal autonomy for India, the committee said that "nothing was more likely to endanger the good relations between India and Great Britain than a belief that India's fiscal policy was dictated from Whitehall in the interests of the trade and commerce of Great Britain." The committee recognized without qualification both the existence of such a feeling at the moment, and the clear necessity for its removal. It recommended, therefore, that "whatever be the right fiscal policy for India, for the needs of her consumers as well as for her manufacturers, it is quite clear that she should have the same liberty to consider her interests as Great Britain, Australia, New Zealand, Canada, and South Africa." Mr. Montagu, who was Secretary of State for India at the time, and primarily responsible for the grant of political reforms, elucidated the position in even more emphatic terms, soon after the inauguration of the Constitution, to a deputation which waited on him on behalf of Lancashire's interests to protest against the enhancement of customs duties in India. He said: "After that report by an authoritative committee of both Houses and Lord Curzon's promise in the House of Lords, it is absolutely impossible for me to interfere with the right which, I believe, was wisely given and which I am determined to maintain—to give to the Government of India the right to consider the interests of India first, just as we, without any complaint from any other parts of the Empire, and the other parts of the Empire without any complaint from us, have always chosen the tariff arrangements which they think best for their needs, thinking of their own citizens first."

At this stage in India's development, political considerations seemed to dominate the purely economic ones. Under Mr. Gandhi's lead and inspiration, a boycott of the new legislatures had been proclaimed in 1921 by the Congress, and the visit of the Prince of Wales (now the Duke of Windsor) had proved, from the point of view of creating an impression, a somewhat dismal failure. It was necessary to revive Indian faith in British fair-play and justice, to demonstrate that the new reforms were not as inadequate and empty as the Congress attempted to show; and, in particular, to win over to some extent at least, Indian capitalist interests from allegiance to Mr. Gandhi's creed. One of the first acts of the newly created Legislative Assembly was, therefore, to sanction, even without much discussion, the appointment of a fiscal commission under an Indian chairman—a new and significant departure. The commission, after an elaborate enquiry, recommended, and the Government of India accepted, the principle of discriminating protection. Tariff boards have been at work since then and protection has been given on their recommendation to a number of industries such as textiles, iron and steel, sugar, etc.

The conclusion seems inevitable on an unbiassed reading of the history of the post-war period that with the growth of a strong political movement in India challenging the very foundations on which British rule had rested, the need was increasingly felt by the Government for placating the capitalist classes and—within the limits of safeguarding the interests of British industry—of seeking points of contact with them.

This new attitude was evident not only in the recognition of the fiscal autonomy convention, but in the provision, under Mr. Montagu's scheme of reforms, for the special representation of landlords and capitalists in all the legislatures and the distribution of the franchise. The vote was conferred on about seven to eight million persons, an enormous increase, no doubt, in the numbers on the electoral rolls in comparison with the previous Constitution; but so far as the workers were concerned, the proportion enfranchized was negligible. The basis was a high property or income qualification which ruled out all but an insignificantly small number of workers. Moreover, the size of the constituencies was so vast, and the expense of contesting an election so great that no representative of the workers could hope to succeed in an open contest. In these circumstances it might reasonably have been expected that special representation would be conceded, not to those who possessed the influence and wealth with which to capture the seats from the general constituencies, but to the weak and the unorganized, on whose behalf, in 1910, Mr. Montagu himself had spoken so eloquently from his seat in the House of Commons.*

In the Central Legislature, which would have had most to do with labour legislation, no provision was made at all; though in pratice, in the Legislative Assembly (the lower House), there has always, been a nominated member for labour; and since 1927 another on behalf of the Untouchables (now called the Harijans), in a chamber consisting of over one hundred and forty members. But in the Council of State, the Upper Chamber, there has been no representative of either of these classes, since it was first constituted.

At the commencement of the post-war period the Indian capitalists found themselves in circumstances of exceptional advantage, partly because of the phenomenal prosperity created by war conditions, and partly also because the Government was anxious to prevent their joining hands with the Nationalists. In fact, throughout the last twenty years, they have manœuvred for position with considerable adroitness and not a little success. On several occasions, indeed, they have played upon Nationalist sentiment with a shrewd eye to personal advantage. During elections they helped, even if they did not join, the Congress Party. From the Government they obtained substantial assistance—a protective policy, the abolition of the cotton excise duty, and a practical monopoly of such political power as was handed over. From the Congress, too, they exacted concessions, as in demanding the abolition of the cotton excise and passing measures of protection for certain industries. Indeed, suggestions were not lacking from some leading capitalists when the Royal Commission on Labour was appointed in

* A strong case was made out in Mr. Wadia's memorandum to the Joint Committee for giving the Indian workers adequate power to safeguard their own interests in the new legislatures. He submitted that in view of their capacity for understanding and coming to decisions on political and economic issues, they should have direct representation in both the Central and Provincial Legislatures, and summed up their main requirements in the following terms: "Schools for their children, houses for themselves, better wages and shorter hours—as a matter of right and justice."

1929, that following the precedent in regard to Sir John Simon's commission on political reforms, Indian labour should similarly adopt a policy of boycott.

But so far as the worker was concerned, he seemed to have definitely lost one support which all through the previous decades had helped him more than anything else to improve his lot—the active sympathy of Lancashire. It seems one of the strangest features in the evolution of India's industrial system, this solicitude of British chambers of commerce for the welfare of the Indian worker, right up to the end of the Great War. But he found, fortunately, just at this moment another source of help outside his country—the International Labour Organization at Geneva. Largely because of the efforts of the Secretary of State for India, her claim to be regarded as one of the leading industrial Powers in the world was recognized, and her representatives have occupied a prominent place in the counsels of the organization. In comparison with the long-drawn controversies on measures dealing with labour in the pre-war era, the passage of some of the important pieces of legislation, such as the amendment of the Factories Act, the Workmen's Compensation Act, the Trades Union Act, to mention but three notable measures, was effected with surprisingly little opposition.

Indeed, so active for a time was the Government of India in modernizing its labour code because of the moral pressure of the International Labour Organization that the deficiencies of the Montagu scheme of reforms passed for a time almost unnoticed. Geneva had more than taken the place of Lancashire as an urge to the improvement of labour legislation. Lancashire's influence was, at any rate, indirect (through the India Office) though at times effective; and her motives were never above suspicion. But the Government of India showed an eagerness in the early years of its association with the International Labour Organization, to implement its obligations, and a number of measures were placed on the statute book. Moreover, the first few years after the war were a period of unprecedented prosperity for industry in India, and employers were naturally unwilling to allow strikes and industrial disputes to dislocate industrial progress.

"The placid and pathetic contentment of the masses" (a phrase first coined by Mr. Montagu) was disappearing, particularly in the urban areas, at a more rapid pace than the British officials perhaps appreciated. The industrial worker emerged definitely as one of the most significant symbols of post-war India. The trade union movement, encouraged by its initial successes, rapidly assumed an all-India basis, and it seemed (for a time) as though it would grow sufficiently strong to overcome the resistance of employers' organizations in the country and secure for the workers amenities enjoyed in the industrially advanced countries of the West. But progress in subsequent years has been slow and sometimes negligible. Lancashire's interest in the Indian worker cooled down rapidly with the grant of fiscal autonomy to India in 1919. Dictation (through the India Office) gave place to seeking the friendly co-operation of the capitalists in India. The moral influence of the International Labour Organization has suffered an eclipse with the loss of prestige of the League, and the Government of India no longer takes its Conventions seriously. The employers, on their side, have wrung an assurance from the Government of India that there would be no further labour legislation, at any rate so far as large-scale industry is concerned, for some time to come.

In February 1936, in the final debate on the Payment of Wages Bill, the Government Member in charge of the measure declared, in answer to a capitalist warning that the Government of India was "proceeding too rapidly with labour legislation," that after the adoption of the Trades Disputes Bill, he would turn his attention to unregulated factories.

The problems of the industrial worker in India are extraordinarily complicated and formidable in character. In the succeeding chapters, an attempt has been made to describe them from the standpoint of the worker. The outlook would, indeed be dark, except for the existence in India of a political party which is pledged to a far-reaching programme of reform. One of the most hopeful signs of the present is the earnestness with which the new Provincial Governments, especially where the Congress Party is in power, are carrying out their pledges. Whether this will satisfy the workers on the one side; and how far the capitalist class will allow the Congress Governments to proceed along the path of reform—these are questions which cannot be answered to-day. But it is due to the worker to say that he has, by his own efforts and sacrifices, become a force in India which cannot be suppressed or ignored, except at grave peril to the stability of the social fabric.

PART 2

SOME GENERAL FEATURES

CHAPTER IV

INDUSTRY AND AGRICULTURE IN INDIA

THERE are certain general features of Indian life which deserve to be studied in some detail for a proper appreciation of the problems and difficulties of the industrial worker. It is sometimes forgotten, even by those who have an intimate knowledge of conditions in India, that the vast majority of her population continues to be agricultural, and the total number of workers engaged in industry and transport, on the plantations of tea, coffee, and rubber, and in the mines cannot be more than 30 million* of a total population of about 375 million. India, despite the remarkable progress in industry she has made in the post-war period, is still a land of agriculture and of small industries. In 1936 (the latest year for which statistics are available) the number of workers in industrial establishments in British India to which the Factories Act was applicable was 1·65 million in about 10,000 factories. Making a generous allowance for industries in the Indian States and for workers without permanent employment, the number of those who look to large-scale industry as a definite occupation cannot exceed three or four million.

Of course, conditions in India are undergoing a rapid transformation, and generalizations made even a few years ago demand considerable qualification to be made applicable to the India of to-day. And in no respect, perhaps, has the change been so remarkable—and, it may be added, from the standpoint of countries accustomed for very many years to regard India as a sure and expanding market for their manufactures, so disastrous—as in the growth of her industries. Even during the period of the depression which hit India with unprecedented severity, practically every major industry registered considerable expansion, the most striking instance being that of sugar whose production has more

* In the Census Report of 1931 the number given is approximately 26 million.

than trebled itself since 1929. In 1936–37, production reached a total of 1·1 million tons, and India is to-day almost self-sufficient in regard to her sugar supplies, though in 1929 she imported nearly a million tons, Java's share then being about four-fifths of that quantity.

India's most important industry is, of course, the cotton textiles whose growth, too, in recent years has attracted considerable attention. Under the influence of a protective policy, accentuated by the removal in 1926 of the excise duty on indigenous manufactures first levied in the closing years of the last century and the stimulus of a boycott of British goods inaugurated for political reasons, the textile industry has achieved new records for itself, at the expense of both Lancashire and the handloom industry in India. In 1937–38, it is estimated that the total mill manufacture in India exceeded 4,000 million yards, as against nearly 3,500 million yards in the previous year. How rapidly Lancashire has declined in her trade with India becomes obvious from a comparison with the figures for the pre-war year, 1913–14. In that year India imported over 3,100 million yards, Lancashire's proportion being 97 per cent and Japan's only 0·3 per cent. The Indian mills and the handlooms produced almost equal quantities, between them being responsible for just over 2,000 million yards. But in 1936–37, foreign imports had dropped to below 800 million yards, Lancashire's share being 43½ per cent and that of Japan 54½ per cent. On the other hand, the Indian mills had increased their production to nearly 3,500 million yards, or more than three times the pre-war figure, while the handlooms were responsible for nearly 1,500 million yards. Lancashire's imports into India have thus been reduced in less than a quarter of a century to a tenth of her pre-war volume of business, and if the indigenous textile industry maintains its present rate of expansion, the time cannot be far when India will be able not only to meet the whole of the home demand but have an exportable surplus.

Then there are industries such as cement, iron and steel, jute, paper, matches, whose development has been only less rapid than that of sugar and cotton goods. India now imports very little cement, her total production being nearly a million tons in 1936–37, or 80 per cent more than in 1928–29. Her production of pig iron exceeded in that year a million and a half tons, that of steel ingots approximated 900,000 tons, and of finished steel 700,000 tons. The manufactures of iron and steel have increased by 70 per cent since 1928–29.

These examples should suffice to illustrate the rapidity with which India is expanding her industries. It is significant that while along the whole range of manufactured products there has been a steady decline in recent years, only in the case of machinery, implements, instruments, and vehicles has the tendency been in the reverse direction. Discriminating protection, increased revenue duties since the war, and the desire to effect some balance between agriculture and industry, aided by a powerful nationalist sentiment will continue to push India rapidly along that line for many years to come.

Nevertheless, the position of the industrial worker in India's economic system and his problems can never properly be understood without a constant appreciation of the fact that despite this progress in industrialization, India is essentially an agricultural country, with nearly three-fourths of her population dependent on agriculture. The problem in India, as the Famine Commission had observed so long ago as 1880, has always been one of superfluity of agricultural labour. Since that observation was made, the proportion of the population dependent on agriculture has steadily risen from 61 per cent in 1891 to 66 per cent in 1901, to 73 per cent in 1921, while in 1931 (the date of the last census) it stood at 71 per cent. The drop in the last decade, however, is only apparent, since the increase in population during the period was phenomenal, from 319 to 353 million, and has continued since, being in the neighbourhood of 375 million to-day.*

There is abundant evidence even now from many parts

* The basis of occupational enumeration has changed during this period, so that the figures are not precisely comparable, but no other statistics are available.

of India to prove that it is economic pressure, the social disabilities of the outcastes and the lack of a diversified occupation that are responsible for driving the rural population in quest of work into the cities. Writing in 1931, the All-India Census Commissioner observed that it was from those hopelessly in debt, the superfluous population whom the land could not support, the "ne'er-do-wells" and "women of equivocal status" that migration to the industrial centres took place. Those who have had the privilege of being thrown into intimate association with the workers, especially in long-drawn disputes testing their moral fibre, can never accept the implications of such a description. Nevertheless, it is true, as those who have an authentic knowledge of rural conditions in India have for many years pointed out, that it is the precarious nature of agriculture that leads the rural worker to leave the village underfed, more deeply sunk in debt and far less capable than ever before, with the present phenomenal growth of population and the existing methods of cultivation, of obtaining a decent livelihood from agriculture.

Another factor which applies with particular force to rural areas in parts of South India is the tendency (now fortunately on the decline) of a few high caste people to claim right over all lands in the village, including unoccupied areas and even house-sites for the peasants. It is not a coincidence that emigration from villages of this type has been most frequent, as the low-caste workers are generally at the mercy of their landlords and liable to be expelled from the only land available as house-sites if they should offend them. In a significant phrase, the Royal Commission on Labour, which enquired into the conditions of industrial and plantation labour in 1929–30, remarked that the rural workers were "pushed, not pulled to the city." It would be fairly safe to generalize even to-day, that in spite of a rapidly growing population which has come to regard industry as its life-occupation, many workers would still prefer to return to their villages if they could be assured of food, clothing, and a house-site.

From the agricultural point of view, the labour problem

has always been to lessen the pressure on land which exists in the densely populated areas, especially of Bengal, Bihar, Madras, and the United Provinces. Moreover, there are certain peculiarities in Indian agriculture which greatly accentuate the problem for the peasant. The subdivision of holdings is a problem whose dimensions have grown so large that the attention of more than one Provincial Government has been drawn within the last few years to the need for a movement in favour of consolidation, either on a voluntary basis or through legislative action.* Subdivision of holdings does not alone convey the full meaning of what has been happening in India; in a single village, instances are numerous of a holding, perhaps barely an acre, being scattered in two or more sections in different parts of the village. Indian agriculture thus suffers from both subdivision and fragmentation.

Apart from these difficulties, inherent in India's peculiar inheritance laws and social customs, the economic depression (from the blighting effects of which India is only just recovering) resulted in a big drop in the income of the agricultural classes. The decline in the prices of agricultural commodities has been such (in some cases going down to levels known in the very early years of the present century) that agriculture has ceased to pay in several parts of India, and very large numbers of wage-earners in the rural areas, counted in millions, have been thrown out of even the partial and irregular employment to which they were accustomed.

To understand the full effects of the depression, one has to compare the position of the peasant in 1930, when India first experienced it, with his condition to-day. The total rural indebtedness of India was estimated by the Central Banking Enquiry Committee in that year at about Rs.900 crores (£675,000,000). But during these years, the volume

* An economic inquiry in the Panjab conducted a few years ago through about 24,000 villages revealed the fact that 17·9 per cent of the holdings were under one acre; 25·5 per cent between 1 and 3 acres; 14·9 per cent between 3 and 5 acres, and 18 per cent between 5 and 10 acres. In a typical village in the Konkan area of the Bombay Presidency, 12 out of 52 holdings were under one acre; 24 non-agriculturists owned 113 acres, while 28 agriculturists owned 78 acres.

must have increased considerably, and the burden on the peasant, in the shape of interest alone, must be staggering. Mr. Darling,* a British official who devoted his career to a careful study of the Panjab peasants (comparatively better off than those in any other Indian province) came to the conclusion that the bulk of them "were born in debt, lived in debt, and died in debt," and that in hardly any district in the province were more than a third free from debt, while in some districts the proportion was less than a tenth. The problem is even worse in other provinces. Nothing could be more graphic, for instance, than the following description from the report of the United Provinces Banking Committee:

"Everything is against him (the peasant). Because he is a cultivator, he must borrow to secure his crop. Because his holding is small and has to support more persons than it can feed, he must increase his borrowing to keep those persons alive while the crop is in the ground. His caste and his religion compel him to borrow a third time to meet the cost of customary festival or customary ceremony. As the debt grows, the repayment of it becomes more difficult—until at last some calamity comes upon him, repayment becomes impossible, and he sinks into a state of chronic indebtedness from which death alone can release him."

The autonomous Provincial Governments which came into existence under the new Government of India Act in 1937 have been busy with schemes for assisting the peasant in a variety of ways. Debt conciliation boards have been established in some provinces, old debts being either wiped out or scaled down to reasonable dimensions, coercive processes against tenants for enhancement of rent have been rendered difficult if not practically impossible, and ejection from holdings for failure to meet past obligations has been prohibited. On the positive side, credit facilities (both for long-term and short-term) are being increased, the co-operative movement is making headway after a long period of stagnation and land mortgage banks are coming into existence in several parts of India.

But these measures will take time to yield results. And

* See his volume on *The Panjab Peasant in Prosperity and Debt.*

to-day even the most casual observer of India's rural life cannot fail to be impressed with the lack of a secondary occupation to fill the time of the cultivator during the off-season and to add to his income from land—a period which may vary from three to five months of absolute leisure in the different provinces. To ascertain the possibilities in this direction, one has only to look at the condition of the handloom industry, which next to agriculture is the most important cottage industry in India. On a rough calculation there are about 2·5 million handlooms in India, and about four to five times that number of people depend wholly or largely for their livelihood on it.* The question has frequently been discussed whether the handloom industry has a future before it and can survive the growing competition of the Indian mills and from abroad. So long as there was an excise duty on indigenous mill manufactures and handloom products were exempt from the levy, the cottage industry enjoyed to that extent the beneficent effects of protection. But since the war, the increase in import duties on yarn and other materials used by the rural weaver has sent up his costs of production, while the abolition of the excise duty in 1926 has deprived him of the protection he incidentally enjoyed from its levy for about thirty years. And, on the other hand, his handicaps have been increased through the grant of protection to the cotton-mill industry on the recommendation of tariff boards.

Moreover, the handloom weavers have been in a difficult position because of their economic status and lack of education. There is practically no organization for obtaining raw materials at the cheapest rates, and no marketing facilities for the immediate sale of the finished products at remunerative rates. The weavers, having no capital of their own, are still financed by the *Mahajan* (the moneylender), and have to pay a high rate of interest. The yarn is either purchased

* At the beginning of the century, according to Mr. R. D. (now Sir Robert) Bell, who was Director of Industries in Bombay in 1924, the output of the handlooms was roughly two and a half times that of Indian mills; and up to the end of the pre-war period the handlooms kept ahead of the mills in production. Since then, owing to the raising of tariffs and the Government's protective policy, the mills have gone ahead of the handlooms.

at an unfavourable rate or advanced by a middleman (generally a petty or wholesale merchant) who may buy the cloth, dictating his own price; or the weaver must find a purchaser in his own or a neighbouring village. There is not much contact between the weaver and the consumer, and the marketing arrangements are so defective that a large portion of the profits must necessarily go to the middleman. The departments of industries in the different provinces have in recent years done something to introduce improved appliances and teach labour-saving methods with encouraging results. But as a general rule, old methods and primitive looms are still in vogue; inefficient tools, inadequate or crude processes in regard to reeling, winding, twisting, and warping are still very common. Frequently also, it must be said, the manufactures lack finish and precision in measurement, and show little enterprise in design or pattern.

But if in spite of all these defects and obstacles, the handloom industry has not only withstood formidable competition since the war, but actually has made progress, there must be, it is evident, an exceptional amount of virility in the industry. But the protection of the handloom weaver, which is almost as necessary as the preservation of the peasant cultivator, so as to avoid the worst features of industrialization in the larger cities in India, is only now being undertaken by the Central and Provincial Governments. Here again, as in the field of agriculture, the new Provincial Governments have already given abundant proof of an altered outlook. The meagre subsidy given by the Central Government* is

* The Government of India has made a belated and half-hearted admission of its responsibility to the handloom weaver by making an annual grant since 1935 of about five lakhs of rupees (£37,500) to the Provincial Governments to be utilized for his special benefit. This amount, though small for any large-scale effort to improve the conditions of this important cottage industry, which finds a subsidiary occupation, though of a precarious kind, for some millions of workers all over India, is being utilized by the Provincial Governments to remedy the defects referred to above. The difficulty has, partly at any rate, been that after the inauguration of the Montagu scheme of reforms at the end of the war, such subjects as industrial development (especially of cottage industries), agriculture, public health, and education were regarded as the exclusive concern of the Ministers in the province, and the Government of India was most unwilling to accept any sort of responsibility or to evince any active interest in them. It is only within the last few years that a welcome

being supplemented by propaganda, marketing facilities, and other forms of indirect assistance. Mr. Gandhi's special preference has always been for hand-spun and hand-woven cloth (known as *khaddar*); but the Provincial Governments realize that the revival of the handloom industry, as indeed of all cottage industries, is essential for the improvement of the economic conditions of the peasantry.

Another of India's most vital problems, the tackling of which would have most wholesome reactions upon both the agricultural prosperity of the people and their standards of health, is that of livestock and animal products. An authoritative report in 1937 on the development of the cattle and dairy industries of India by Dr. Norman Wright (Director, Hannah Dairy Research Institute, Ayrshire, Scotland) has emphasized the importance of cattle in India's economic life. According to his statistics India possesses nearly a third of the world's cattle population, approximately 215 million of a total of 690 million.

Adverse climatic and economic conditions and age-long superstitions have imposed a severe restriction on the productive value of the cattle industry. But even under existing conditions it is estimated that milk and its by-products are valued at about 300 crores of rupees (£225,000,000). This, as Dr. Wright observes, is roughly equivalent to the value of India's total output of rice (330 million tons) and three to four times the value of her wheat (9·5 million tons). But there are other miscellaneous products, such as hides and skins. India is still the largest exporter of hides and skins in the British Empire; her products, representing one-third of the total Empire exports, bring to the producer roughly 40 crores of rupees (£30,000,000). Though these are, comparatively speaking, only minor by-products of the cattle industry, they have a greater monetary value than the total Indian output of sugar valued at Rs.30 crores (£22,500,000). Again, as is generally admitted, cattle labour represents the most impor-

change of outlook has come over the attitude of the Central Government, and both research schemes and relief measures have been undertaken to afford assistance to these "nation building departments," as they are called in India.

tant contribution of livestock to Indian agriculture. Without the ox in India, no cultivation would be possible and very little produce could be exported from the villages to the urban areas. On the assumption, which has official support, that the total value of India's annual output of agricultural produce approximates 2,000 crores of rupees (£1,500,000,000) the share of cattle labour alone would be about a fifth of this amount.

Another indirect source of income attributable to cattle is their contribution to the fertility of land. Figures for this must necessarily be very rough, but Dr. Wright accepted a provisional figure of 270 crores of rupees (over £200,000,000). A great deal, however, of cattle-dung is burnt up in the Indian villages as fuel and what would be most valuable manure is thus lost to the agriculturist. Dr. Wright's conclusion was that in actual value, including the value of dairy products, the cattle industry contributes at a very rough estimate about 1,000 crores of rupees annually (£750,000,000) or about half of the total agricultural income of the country.

As another illustration of what may be done to relieve unemployment in the rural areas and reduce the exodus of the superfluous population into the towns and cities, it may be said that there is hardly any country in the world which would benefit so materially from a policy of road-building as India. It has been estimated that the cost of transport for agricultural products in India could be reduced by at least 25 per cent if metalled roads could take the place of earth roads. The lack of suitable communications imposes a heavy strain on the cultivator and limits his market.

One difficulty is that road-making is exclusively a provincial subject under the control of the ministers. About four-fifths of the roads in British India are under district boards, the rest being under the direct supervision of the provincial public works departments and the military authorities. A road development committee reported in 1927 on the great need for a rapid development of the road system for the better marketing of India's agricultural produce and for the social and political progress of the rural population. But the fear of competition with the railways which has become real with a considerable drop in their revenues is inducing the adoption of a policy towards motor transport, which Provincial Governments have no hesitation in describing as shortsighted,* while their own expenditure on roads has been severely reduced in the last five or six years as a measure of economy. One of India's most urgent requirements to-day is a comprehensive road development policy which would pay due attention to the needs of agriculture and industries.

Yet another direction in which large-scale expenditure would result in enduring results, both in assisting agriculture and in securing employment for the millions who cannot find work, is irrigation. The total amount spent by the British Government on irrigation schemes in India during the past eighty years exceeds £110,000,000. But much more could be done if the hampering condition, as the president of the board remarked at the annual meeting of the Central Board of Irrigation in 1936, that a project should be capable of showing a minimum return of six per cent on the capital invested within ten years of its completion, were relaxed by the financial experts of the Government of India.

And it is not only for helping agriculture that a more liberal irrigation policy is required. From the standpoint of population, it is of the utmost importance; for the problem of population is intimately connected with that of food supply. The total acreage under food crops in India amounts to about three-quarters of an acre per head of population in British India. Manifestly it would be impossible to provide a sufficiency of food for the present population of India from an average acreage of this dimension, unless more intensive methods of cultivation are adopted and land which has hitherto lain fallow is brought under cultivation.

* The Government of India's Motor Vehicles Bill, which will become law in 1939, is a fairly satisfactory compromise between the two points of view.

CHAPTER V

POPULATION

THE problem of numbers is one of the most fascinating, if also one of the most baffling in India. Since the devastating influenza epidemic of 1918–19, which was responsible for a loss of not less than 12 million lives in a year, India has been free from epidemics of a major character, and the result is to be seen in the phenomenal growth of population from 319 million at the time of the census in 1921 to about 375 million at the present moment. One point which has to be remembered in this connection is that the influenza epidemic was particularly destructive among young women, with the consequence that birth-rate fell to below normal for some years following its appearance, and the actual increase of population during the post-war period has occurred really within the last twelve or thirteen years.

It is instructive to look back to India's birth and death rates during the last forty years and watch their reactions on the population. While the birth-rate has remained fairly steady, especially since the commencement of this century, at about 35 per mille (in 1934 it was 34), the death-rate has been brought down from 34 to about 22 during the same period. The rate of annual increase in population has, in consequence, risen from about a million to 4 or 5 million.

The fact is that both medical research and the growth of public health organizations have made much progress in the post-war period in India. Extensive work is being carried on against disease, and medical science will undoubtedly claim new fields of achievements. Moreover, with the growth of irrigation and the expansion of railways and other forms of communications, famine, which exercised such a severe check on population has become rare in the sense in which it existed in previous centuries, if not altogether impossible.

Cholera, plague, and smallpox, which have long been associated with India, cannot really be regarded as major scourges, for they are responsible in the aggregate for less than half a million deaths in a normal year. So far as danger to human life is concerned, India has far more reason to be on her guard against other diseases, more insidious in their effects, if immediately less dangerous, such as malaria, tuberculosis, venereal disease, leprosy, and hookworm (the details of which are discussed in a later section).

Infant mortality has been brought down by persistent effort to a low record, being only 164 per mille of live births in 1935; but even so the annual number of deaths among children below the age of one year exceeds a million and a half, while about 150,000 women die in child-birth or from causes associated with it.

There is, in spite of much progress in recent years, a terrible wastage of life in India, particularly of child and maternal life. It has been established by medical testimony that barely half the number of children born in this country reach the age of ten years, as against a 12 per cent rate of mortality in that age-period in Britain. These striking differences, as the highest public health authorities in India recognize without hesitation, point to the necessity for comprehensive planning, not only in regard to ante-natal care, midwifery, and infant welfare, but over a far vaster field of general public health service. There is not the least doubt that pure water supplies in the villages, better conservancy and sanitation will have a great effect in reducing the appalling infant and child mortality still taking place in this country.

The point, however, to be noted from the standpoint of population is that with the progress of such schemes for combating child mortality, the death-rate in India will come down still farther; for at least a fourth of the total mortality in India is among children, and determined efforts are being made in all the provinces to reduce it to the level attained in other countries. But as the gulf between the birth and the death-rates widens, the increase in population must necessarily become more rapid. There is general agreement among those who have devoted time and attention to the problem that by 1941 when the next census is due (provided that the immunity from major epidemics continues) India will probably touch, if not exceed, the 400 million mark.

The question is, whether there are any outlets for this enormous population. Apart from the growth of new industries, whose extremely limited possibilities for absorbing some of the surplus population have already been indicated, overseas migration affords a way out for an insignificant fraction in India's congested areas. The total number of emigrants to Ceylon, Burma, the Federated Malay States, South and East Africa, and British Colonies like Fiji, British Guiana and Trinidad, is less than 3 million; and between 1921 and 1931 the outward balance of migration was only about a million and three-quarters, or 5 per cent of the total increase of population of 34 million during that decade. Even this means of escape for our population is now practically ruled out, for some of the chief centres of migration have reached a point at which they are unable to absorb more than a very small number. Moreover, the imposition of civic or economic disabilities on Indian settlers abroad has led in more than one instance to schemes of repatriation being adopted by the Government of India,* or at any rate to the stoppage of assisted emigration.

Inter-provincial migration stands, of course, in a different category. There is probably some scope even now for greater mobility than India's population has so far shown, for while India as a whole has an average density of 195 per square mile, Bengal reaches an average of 646 per square

* As an interesting sidelight on the conditions of the emigrant workers it is worth noting that while India's political leaders insist on minimum wages being paid to those who go out to Ceylon or the Malay States for working on the tea or rubber plantations in these colonies, there are no provisions of a like nature within India either for agricultural or industrial labour. The imposition of civic or personal disabilities on Indian emigrants is resented by all sections of public opinion in India, and under the Emigration Act of 1922 the Central Government restricts emigration whenever the pressure of the non-official elements in the Legislature becomes vocal. Planters in these colonies cannot do without Indian labour, because of its cheapness. An adult male worker would be willing to work for 8 or 9 annas a day, and a woman for 5 or 6 annas. As against these rates of wages may be compared agricultural wages in many parts of India, 2 annas a day for an adult man, and an anna and a half for a woman. (An anna is equivalent to just over a penny in English money.)

mile, Bihar 379 per square mile, Madras 329 per square mile, and the United Provinces have a density of 442 per square mile.

Taking the other aspect of the question, from the standpoint of provinces with a surplus population, Bihar lost during the decade 1·2 million, of which the bulk went to Bengal; the United Provinces lost a million, and Madras 0·9 million. The bulk of the overseas migration is from Madras, over 90 per cent of the labour going to Ceylon and the Federated Malay States, the main cause being chronic poverty or seasonal distress. Burma also gets a considerable proportion of its labour from Madras, Bengal, and the United Provinces. But inter-provincial migration, while it may temporarily relieve the pressure of population in the more densely inhabited areas by the transfer of a certain number to neighbouring provinces, only provides a palliative and does not solve the problem.

Such in brief are the circumstances under which the population crowds into India's towns and cities. Agriculture is incapable of supporting even the numbers who depended on it for a livelihood (however meagre or precarious) when prices ruled generally higher; there are no village industries worth mentioning or unemployment relief schemes like irrigation or road-building as alternative occupations; and the outlets beyond the seas, the colonies in India's immediate surroundings or even farther, are practically closed.

It need hardly be argued that the growth of population is one of vital concern to the worker. Any one who watches the growing crowds of the unemployed clamouring for work outside the gates of almost every factory or mill in any part of India can appreciate, without reference to statistics and reports, the difficulties of the worker. "For every one who goes out of this gate," said a mill manager to me three years ago, in discussing the demand for higher wages, "there are nine waiting outside who would be grateful for the wages I am paying." In another industrial centre, the workers in a textile mill had obtained after a prolonged dispute and on the intervention of the Government, a substantial enhancement in their earnings. But so great was the pressure of the unemployed from outside that the employer had little difficulty in obtaining fresh recruits willing to work on the original rates of wages. For the worker, though he may not himself often realize it, there is no problem of greater significance than the rate of expansion of the population. Indeed, its influence is so overpowering that no measures, legislative or otherwise, will enable him to maintain even his existing standards, pitifully low as they are; and it will be felt with greater and increasing pressure in the coming years, in spite of the presence of other factors which may relieve it to a certain extent and for a time.

It is not surprising in the conditions described above that India's urban population should have grown rapidly since the end of the war.* In proportion, it is perhaps not impressive, being only 11 per cent of the total, and showing an increase of but 1 per cent during the decade 1921–31. But in numbers, the increase was by 6·5 million and the total stood in 1931 at 39 million. Calcutta increased its population during the last decade by 12 per cent, Rangoon by 17, Madras and Karachi each by 23, Patna by 33, Delhi by 40, Bangalore by 45, Nagpur by 48, Lahore by 53, and Amritsar by 65 per cent.

These figures have naturally a serious reaction on the state of congestion in the cities, especially in the working-class areas. The average density of Calcutta Municipality is 37,120 per square mile, and of the neighbouring industrial centre of Howrah across the river Hooghly, 22,400 per square mile. But in entering working-class areas the acuteness of the problem becomes at once apparent. Six wards of Calcutta have an average density of 112,000 per square mile, and another five exceed 100,000. Bombay is far worse; in three wards the average density is 385,000, 407,000, and 465,000 per square mile respectively. One has only to undertake a midnight tour of the central portions of Madras or Bombay and see the large numbers of people sleeping on the

* Bombay is the most urbanized province, with 22·6 per cent of the population in the urban areas. There were in India at the time of the last census 38 cities with a population of over 100,000; 65 towns with over 50,000; 268 with over 20,000; 543 with over 10,000; and 987 with over 5,000.

pavements to realize what congestion means; and some of them have lived on street pavements for over twenty and twenty-five years!

It is not merely congestion and the terrible housing conditions, to which a more detailed reference will be made later, that is the trouble: migration from the village to the city or to a different province creates problems of another kind. In most cases the worker goes alone in quest of work, and the result is seen in the great disparity in numbers from the standpoint of the sexes.

The sex ratio in some of the bigger cities is a problem worthy of serious attention,* for in many of the bigger industrial centres, the disparity is striking, being as much as two men to a woman. In the working-class areas, the position is even more unsatisfactory. The effect of this is to be seen in the alarming spread of tuberculosis and venereal disease from the industrialized urban areas to the countryside, to which a detailed reference is made in a later chapter (on public health).

The uncontrolled growth of population in India is beginning to receive at last serious attention from her leaders, and a movement has been inaugurated within the last two or three years on an all-India basis to study the various problems connected with it. There is general recognition of the fact that a half-starved population, stricken with disease and increasing at a rate which is far in excess of the standards of living (if such a phrase has any real meaning in India) constitutes a menace of increasing gravity for the future. Birth-control is a subject of frequent discussion, not only in the universities but at women's conferences, several of which have adopted resolutions urging the establishment of clinics to teach methods of contraception. New forces are at work in India, and there is evidence, especially among the youth

* The following table is instructive:

City	*Women per 1,000 men*	*City*	*Women per 1,000 men*
Calcutta ..	.. 468	Amritsar ..	.. 666
Bombay ..	.. 554	Lucknow	.. 722
Lahore ..	.. 565	Karachi ..	.. 688
Rangoon ..	.. 477	Howrah ..	.. 550
Delhi ..	.. 694	Cawnpore	.. 694

and the women, of a spirit of challenge to the traditional outlook on life and its problems.

It is not to be imagined, however, that the forces of orthodoxy and conservatism will yield without a struggle. In assessing the possibilities of social progress in India, one can never afford to overlook the fact that education is still in a backward condition, and literacy is confined to less than a tenth of the population. The vast majority cannot even read or write, and among the Hindus, especially, who form the bulk of the population, there is a pronounced prejudice based on religious sentiment in favour of large families.

How far birth-control will succeed in checking the growth of population in India is a matter on which practical experience can give little guidance, for the number of clinics is negligible and it would be difficult and even hazardous to draw any general conclusions. Propaganda is undoubtedly on the increase, especially among the middle classes in the urban areas. A neo-Malthusian league has been in existence for some years in Madras with a commendable record of activity. But so far as the masses and even the industrial workers in the cities are concerned, there will be two formidable difficulties to encounter. One is that of prejudice fostered by habits and practices thousands of years old. How often does not one come across instances of a poor worker with a large family explaining the phenomenon with an air of unshakable conviction as though it were not an arguable matter: "But so it is said in my horoscope"! I can recall the vehemence with which the members of the executive of a trade union of which I was the president—all workers themselves—attempted to dissuade me from participating in a propaganda meeting in support of birth-control. Their general view was summed up in a question which one of them addressed to me: "Who are you to interfere with the number of children God has chosen to bestow on us?"

The other difficulty is that in a country so extremely poor as India is, the cost of contraceptives is bound to be prohibitive, except for the middle and upper classes. In a very interesting note appended to the Census Report of 1931, on the population problem in Bengal, the census commissioner observed: "Attempts to effect a retardation of the rate of increase by voluntary limitation of the birth-rate are almost certainly doomed to failure, particularly in Bengal. They are repugnant to common sentiment in this country, the methods adopted are so expensive as to be beyond the reach of the great majority of the inhabitants, and it is probably true to say that there are, as yet, none which can be relied upon as being absolutely certain and satisfactory. Figures from the different strata of society . . . show that there is no evidence to believe that contraceptive measures are used by the upper classes or those engaged in professions and the liberal arts; and it is certain that they are not practised at all in the lower strata of society. . . . It is possible to expect that a reduction of the birth-rate by the adoption of improved measures of public health, accompanied by an improvement in the standard of living, an increase in the spread of education and perhaps principally by a further emancipation of women and their introduction to spheres of usefulness and activity from which they are now in Bengal generally debarred by social customs and by the institution of *purdah* (seclusion) will in due course result in a decrease in the birth-rate corresponding with the decrease in the death-rate which it is the object of public health measures to bring about."

For practical results, India is thus reduced to the expedients of mass education and the gradual effects of the raising of the age of marriage for both boys and girls through legislation, aided no doubt, by positive action on the part of a small minority of social reformers. The apathy of the educated classes towards the problem of population has often been a subject of sharp comment in official documents and reports. What is not stated in these publications is that the policy of the British Government itself has been one of drift. The Government of India seems to be afraid of wounding the susceptibilities of the orthodox elements who are generally its most loyal supporters. Action on the report of the Age of Consent Committee which recommended legislative enhancement of the age of marriage was undertaken with the greatest reluctance and in such a manner as to reduce it in practice to a farce. In 1936 on a resolution in the Council of State (the Upper Chamber of the Central Legislature) which a Moslem non-official member brought forward to urge action for restricting the growth of population, the Government's official spokesman, Mr. M. (now Sir Maurice) Hallett, seriously suggested that floods, famines, epidemics, and earthquakes (as in Bihar and Quetta) could be depended upon to supply the necessary checks! There has been, however, within the last twelve months, a welcome change in the official attitude towards measures of social reform of which tangible proof was forthcoming in the support accorded to two measures in 1938 designed to tighten up the provisions of the Act relating to the age of marriage.*

* Though the Child Marriage Restraint Act of 1929 was almost a dead letter because of the many avenues for escape from its provisions, certain amendments made in 1938 have had the effect of tightening the law. It has now been laid down that marriages performed by British subjects in contravention of the law (the minimum age is fourteen years for girls and eighteen for boys) in any part of India—including the Indian States and French and Portugese India—are liable to be penalized. Another useful feature introduced this year is that a court may, on satisfactory evidence that a marriage is likely to take place in violation of the law, issue an injunction prohibiting it. Instances of such action afford proof that the reality of the law is at last being brought home to the orthodox elements.

CHAPTER VI

NUTRITION AND FOOD SUPPLY

AMONG the problems connected with the growth of population, one of the most important is undoubtedly that of food-supply. Ever since political consciousness began to be roused among India's educated classes about half a century ago, the impoverishment and starvation of the masses has been a popular theme. But official recognition of the existence of such a problem is only of very recent origin. A valuable enquiry was held in 1933 under the direction of Major-General Sir John Megaw, who retired as Director-General of the Indian Medical Service after a long and distinguished record of medical service in India. The enquiry was mainly concerned with certain public health aspects of village life in India. The method adopted was to distribute an elaborate questionnaire among several hundred village doctors in typical agricultural villages selected from every province of British India. Some questions were purely test ones, included in the questionnaire for the purpose of ascertaining the degree of care and precision employed in obtaining the information. After rejecting those which betrayed signs of inherent unreliability, the remainder (nearly six hundred in number) formed the basis of certain general conclusions as to existing conditions in the rural areas.

The average size of a family was found to vary from five members in the Central Provinces and Madras to 6·4 in the Panjab. In the other provinces, it ranged from 5·2 to 5·8, the average for all-India being just under 5·5. The average area of land per head of the population ranged from 0·72 acre in Bengal to 2·63 acres in the Central Provinces.

Of particular interest were the data in regard to the physical conditions of the villagers. The report itself opened with a note of caution that village doctors were unlikely to have adopted a high scale of standards, and that the conclusions would have been even more unfavourable if the enquiry had been entrusted to men with European knowledge and experience. In many cases, it observed, in which the food-supply had been stated to be sufficient, there was plenty of evidence in the replies to the other questions that this was far from being the case. But even on the low standards adopted by the village doctors, it was established that only 39 per cent of the people were well nourished, 41 per cent poorly nourished, and 20 per cent very badly nourished. The most depressing picture was that of Bengal, where the proportions were 22 well nourished, 47 poorly nourished, and 31 very badly nourished. In nearly 40 per cent of the villages the population was considered to be excessive in relation to the food-supply. The position was worst in Bihar and Orissa, where 60 per cent of the villages were over-populated, Bengal and the Panjab coming next with 46 per cent each. These figures have, of course, to be accepted with the qualification that the standards of life vary widely in the different provinces.

The conclusions of the medical survey are of the greatest importance: (1) India has a poorly nourished population; (2) the average span of life is less than half of what it might be; (3) periods of famine or scarcity of food have been occurring in one village out of every five during a ten-year period in which there has been no exceptional failure of the rains; (4) in spite of the excessively high death-rate, the population is increasing much more rapidly than the output of food and other commodities.

Worst of all, said the report, there was little evidence that the educated classes in India realized the full gravity of the situation. How serious it is, is obvious from the following words: "It is clear that the growth of population has already begun to outstrip the increase in the production of the necessities of life, so that even the existing low standards of economic life must inevitably become lower still unless some radical change is brought about. The outlook for the future is gloomy to a degree, not only for the masses of the people who must face an intensified struggle for bare subsistence, but also for the upper classes whose incomes depend on the production of a surplus of crops and other commodities. If the entire produce of the soil is needed to provide for the urgent needs of the cultivators, nothing will be left for the payment of rents or revenue, nothing to exchange for other commodities or even for the purchase of railway tickets, and the whole social structure of India must inevitably be rudely shaken if not completely destroyed."

Investigations in regard to food, from another standpoint, namely of its quality, came much earlier, though until about three years ago they were confined to the laboratory, and no practical efforts were made to link research with propaganda and bring scientific knowledge within the reach of the ordinary people. In this field of research a great deal of credit is due to the work of pioneers like Colonel McCay and later of Colonel (now Sir Robert) McCarrison. They showed by patient study and observation how the stamina and physique of the rice-eating classes of Bengal and Madras could not compare with those of the northern races who live on wheat, milk, vegetables, and fruit and meat. Attention is only now being directed in India to the necessity of a balanced diet. But Colonel McCay, who, more than twenty-five years ago studied Indian diet problems with minute care, came to the conclusion that with a deficient supply of nitrogenous food, mental and physical degeneration was inevitable. The production of milk in India has been so grossly neglected (as Dr. Wright proved in an authoritative document in 1937) that the quantity of milk available is utterly inadequate, and its price is beyond the reach of all but the comparatively well-to-do. Colonel McCay noted that as one passed from the north-west regions of the Panjab, through the Gangetic plains to the plains of Bengal, there was a gradual fall in the stature, body-weight, the stamina and efficiency of the people. It was of significance that there was also a corresponding fall in the nutritive value of the dietaries of these areas and more especially in the average level of protein metabolism attained by the people of the Panjab, the United Provinces, Bihar, and Bengal.

Sir Robert McCarrison's work on the nutritive value of foods came into prominence within the last ten years before two Royal Commissions, the one on agriculture and the other on labour. How important such research is one can realize from the spread of diseases in India due to malnutrition and diet deficiency. In fact, he regarded these two as being the most potent causes of the low efficiency of the workers. Malaria has such a powerful hold on the country only because of the malnourished condition of the masses. Leprosy also increases from north to south in a manner suggestive of an increasing degree of malnutrition. Singularly little heed was paid for a long time to his strong plea for the establishment of institutes for the study of nutrition problems, the survey of food resources and the study of malnutritional diseases. Basing his conclusions on experiments with food of the different provinces, he established that the Sikhs, the Pathans, and the Rajputs, all wheat eaters, and some of them also great milk drinkers and consumers of vegetables and fruit in adequate quantities, were among the finest races, not only in India, but of mankind.

The basis of all diet in India is generally a cereal of one kind or another, supplemented by the other food-products. The grains of higher nutritive value are wheat and certain millets, known in India as *ragi*, *kambu*, etc., while of a lower order are maize and rice. Apart from their intrinsic food values, much depends on the manner of their preparation. Thus, white flour from wheat and mill-polished rice lose a great deal of their nutritive value; but unfortunately, both are gaining ground in India. Wheat and barley are the staple articles in Northern India, and rice in Bengal, Madras, and parts of Bombay. But in many parts of rural India, the staple cereal is one of the millets, some of which are more nutritious than rice.

Sir Robert McCarrison found that the physical efficiency of the Indian workers was greatest among the wheat-eaters, least in the rice-eaters, and intermediate in those living on one of the millets. An experiment on groups of albino rats which was conducted some years ago in the Nutrition Institute at Coonoor in South India deserves to be mentioned as of great interest and value. He chose rats, all of the same age, size, and body-weight, segregated groups of them in different cages, and fed each group on the common diet of the provinces. On the eightieth day of the experiment, they were weighed, and the average weights were as follows:

Sikh ..	.. ..	235 grammes.
Pathan	.. ..	230 ,,
Mahratta	.. ..	220 ,,
Gurkha	.. ..	200 ,,
Kanarese	.. ..	185 ,,
Bengali	.. ..	180 ,,
Madrasi	.. ..	155 ,,

The experiment confirmed in a remarkable way the view that as rice replaces wheat and the quantity of milk consumed gets less and less, as in Bengal and Madras; further, as the animal fats in the food are reduced to a low level and the vitamin contents of the food drop, there is a corresponding and even marked fall in the level of physical efficiency.

Dr. Wright in his report on the development of the cattle and dairy industries of India (to which reference has already been made) came to the same conclusion in 1937, with particular reference to milk. In India, he said, the climate being sub-tropical or tropical, and the ordinary diet of the large mass of the population being vegetarian, milk was the only available source of first-class protein and capable of supplying a considerable proportion of the mineral constituents and vitamins of the diets.

The essential point in his report was that the amount of milk available for the needs of India's huge population of 375 million is extremely inadequate.* From a tabular

* Dr. Wright cited in his report the results of two milk-feeding experiments, one in Simla and the other in South India. A pound of milk was added in the first instance as a supplement to the ordinary diet of children for a period of three months. Their heights and weights, as well as of those groups to whose diet no such addition was made, were recorded both at the beginning and at the end of the feeding period. It was noticed that the children receiving milk showed markedly greater increases in both weights and heights over those who received no such supplement. In the second experiment, conducted in certain residential institutions for children in South India, skim milk was given reconstituted from milk powder for a period of three months, at the end of which the children fed on skim milk showed a great increase in weight and height over those receiving no milk supplement. The same children were later used in an identical experiment; but in this case the groups were reversed,

statement of milk consumption in the different countries of the world, he drew the conclusion that while six countries could show a production of between 30 and 40 oz. per head per day and nine countries (such as Australia, Canada, New Zealand, and the Scandinavian nations) exceed 40 oz. per head per day there are, on the other hand, rural countries like Poland, Italy, Rumania, and India who can neither afford to import milk products nor produce an adequate supply to meet their nutritional needs. India's consumption he estimated at 7 to 8 oz. per head per day, which is less than a quarter of that of the self-supporting countries.

Dietary surveys in different parts of India within the last two years have disclosed even more unsatisfactory conditions. In a survey of the food consumption of tenant cultivators in the western Panjab (a part of India where much more milk is consumed than in the other provinces) it was ascertained from the details of milk consumption of thirty-nine families that the average daily *per capita* consumption of milk products was just over 14 oz. But domestic servants and the poorer sections of the non-agriculturists consumed much less; for instance, in the Sialkot District of the Panjab the milk consumed by sixty families averaged between 5 and 5½ oz. per head. In South Indian villages a survey of milk and its products consumed showed that they were entirely absent from the diets of thirty-one out of forty-four families whose dietaries were investigated, and in the remaining thirteen, of 7 oz. per head daily. The consumption of milk and milk products throughout India is in fact markedly lower in urban than in rural areas. An enquiry conducted in nearly 2,500 working-class households in Bombay showed that the average quantity of milk consumed per head daily was less than ½ oz., supplemented by 0·05 oz. of *ghee* (melted butter). A similar enquiry among ninety-seven families of jute mill workers in Bengal gave a *per capita* daily consumption of just under 0·01 oz. of *ghee*.

Of course, poverty of a kind inconceivable in the West is

those who had previously acted as controls receiving the milk supplement. Once again the result showed the value of a supplement of skim milk to those children who received it.

at the root of the food problem. Sir John Simon's Commission in 1930 said that what struck it with peculiar force in India was the extreme poverty of the people, the average income per head of the population being estimated at £8 per year, as against £100 in Britain. The Banking Enquiry Committee, which held its investigations about a year or two later than the Simon Commission, took the view that the income of the agricultural population per head could not be more than Rs.42, or just over £3 a year. Since these enquiries were held, prices have registered a further drop, and estimates of average incomes at present should be very much lower than four or five years ago.

A large part of the population in India really lives on one meal a day. In several parts of Northern India, the industrial workers cannot afford anything more than parched gram and coarse sugar for the midday fare, the evening meal generally consisting of wheat-flour cakes and lentils. Vegetables, oil, *ghee*, and fruit enter but little into their dietaries. In the rice-eating areas, as in Madras, the position is not substantially different: a meal of cold rice (boiled the previous night) with salt for breakfast, rice and lentils at midday and repeated at night; with very few vegetables, practically no fruit, milk or *ghee*. Out of about eight hundred family budgets prepared by the Madras Labour Union in 1927, only about two per cent contained any reference to milk or its by-products. A social service organization in Madras went into the question of diet in one of the slums in the city in 1933 and came to more or less the same conclusions. Rice, lentils, vegetables, oil and tamarind, and occasionally a little fish formed the dietary of a family of seven adults and two children, though in this case poverty could not be pleaded, with a total income of Rs.67·5 (about £5) per month for the whole family. In a second case, a family of three adults and a boy lived on *ragi* (a millet), rice, lentils, oil and vegetables worth less than an anna (about a penny) per day, the expense on food for the entire family being 7 annas per day (about 8d.). Considering the money available for food, perhaps it was the best use the family was making of it, *ragi* being much more nutritious than mill-polished rice which is driving the hand-pounded variety (so much better from the health point of view) out of use.*

The same indications of widespread distress come from the rural areas. A recent enquiry into the economic conditions of a typical village in South India, the great majority of whose residents were depressed class agricultural workers, revealed that most of them lived on one full meal a day, supplemented by a course porridge of *ragi* (a millet) in the morning. But in the case of a substantial minority it became difficult to obtain during the periods of unemployment which invariably followed a harvest. For three months, perhaps, a full meal was possible; but later, it was impossible to live without getting into debt on high rates of interest.

I was much struck, in visiting a large central prison in the Madras Presidency, with the steady increase in weight of the prisoners whose diet was a combination of rice with *ragi*.† In fact, it is true to say that from the standpoint of food, criminals in prisons are much better off than the working classes; more attention is paid to the subject than the workers bestow on it, and with uniformly favourable results.

The subject of nutrition has come to the fore since 1936, mainly because of the active interest of the Viceroy, Lord Linlithgow. But the position in India cannot be described better than in the words of the Public Health Commissioner of the Government of India, who pointed out in his report for 1935 that the conclusion was irresistible that a considerable proportion of the population in India revealed malnutri-

* One of the many services rendered by Mr. Gandhi to India is his campaign in favour of hand-pounded rice which has met with an encouraging response.

† We made some years ago an attempt to start a Workers' Club in Madras, in the hope of providing some social amenities and, incidentally, of introducing some reform in diet. I spoke to the members of the trade union about the desirability of gradually eliminating mill-polished rice in favour of the hand-pounded variety, with some wheat and *ragi* as an addition, the latter especially being within reach of the lowest-paid workers. They listened to my observations on the results obtained in prisons and the comparatively better physique of villagers, many of whom still cling to their traditional *ragi* porridge. One of them said at the end, with the evident approval of the rest, "But we are neither prisoners nor villagers." That seemed to them a conclusive answer!

tional conditions, due for the most part to qualitative defects in the ordinary diet of the people. He added: "No preventive campaign against malaria, against tuberculosis or against leprosy, no maternity relief or child welfare activities are likely to achieve any great success unless those responsible recognize the vital importance of this factor of defective nutrition and from the very start give it their most serious attention. Abundant supplies of quinine and the multiplication of tuberculosis hospitals, sanatoria, leprosy colonies, and maternity and child welfare centres are no doubt desirable, if not essential; but none of these go to the root of the matter. The first essentials for the prevention of disease are a higher standard of health, a better physique, and a greater power of resistance to infection. These can only be attained if the food of the people is such as will give all the physiological and nutritional requirements of the human frame."

CHAPTER VII

PUBLIC HEALTH IN INDIA

Closely connected with the problems of population and food-supply is that of public health in India. The Indian Industrial Commission, supported by the powerful testimony of Major Norman White (then Sanitary Commissioner of the Government of India), came to the conclusion during the war that an improvement in public health was of fundamental importance for increasing the efficiency of labour. Within a year of the publication of the report came the influenza epidemic to whose disastrous effects reference has been made in an earlier chapter.

Unfortunately, public health has never been considered by those responsible for formulating policies in India as of major importance to national welfare. It is significant that while there have been commissions and committees on every subject, political, educational, social, and economic, there has been none on health since 1863. The outbreak of plague in 1896 led to the appointment of a plague commission—a solitary exception to the general rule of neglect—and on its findings was appointed the Sanitary Commissioner with the Government of India. Major Norman White, who occupied that post during the war, declared with perfect justice:

> When a military force, however small, takes the field, the necessity of a sanitary organization and precautions to safeguard the health are never overlooked. It is realized that their neglect is certain to lead to disaster. Quite as elaborate precautions are called for in many of our large constructional works; but, with few exceptions, the measures taken in the past have been most inadequate, or altogether wanting, a neglect that has involved much waste and sometimes disaster. Large projects of the nature alluded to are rarely referred to a health expert at any stage of their inception; their probable financial cost is estimated to a rupee; but their probable cost in human life receives no consideration whatsoever. The Panama Canal was a triumph for the engineer; it was a still greater triumph for preventive medicine

which made the engineer's work possible. For once the health official was not subordinated, but given plenary powers; and he made good. Is it not an irony that the most important research (in regard to malaria) of which the results were applied with such profit in Panama was research work done in India, work which has done so little for India as yet?

While the position has undoubtedly improved in some respects since Major White made this criticism, there is still considerable room for improvement. Funds for medical research and investigation are generally among the earliest items to come under the axe of retrenchment during periods of financial stringency. After the introduction of the Montagu Reforms in 1920, when public health became transferred to ministerial control in the provinces, the Government of India was at first inclined to take the view that a central institute of public health was essential for co-ordinating the health policies of the various provinces and for providing facilities for research. All the preliminary formalities of sanction were, in fact, gone through for a scheme which would have cost no more than about £150,000 at the start and involved a recurring annual expenditure of about a fourth of that amount. But just at that time came a crisis in the finances of the Government of India, and the scheme (on the recommendation of Lord Inchcape's committee on retrenchment in 1922) was held in abeyance until the return of better times. But those better times never came. A more modest effort was made instead, by a grant of less than half that sum for research work, until the axe fell again heavily in 1931, reducing it to insignificant proportions.

The excuse cannot be put forward that the Government of India has had no warnings from its expert advisers that public health deserved far greater importance than it was receiving. Almost every year, from 1924, a conference of medical research workers, presided over by Sir John Megaw, who later became the highest authority in the Indian Medical Service, has pointed out that the number of deaths in the country every year from preventable diseases alone was five to six million. The number of days lost by each worker for the same reason was estimated at two or three weeks in a year, and the loss of efficiency from preventable malnutrition and disease at not less than twenty per cent. The view was authoritatively stated by the conference that preventable disease was the greatest cause of poverty and financial stringency.

The Royal Commission on agriculture, quoting this view* with approval, referred to the devitalizing effects of malaria, plague, cholera, hookworm, and other epidemics, and said

* An interesting experiment was conducted some years ago in the Assam tea plantations, the results of which were embodied in a paper read before the Far Eastern Association of Tropical Medicine. The observations, which were based upon an examination of 7,000 men, women, and children, said: "For 972 children alive, there were 931 dead, a ghastly legacy of ignorance or indifference." The height, weight, chest and girth measurements were considerably below Western standards, due "to adverse economic conditions and a poor state of health." What was found particularly of value were the suggestions obtained from Sanitary Commissioners and carried out in the plantations. Some houses were rebuilt on an improved plan. The water supply was looked after, and a better system of conservancy introduced. Sanitary gangs were started to work and maintain earth-drains and clear away the rubbish. Other preventive measures included emergency medical boxes and surgical apparatus installed at convenient parts all over the gardens and replenished every month. Every fortnight the workers were examined and put under treatment. Their education in matters of health was not neglected; by means of placards and posters and frequent demonstrations they were made to appreciate the advantages of preventive work. Expectant mothers were given at least four months' leave with extra food, milk, cod-liver oil, malt, and tonic mixture three times a day. Babies were brought to the hospital daily for two or three months. A central hospital was constructed on up-to-date lines.

The most significant result of this work was the increase in the number of workers who turned out to work daily. While before the introduction of these improvements, during the most busy season, 76 per cent of the total labour force turned out for work, in places where these changes were in full action, the number was raised to 83 per cent, and was still on the increase. In time, the proportion was expected to reach 90 per cent.

As regards disease, smallpox had become almost unknown; malaria had been reduced by 50 per cent; spleen index was below 10 per cent, whereas three years previously it was over 20 per cent. There was only one case of cholera during the year, although it was widespread in the district. Dysentery had been reduced by 40 per cent; hookworm was rapidly disappearing. There had been a big rise in the birth-rate and a fall in the death-rate.

As the medical authority in charge remarked, "The cost of disease is enormous, necessitating, as it does, the recruiting of new labour to replace wastage, outgoings in sick pay and attendance and lack of labour just when much health is needed to assure a large crop." He estimated the cost of disease at Rs. 3 per head per month, while the cost of prevention did not amount to more than one rupee.

quite truly that any enquiry into the general condition of agriculture and the position of the cultivator was bound to take into account the public health aspect of his life, the suitability of his diet, the sanitary conditions under which he lived and his general rural environment.

There is not the least doubt that malaria continues to be the gravest menace to the health of India's population. According to Colonel Sinton, who was for several years director of the malaria survey of India, there is indisputable evidence to show that at least a 100 million individuals suffer yearly from malaria in British India alone; and this, he added, was probably a moderate estimate. There is, further, an indirect morbidity caused by malaria which may affect between 25 and 75 million additional cases. Not more than a tenth of the cases of malaria actually receive treatment in hospitals, the plain and terrible fact being that the amount of quinine available in India is far too inadequate. The highest medical authorities in the country have pleaded for years for a definite official policy to increase the supply of quinine so as to bring it within the reach of the masses. Under existing conditions and at present prices quinine is a costly luxury for the vast majority of those who are chronic victims. As a result of continued pressure on the Government of India a small amount was allotted in the budget of the Central Government in 1937 towards anti-malarial operations, commencing with a drive against the disease in the Imperial capital. But until quinine is produced in India in sufficient quantities,* it is to be feared that the conditions so vividly described by Colonel Sinton will continue, inflicting enormous losses on the country.

Major Bentley, who made a special study of malaria during his official life in Bengal, wrote some years ago a striking book entitled *Malaria and Agriculture in Bengal.* Eighty thousand villages in the province, he estimated, at that time were stricken with malaria, and the number of people suffering from the disease in Bengal alone he reckoned at 30 million. In certain areas (like Burdwan and Hooghly)

* A special officer was appointed by the Government of India in 1937 to investigate the possibilities of extending cinchona cultivation in India.

malaria has been devastating. So long ago as 1881 the census report had drawn attention to the fact that the population in these areas was on the decline owing to the ravages of the disease and the consequent abandonment of agriculture.

Major Bentley said in his book: "Since the flushing of the country has been prevented, agriculture, health and prosperity have suffered, millions of lives have been sacrificed, thousands of crores of rupees have been lost, the people are sunk in poverty, and a vast proportion have suffered in each year from a recurring attack of malaria."

The estimates of the incidence of disease in the rural areas are bound to be rough; but in the absence of detailed surveys, they must be accepted and verified wherever other data are available. The figures given in this chapter are from Sir John Megaw's report (published in 1933) and may be accepted as sufficiently accurate for general conclusions. Rickets, a disease caused by a deficiency in the diet, was far more prevalent in Bengal than elsewhere, and least common in the Panjab, the total number of cases in India being 2·3 million. Night-blindness, another "diet-deficiency" disease, extremely common in the United Provinces and less so elsewhere (except in Bombay, which seemed to be on the whole free from the disease), claimed 3·6 million victims. As regards venereal disease, to which reference has already been made, the estimate for all India is 13 million, though according to the report, if all those who have suffered from syphilis at some time or other but lost all obvious signs are to be included, 10 to 15 per cent of the people "would probably be well within the mark."

Tuberculosis has rapidly grown into one of the worst scourges of India. Sir John Megaw had observed in 1933 that the estimate of just over two million cases of tuberculosis in India as a whole was much too low. Every large town was known to be very heavily infected, and, therefore, an estimate based solely on the incidence of the disease in the agricultural areas was likely to be unduly favourable. From a detailed survey made in 1937, in connection with Lady Linlithgow's anti-tuberculosis campaign, the number of cases in India was estimated at approximately five million.

The most gloomy view is expressed in regard to the future. The population of India is considered to be highly susceptible to tuberculosis and among most people, especially in the rural areas, the disease takes a virulent form and runs a rapid course. It is generally agreed that housing conditions in many towns are favourable to the rapid spread of the disease. Competent observers hold that the problem resolves itself into one of improving housing conditions in urban areas with all that it implies in regard to space, sunlight, and fresh air, and sustained propaganda in favour of good nutrition.

Sir John Megaw's conclusions were: "Tuberculosis is evidently very widespread throughout the villages of India, but is specially serious in Bengal, Madras, the Panjab, Bihar and Orissa. Pulmonary tuberculosis seems to be much more common than extra-pulmonary, except in the United Provinces and Bombay. The low incidence in the Central Provinces is remarkable and is perhaps associated with the sparse distribution of the population and with defective means of communication.

"Tuberculosis is well known to be exceedingly prevalent in the cities and large towns, but little is known as to its incidence in rural areas. The evidence of dispensary doctors goes to show that the disease is very widely disseminated throughout India. From other sources of information it seems likely that the disease is increasing steadily and rather rapidly.

"Tuberculosis is a disease which has very special importance in India for the reasons that (1) it is likely that many villagers have never come in contact with infection and therefore are virgin soil on which the disease is likely to thrive, (2) the infection is being steadily spread from the large towns to the villages, (3) the disease constitutes a reliable index of the standards of life which prevail in countries in which it has become established for long periods of time; it spreads rapidly among ill-nourished and badly housed populations and correspondingly diminishes when the people are well fed, well housed, and cleanly in their habits."

With regard to blindness, the medical survey is positive that the 1931 census figures are unreliable; in every case in which they were checked by detailed investigation, they were found to be far too low—Nasik District in the Bombay Presidency, for example, returning three times as many blind as were recorded in the census report. The estimate for all India is nearly two million—cataract, glaucoma, smallpox, and trachoma being the chief causes. The explanation, however, given in the census report is worth noting: "Much of the blindness in India," it said, "is curable and more is preventable. One serious difficulty is the economic one. Cultivators suffering from eye complaints cannot afford to leave the work on their fields for a prolonged stay in hospital, either for themselves or to look after their children there."

What is true of blindness is also true of leprosy, census figures being in nearly all cases gross understatements. The census commissioner for India regarded the view of medical authorities in Bombay City, that the census statistics were not more than one-tenth correct, as being capable of more or less general application. In one small area in Bengal, the census figure was 30 while a medical survey returned 274; in Hyderabad State it was just over 3,700, but the medical estimate was 60,000. Similarly, in Orissa, the census return for 450 villages gave 179 lepers per 10,000 of the population, against 1,344 found by a medical survey. Sir John Megaw's estimate, qualified by the observation that "it is probably on the low side, although it is far higher than the census figures," is three-quarters of a million for the whole of India. "Leprosy shortens life," the census commissioner remarked, "and the age curves of leprosy show steady increases after maternity until the period of old age is approached, when they fall rapidly." The experience of Madras may be taken as typical where the peasants and the industrial workers provide the bulk of the victims. The Public Health Commissioner of the Government of India, in discussing the predisposing causes of the disease, in one of his reports, said that a high leprosy rate was associated with a poor soil where vegetables and fodder did not thrive and the cereal crops were therefore apt to fail; also, with an inadequate consumption of vegetables and milk, and the consumption of food of bad quality, such as spoilt rice and rotten fish.

Hookworm is worst in the Madras Presidency, the incidence in certain districts being incredibly high; thus, in Trichinopoly, South Arcot, Salem, and Tinnevelly districts, over 90 per cent of the population are believed to be infected, according to the statistics collected by the provincial department of public health. In six other districts the proportion exceeds 80 per cent; in seven it is over 70 per cent. The remarks of the census commissioner for all India in the report for 1931 are of interest: "It is not generally understood how great are the economic effects of this disease, not merely in respect of poor out-turn and lethargic work, but in the creation of large numbers who are, in fact, parasitic on their less infected fellows. Hookworm produces habitual criminals and village pests of the petty pilfering order and probably innumerable beggars, and the writer, when in charge of one of the smallest jails in India, found by deliberate experiment that habitual pilferers and village parasites could, by being tested for hookworm and by treatment in jail, be made into useful members of their communities."*

Lack of medical assistance in India is, of course, a factor of great importance. Even now with the constant pressure of non-official majorities in the legislatures, and the extension of medical relief and public health organizations only a very small fraction of the total revenue of the country (less than five per cent) is available for this vital need. Indigenous systems of medicine, both Hindu and Moslem (known as the *Ayurvedic* and the *Unani* systems respectively), are very much cheaper than the Western, and, so far as experience shows, at least as effective. In one or two provinces the Provincial Governments have established medical schools to impart education and training in these systems, and local bodies are running several hundred rural dispensaries in charge of trained doctors with marked success and at an extremely

* It is of interest to note that tea garden experts estimate a 10, 25, or even 50 per cent increase in labour efficiency under effective hookworm control.

low cost. The masses of the population have more faith in the indigenous than in the Western system of medicine and, given the choice, would in most cases prefer the former. Even if more funds were not forthcoming, greater expenditure on these would be a much more useful investment than up-to-date hospitals on Western lines.

Apart from this, the idea has yet to spread sufficiently in India that preventive work is even more important than medical relief. Sir John Megaw complained in his medical survey that too many village doctors (to whom the task of surveying was entrusted) regard themselves as being responsible only for treating the sick who come to them for medical relief instead of being, as they should primarily be, missionaries of preventive medicine in their areas of work. It is only within the last fifteen years that public health organizations have grown up in some of the provinces.

There is no difficulty at all in suggesting a solution for India's problems of public health—apart, of course, from lack of funds. The Simon Commission was so impressed with the absence of a clear-cut policy that it advocated the formation of a central board of public health, a reform which was not carried out until 1936. But it is not only direction from the centre that is wanted. The administration of public health in the provinces has been so complicated by lack of consolidation of the various public health enactments contained in a number of measures that it is extremely difficult for a health officer to know precisely what his functions and powers are.

There is urgent necessity for a consolidated Public Health Act* in the provinces, and the creation of a Ministry of Health, both in the provinces and at the centre. Since the creation of the Imperial Council of Agricultural Research, following the report of the Royal Commission on Agriculture, it has been demonstrated in practice that not only is there no divergence of interests between such politically distinct areas as British India and the Indian States, but that co-operation is both possible and to mutual advantage.

* This long-needed reform has been effected in Madras, and is likely to be copied in the other provinces.

States like Hyderabad and Mysore make annual contributions towards the expenses of the Imperial Council and derive benefit from their co-operation. The precedent in the realm of agriculture should enable a similar organization for public health purposes to function with the same satisfactory results.

CHAPTER VIII

UNTOUCHABILITY

No account of the general conditions of India from the standpoint of the workers can be complete without a reference to the problem of untouchability into the solution of which Mr. Gandhi has thrown the full weight of his magnetic personality. Caste among the Hindus, although it has lost much of its force in the urban areas, is still a dominant influence in rural India, and makes itself felt in a variety of ways. The ordinary caste Hindu worker would prefer unemployment to work, for instance, in the tanning industry—so great is the prejudice against handling leather. In many factories there is insistence on separate arrangements being made for the midday meal for the caste workers and the untouchables, inter-dining in India being a mark of social equality. But, speaking generally, the rigours of untouchability are far less in evidence in the industrial and urban areas than even ten years ago. In addressing workers' meetings, one would find it impossible to-day to differentiate between caste and untouchable workers: common economic interests are forging bonds of unity which are gradually proving stronger than these traditional distinctions. Education and modern methods of travel by railway trains, tram-cars, and the motor omnibus are also helping to break down the barriers of caste. But the complex is almost universal and has unsuspected reserves of strength. There are Christian churches in parts of South India (which is the home of untouchability) where "caste" and "non-caste" Christians faithfully observe the rule of sitting apart for congregational worship almost as rigidly as though they were Hindus.

Precisely what constitutes untouchability it is not always easy to tell—whether it is birth alone, or the following of an unclean occupation (such as scavenging and tanning leather), or the eating of unclean food (particularly beef and pork). Conditions differ so widely in the different provinces that generalizations are wellnigh impossible. Committees appointed by the Government have been unable to agree in the past as to the line of demarcation to be drawn, and in consequence estimates as to the number of untouchables in some provinces show extreme variations. In some parts of India (especially in Madras and large parts of Bombay) the untouchables are also the depressed classes; and the two, in fact, are interchangeable terms. But in the United Provinces the Government, in a note which it supplied to Lord Lothian's Franchise Committee in 1932, said that if the sole test of untouchability was pollution by touch or approach, the number would be slightly under half a million. The census commissioner's estimate in the previous year of 12·6 million consisted of two categories, (*a*) untouchable and depressed (11·2 million), and (*b*) touchable but depressed (1·4 million). There has been, it would appear from an official report, a growing tendency in recent years to regard untouchability as a personal rather than as a caste attribute. Any caste (or a member thereof) who abandons the hereditary occupation carrying with it the stigma of untouchability could, by that means, acquire a higher caste status. Thus, a *chamar* (a worker on dead animals) by becoming a saddler, or a cobbler, or a groom would become a touchable; or a *bhangi* (a scavenger), by rising to the rank of a *jemadar* (the supervisor) of scavengers, would acquire a new status among his fellow citizens. Similarly, in Bengal, for more or less the same reasons estimates have varied between 11·2 million on the one hand by the Government, and 0·07 million on the other by the provincial franchise committee. For all India, Sir John Simon's Commission practically agreed with the estimate of the census commissioner for 1921 (43 million), while the Provincial Governments in their reports to the Franchise Committee in 1932 gave the figure as 37·5 million, and the provincial franchise committees only 18·6 million.

It is not to be imagined that within the circle of untouchability there are no subgradations, and that all untouchables are equals among themselves.* In the Madras Presidency

* The following statement is taken from an address of welcome presented to Mr. Gandhi during a tour in Orissa, which he undertook four years ago. "All the various grades of untouchables are untouchable among themselves,

alone (where at any rate there is no dispute as to numbers, about 7 million), there are, it is said, no less than eighty subdivisions, those at the top regarding the less fortunate of their own brethren as untouchable. At the bottom of the scale come some classes, like the *Nayadis* of Malabar, whose very shadow is pollution.

But whatever their actual number, it is beyond doubt that within the last twenty years much progress has been made in awakening the social conscience of India to the disabilities of these outcastes. It is to the credit of the various legislatures that under the Montagu Reforms there was not a single instance in any province of refusal of educational facilities to the members of the depressed classes. The growth of education among them has been in many provinces more rapid than the general rate of expansion—a tribute to the anxiety of Ministers of Education, whatever their political views, to pay special attention to their needs. A number of social service organizations and individuals have been doing fine ameliorative work for a number of years; but there was no strong nation-wide incentive until Mr. Gandhi appeared on the scene in 1920 and made the abolition of untouchability an essential and prominent item in the achievement of India's freedom. There was some controversy at the time as to the wisdom of bringing in a measure of social reform, however desirable in itself, into a political programme. But Mr. Gandhi's extraordinary influence overcame all hesitation and the Congress, under his leadership, has associated itself actively and prominently for over fifteen years with uplift work.

each superior grade considering the inferior grade as polluting as the highest class of the caste Hindus regard the worst grade of untouchables. Further, among the same grade of untouchables there are sections, each considering itself different and distinct from any other, prohibiting inter-dining and inter-marriage. Thus, there are four distinct sections in the *Chamar* grade, two sections in the *Hadi* grade, though in our village there is only one section from each of the grades. These worst classes of untouchables undergo the same social disabilities as are prevalent elsewhere, namely, they are prohibited the use of temples and wells. Schools, bathing *ghats*, and roads are not prohibited to them; only, they must not touch the touchables or the superior grades of untouchables while making use of them. They are segregated in uncomfortable regions of the village where no caste Hindu can have access without polluting himself to a degree beyond the capacity of mere ablutions to retrieve."

It is abundantly clear that no one but Mr. Gandhi can lead a movement against untouchability with hopes of striking success. Beyond question he wields a far greater influence over the masses than any other leader has ever done, and it is all to the good that such unsurpassed power should be harnessed to a purpose so noble and humanitarian as the uplift of the depressed classes. When India has shed the last vestiges of untouchability, it will be Mr. Gandhi's name which will stand out as the liberator of these oppressed millions. He has concentrated his main attention on getting the ban on temple-entry for the depressed classes removed, and makes no secret of his view that Hinduism must reform itself by proclaiming the equality of man—high-caste Brahman or the lowest of the untouchable. He could not, consistently with the circumstances under which he commenced this work, ignore the religious aspect of the problem; and probably, also, he takes the view that once the most formidable barrier is broken by permitting free entry into Hindu temples, social and economic reforms must inevitably follow in its wake.*

But so far as the untouchables themselves are concerned, many of their leaders view the problem in a different light. They are, comparatively speaking, little worried about temple-entry; but they attach far more importance to the removal of disabilities in the social and economic spheres. They would be perfectly content if village roads, wells, and schools could be opened to them without restrictions, and they were not reminded in their daily lives of their badge of inferiority.

It should not, however, be supposed that because Mr. Gandhi's stress is greatest on temple-entry the other aspects of the work are in the background. One has only to read the issues of his weekly journal called *Harijan*, to see how many-

* The State of Travancore, regarded for generations as a citadel of Hindu orthodoxy, adopted the bold course in 1936, under the generous impulse of its young but enlightened ruler, of throwing open all State temples to the untouchables. His proclamation created a profound impression in India. This example was followed two years later by another State, Indore. Provincial Governments, especially those under Congress control, are making much larger grants for Harijan uplift schemes.

sided the awakening is; not a single month passes without some temple being thrown open, new schools constructed or existing schools admitting the children of the untouchables and some fresh and tangible evidence of a "change of heart" (a phrase dear to him) on the part of the Hindus. A new organization, originally known as the Servants of the Untouchables Society, now styled as the "Harijan Sevak Sangh"—meaning the Society for the Service of "the Harijans," Mr. Gandhi's new name for the untouchables—has completed four years of its existence and is full of promise for the future. Its many branches all over the country have attracted a number of young men who went to prison under Mr. Gandhi's leadership during the civil disobedience movement and are now devoting themselves to the cause of the untouchables. But it is not only Congressmen who have taken to this work; many of the responsible office-bearers in the new organization are non-Congressmen in their political views who find much in common with Mr. Gandhi in his present activities.

It is extraordinary how the term "Harijan" (which literally means the people of God) is gaining currency all over the country. All the old nomenclature—Adi-Dravidas, Depressed Classes, Untouchables, Panchamas, etc.—is quickly going out of fashion. Mr. Gandhi, with characteristic sensitiveness of feeling, realized that the use of the term "Untouchables" or "Depressed Classes" carried with it a stigma and promptly adopted the new epithet early in his present campaign.

Fascinating as the subject is, one must turn from it to the economic aspects of the movement against untouchability. These unfortunate millions are practically all workers in the agricultural areas, in the plantations of tea, rubber, and coffee, and to some extent in factories also; for the reasons already stated, they have almost a monopoly of labour in the tanning industry. The right of admission to schools, of the free use of roads and wells touches vested interests less than the assertion of economic rights. Organizations of the untouchables are, however, placing it in the forefront of their programme; in the United Provinces, for example, the demand has been made for the abolition of all forms of forced labour; and already several Provincial Governments have taken stringent action warning public servants against impressing forced labour or free services of any kind.

In regard to the problem of housing of the untouchables, it is true of many parts of India that overcrowding is at least as bad in villages as in the urban areas. In the United Provinces, for example, if village densities were calculated on the areas of the sites actually inhabited, leaving out the village lands, they would probably be as great as in many towns. From Madras comes the same tale. Some of the worst specimens of housing in the province are to be found in certain rural areas, especially the wealthy delta tracts round the irrigation systems of the Godavari, the Krishna, and the Cauvery rivers. Where land is dear, as in these deltaic districts, housing tends to be congested and even a comparatively well-to-do landowner may be content to live in conditions that may be surprising to a stranger.*

A recent enquiry in a large and typical agricultural district in South India conducted by a rural reconstruction society revealed their deplorable conditions. The area selected contained about 18,000 untouchable workers, some of whom were able to supplement their meagre incomes as landless labourers by taking to non-agricultural labour, such as road-making, railway construction, work on bridges and dams. But being untouchables, they were not allowed to undertake repairs or construction of the houses of the caste people, nor to sell milk and vegetables to them. A major complaint in the area was that liquor was sold in the toddy shops in contravention of all the rules of licensing made by the Excise Department. Banking facilities were practically non-existent, and such of the untouchables as were inclined to be thrifty were often the victims of speculative organizers of unsound credit institutions. Nevertheless, some had

* The *Madras* Census Report observes: "If this is so with the actual owner of the land, it can be imagined what will be the condition of the farm labourers who, in many cases, also belong to the depressed classes. In Tanjore, these last form the backbone of the agricultural labouring population, and are even yet little removed from a state of agrestic serfdom. . . . The *paracheries* (slums in which the depressed classes live) of this Presidency may safely be counted upon to produce the worst examples of housing." (Part I, pp. 71, 72.)

managed to acquire a few plots of land and thus rise in the social scale. But these men, instead of becoming the natural leaders of the less fortunate members of their own class, were combining with the higher castes, it was found, in perpetuating their serfdom. Caste landlords collected their dues and produce through them; money-lenders lent both money and cloth to the workers on the security of these comparatively better off men; contractors for road and bridge work made them their intermediaries for obtaining labour; and even the police found it useful on occasions to utilize their services for their own purposes.

The untouchable workers in the fields, who formed more than half the total population of the area, owned in a number of cases tiny fragments of land, and some of them also a few cattle and sheep. But the bulk of them could not get regular incomes and lived a precarious existence. A few had taken to village industries like mat-making and weaving rough cloth; the more adventurous sought escape from the hard life of the village by migration to Ceylon, or the Straits Settlements, or to some urban area; but the others lived in pitiable circumstances. How low their standards were may be gathered from the fact that an average family of five people, whose occupation was sewing and repairing leather buckets for ten or twelve wells, had a total income of Rs.70 per year (about £5).

This carefully conducted economic enquiry is of interest as disclosing the conditions of the untouchables. More reference will be made to their plight in the industrial areas, particularly in the tanning industry, in a later chapter. But it is well to bear in mind that the governing consideration in their case—as, indeed, in that of all industrial workers—is the economic exploitation in the rural areas and the practical denial of all hope of redemption.

PART 3

SOME PROBLEMS OF THE WORKER

CHAPTER IX

RECRUITMENT

It is against the background, the main features of which have been described briefly in the previous chapters, that the problems of the worker in industry have to be viewed and studied. One cannot afford to forget his social and economic status when he leaves the village in search of employment in an urban area. It may be near his village—or at any rate not so far that he is unacquainted with the language, customs, and habits of the people. Or, it may be many hundreds of miles away, involving a long journey. He comes to the city as a stranger generally alone, with little knowledge of its conditions and hardly any equipment; he has probably contracted debts and finds it embarrassing to remain in the village, or for some other reason would prefer to be in a place where he is less known and therefore migrates to the city.

With regard to recruitment, it may at once be said that there are no State agencies for the engagement of industrial labour. As a rule, each concern engages the labour it requires, and so far (except during brief periods following the outbreak of a violent or widespread epidemic) there has generally been a plentiful supply of labour. India has moved far from the stage in her industrial development (unfortunately for the worker) when an employer could feel the difficulty of finding a sufficient number of workers for his factory. Even so recently as 1921 the census report observed that the progress of industry in the country was limited in one vital respect, namely the problem of obtaining and retaining labour. But that was because of a temporary shortage created by two successive waves of influenza in 1918 and 1919. Since then, owing to the enormous growth of the population, and the other factors already described—unemployment in agriculture, the lack of other forms of occupation in the rural areas and the closing down of outlets beyond the borders of India—there has been, as a general rule, no special effort required to recruit new workers. Outside the gates of a factory in an industrial area in any part of India are hundreds, if not more, of the unemployed, waiting every morning to be taken on as *badlis* (substitutes) in the place of those who are absent for shorter or longer periods.

In a number of industrial establishments it used to be the practice until a few years ago to keep a certain number of workers on a waiting list, and offer them a small daily allowance even if there was no work for the day. But this practice, adopted in times when workers were not always easy to obtain, has practically disappeared. Indeed, certain mills are now not only not paying any waiting allowances to the *badlis*, but enter into an agreement with them that no wages will be paid while they are learning work. There is such keen competition to secure even temporary work, that the workers (the vast majority of whom are illiterate) do not hesitate to sign any agreement that is put before them, in the hope that at least after serving their apprenticeship for a few months, they will be entertained as regular workers with a fixed wage.

When a worker arrives for the first time in a city in search of employment, he is generally without any money, skill, or influence. He spots out a relation, near or distant, or an acquaintance in a factory and works through him. Recruitment of new workers is practically everywhere left to the *maistri*, or the *sirdar*, or the *mukadam*, or the jobber (as they are called in different parts of the country). Even to get inside the mill to be employed as a substitute is not easy; the jobber must be paid for this piece of service, and the bribe may be in cash—a few rupees, perhaps the first month's earnings, supplemented in many cases by personal service in the house of the jobber, or a supply of vegetables, milk or *ghee*. The jobber is not the only one to be satisfied; there is the time-keeper, an important functionary in many mills and the muster clerk. Especially in the early stages, while the raw recruit is still learning his work—making mistakes, some of which may be at the expense of the employer—it is essential that he should maintain harmonious relationships with the subordinate staff, and in particular with the jobber. Even later, when he has been placed on a permanent footing, he is dependent on the jobber for leave, promotion or transfer from one piece of work to another. Nothing, in fact, can happen in an Indian factory without some price being paid, and it is a common practice to follow a definite schedule in regard to payment. A jobber is generally a well-paid man in a mill, and it is not unusual for him to receive a wage ranging from Rs.60 to Rs. 120 a month—and even more in a number of cases. But what he earns through bribes is much more than his wage. After a few years of service as a jobber he has enough money for purchasing his own house and jewels for his wife and children; and very frequently he also becomes a moneylender to the workers in his mill and builds quarters for them which he rents out at exorbitant rates.

The jobber in the factory is primarily a chargeman, responsible for the output in his department and supervision of the workers under him. He acts sometimes as a mechanic and generally assists the unskilled worker. But quite apart from his normal and legitimate duties, his importance is due to his being an intermediary between the employer or the factory manager and the body of the workers. It is more convenient for the management to deal with a handful of jobbers who know their work and in many ways are capable men than to establish direct contact with the workers. In a number of factories the manager and many of the heads of departments are Europeans, ignorant of the ways and habits of the workers; the gulf is so wide that even after many years of life in India, they know very little about them and find it almost impossible to understand, much less appreciate, the workers' ways and habits and difficulties. The jobber thus becomes an indispensable link in the chain of officials. He interprets the workers' requirements to the manager and conveys, in turn, the latter's directions and instructions to the rank and file. If there is trouble of any kind, the jobber's co-operation is essential for the restoration of normal conditions. "A clever rascal" is generaly the expression used by a manager in respect of the jobber. Through anonymous petitions, written in quaint English, the manager is acquainted with the iniquities practised by the jobber on the workers —with, generally, though in varying degrees, a solid substratum of truth. But even then a sympathetic and conscientious manager (or head of a department) finds it too embarrassing to follow up the particulars in any case to their logical end. He knows that the smooth working of the factory is dependent on the goodwill and the hearty co-operation of the jobber. If in his anxiety to do justice to the workers he should alienate the sympathies of the jobber, the work of the factory as a whole can and will be made extremely difficult for him.

It would, of course, be unjust to generalize against a whole class of workers. I have come into contact with many jobbers who, given the opportunity, would make fine leaders of trade unions. But it is impossible at this stage of the movement. Even if a jobber were capable and willing, it would be risking too much for a person with a wage of Rs. 60 to Rs. 100 or more a month to come into the open and associate himself with a union. Dismissal in his case would mean an amount of hardship for himself and his family which no union can relieve; he contents himself, therefore, with maintaining a semblance of aloofness from the union so as to satisfy the employer.

The Royal Commission on Labour paid a great deal of attention to this problem of bribery, especially at the stage of recruitment, some years ago and suggested that by systematic efforts bribery could be substantially reduced if not eliminated. The methods advocated were that the jobbers should be excluded from the engagement and dismissal of labour, and suitable labour officers appointed directly subordinate to the general manager—not necessarily equipped with technical qualifications, but rather men of integrity, an attractive personality, and endowed with a sympathetic imagination. The Commission was so impressed with the necessity of stamping out bribery and corruption that it recommended that employers should seek the co-operation of trade unions (wherever such existed) in achieving this worthy end.

The recommendation, based undoubtedly on excellent intentions, is contrary to the experience of practically all trade unions in the country and implies an imperfect reading of the psychology of the situation. A trade union, as will be explained in the chapter dealing with the organization of the workers, is as a general rule not welcome either to the jobber or to the employer. The former objects to it because his income and influence are thereby affected and imperilled, while the employer regards it frankly as a nuisance from every point of view. To weaken a union, to break its power in normal times, to smash a strike, if the workers should go so far, through the recruitment of blackleg labour—in all this the employer must depend on the support of the jobber at every stage. How can he, in reason, be expected to throw overboard an ally who, if unscrupulous, is certainly very helpful, in favour of an organization of the workers which will advance claims to which he is unaccustomed, and the concession of even one of which will weaken him in resisting the rest? It is impossible, so long as the other features of the industrial system in India remain unaltered.

The difficulties in regard to the recruitment of women workers* are naturally accentuated under the conditions described in the preceding paragraphs, as they are prone to suffer in silence injustice and tyranny of many kinds at the hands of the jobber. In some factories, in recognition of this fact, women jobbers, known as *Naikins*, have been appointed; but though some of the evils associated with men jobbers supervising the work of women may have been diminished, it is still true that women are even more exploited than are men in similar circumstances. The Labour Commission suggested the appointment of educated women to take charge of the supervision and welfare of women workers. It may be that in some isolated instances the experiment has been successful. But for appreciable results, one must look to educated women's organizations to rouse public opinion on some of the scandals generally prevalent in industries employing women workers. It is a hopeful sign that women's

* There are few women workers in industry, about 234,000 of a total of 1·65 million working in registered factories in 1936

conferences in several provinces are now devoting special attention to their problems.

The methods of recruitment mentioned above obtain in most of the perennial factories, and within recent years, owing to the rapidly increasing pressure of the population, in the seasonal factories also in varying degrees. But labour for the plantations, mines, and large public works has still to be recruited through contractors and overseers, known in the plantations as *sirdars* in the north and *kanganies* in the south. The contractor is greatly assisted in his work by the extreme poverty and the indebtedness of the peasant and, of course, a bad harvest or an unfavourable agricultural season serves as an additional incentive. It is pathetic to see the child-like credulity of the workers and the frauds and misrepresentations of which they are frequently the helpless victims.

Plantation labour in India, which gives employment to nearly a million and a half people, presents peculiar features of its own. In the main it is agricultural, though the actual processes of manufacture bring a very small proportion of the workers under the Factories Act.

It is undoubtedly in the tea plantations that serious abuses have occurred in regard to the recruitment of labour. Their inaccessibility, coupled (at any rate until the inauguration of provincial autonomy in 1937) with the somewhat ready use of the prohibitive sections of the Criminal Procedure Code in order to shut out those interested in the workers' welfare, prevented the light of public opinion from playing on these remote areas. The Government of India admitted before the Labour Commission that recruitment for the Assam tea plantations*—by far the largest in the country—was always regarded with suspicion by Indian public opinion,

* The greater portion of the tea grown in India comes from Assam and North Bengal known as the Dooars, while South India, round about Coorg, the Nilgris district, and the highlands of Travancore, produces a smaller proportion of tea and practically all the coffee grown in India. Ninety per cent of the total plantations in North India and an even larger proportion in the South are controlled and managed by Europeans. It is only in the small province of Coorg where coffee is grown that the Indian planter predominates. In 1936, on the Assam tea estates alone, there were 615,000 adults and 527,000 children at work. (Annual Report on the Working of the Tea Districts Emigrant Labour Act of 1932 for 1937).

and the official memorandum referred to "the mystery" surrounding the plantations. The bulk of the recruits are from the aboriginal areas of Chota Nagpur (in Bihar), the Central Provinces, and the agency tracts in the Northern Circars of the Madras Presidency—a distance of several hundred miles, much of it by rail with some changes *en route*, and involving a crossing of the Brahmaputra, the last stage being up the hills in motor lorries.

The Government of Bihar, which was primarily concerned with the recruitment of labour for Assam, declared in its evidence that for the aboriginals the fact that a man had gone to Bhutan or Assam was synonymous with his total disappearance. Recruiting is an expensive item for the tea industry (about Rs.84 per adult, or Rs.64 per "soul," including both adults and children, in 1937), because of the great distances to be traversed and the necessity of maintaining a staff and depots in the recruiting areas. This, of course, is bound to add to the costs of production; and with the decrease of prosperity in the tea industry and the drop in prices on the one hand, and growing distress consequent upon agricultural unemployment on the other, it is inevitable, in the absence of a wage-fixing machinery, that the planters should reduce wages in order to minimize their costs.

Recruitment of labour for the plantations, whether in the north or in the south, presents certain common features, although the difficulties and complexities are much greater in the case of Assam and only less so in the case of Dooars in North Bengal. The South Indian plantations have their recruiting grounds very much nearer than those of the north. But the Madras Presidency has always had a large superfluous agricultural population which has supplied without difficulty all the labour required for the plantations. The planters have an organization with a network of branches in several of the surrounding districts from which labour is drawn, and recruitment is effected through agents called *kanganies*. Money is advanced to the *kanganies* in order to induce workers to come to the plantations. Abuses have been common in connection with the system, in many cases only a portion of the amount being actually given.

Until 1929 there was in force the Madras Planters' Labour Act under which penalties could be imposed for breaches of contracts by the workers. Though it was repealed in that year, the fact was not generally known among the workers for some years. The claim of the planters was that because labour went to the same estate year after year the workers were satisfied, or at any rate could have no serious causes of complaint against the treatment meted to them or their conditions of service. But the pressure of population and the lack of employment are causes which compel the superfluous population of the plains to seek a livelihood somewhere and under any conditions. A failure of the rains, agricultural distress and the treatment given to the untouchables in the rural areas are factors helpful to the plantations.

In regard to Assam and the Dooars in Bengal, recruitment presents a more formidable problem because of the very long distances from which labour has to be brought and the substantial costs involved in the process. European missionaries pointed out in their evidence before the Labour Commission that the cause of emigration was extreme poverty. They complained that young unmarried girls were enticed and disappeared, and married girls were decoyed by false promises. The *sirdars*, as the recruiting agents are called in the north, did not hesitate, if pushed to the necessity, to use sometimes even illegal means to obtain labour: agreements were in many cases signed not at Ranchi, the recruiting centre in Chota Nagpur, but in the tea estates in Assam. Girls, whether married or unmarried, were taken by devious ways to the depot by the *sirdar* who, in order to avoid detection, changed the names of his victims; and a number of cases were on record in which the *sirdars* had supplied alcohol or drugs to their victims before enticing them away.

Similar evidence came from the agency tracts of the Madras Presidency, also from European missionaries, who spoke in strong terms against the methods adopted for recruiting workers for Assam. Family life, they observed, was being broken up, and one of them referred to "selling men" to Assam. Among the chief reasons which, they alleged, led to emigration from those areas were a desire to earn more money or the indebtedness of emigrants without any other way of paying off their debts, family quarrels—one man taking away the wife of another, or perhaps the daughter not wanting to marry the man of her father's choice—or the commission of some crime.

As in South India, the planters of Assam sought protection for themselves in the early days of the industry through the Workmen's Breach of Contract Act which was passed in 1859 and repealed only in 1926. With the earlier abuses (to which the system lent itself), grave as they were, one need not concern oneself, except to point out in passing how utterly unjustified was the cry raised by interested parties that the discontent among the tea-garden workers in 1921 which flared up into a sort of general strike was due to the mischievous activities of political fomentors of unrest.

In 1921 there was serious trouble in the Assam tea gardens as a result of which there was a wholesale exodus from some gardens. The Government of India set up the Assam Labour Enquiry Committee to enquire into the conditions of labour on the tea gardens and to ascertain whether wages were adequate in view of the rise in prices. The conditions were so bad, according to the committee, that they afforded ample explanation for the reluctance of the workers to remain in the industry. The chief problems centred round the question of wages, the freedom of movement of the workers, and the relations of the workers with their employers.

Although it is true that the Workmen's Breach of Contract Act, under which criminal penalties (of imprisonment or fine) could be imposed on workers breaking their contract, had been repealed in 1926, there were reasons for the conclusion that very little effort was made either by the Government or by the planters to acquaint the workers with that vital change. There was, in fact, evidence before the Labour Commission that cases were instituted against minors, and children of eight years of age and upwards were placed under agreements and punished with imprisonment, although the Act of 1901 forbade placing minors under sixteen under contract, and the enquiry committee in 1921 had expressed its strong disapproval of the practice of placing workers under long-term agreements, and condemned the illegal arrest of absconders and the practice of taking contracts from minors.

Incredible as it may seem, the Government of Assam admitted before the Labour Commission that among a considerable portion of the workers the impression was still prevalent (three years after the repeal of the obnoxious law) that they were not free. It referred to cases of workers affixing their thumb-prints to agreements absolutely identical in terms with the old agreement, with the exception of the penal clauses. But with illiterate workers, it is easy to understand how they would not be in a position to compare the old agreements with the revised ones. The Government of Assam thought that there would be grave risks if steps were taken to make it known to every tea-garden worker that he was not bound by any agreement and was perfectly free to move!

In the evidence taken from the workers, it was clear that they were afraid to leave the plantations. One of them said, "If I go away, the *chowkidar* (watchman) will catch me and bring me back." Another said, "The manager and *chowkidar* keep us back. We are kept here by the *chowkidar* and sometimes beaten. The *chowkidar* goes at night round with a lamp, and even opens the door to see if we are there." The Commission put it mildly when it said that it was a matter for regret that when a vital change was made in the law, by which penal contract became illegal, little was done to bring it to the notice of the workers, and recommended that immediate steps should be taken in this direction.

Another difficulty which made recruitment unpopular was that the workers in the tea gardens had no facilities for maintaining contacts with their homes even by correspondence. A woman worker told the commission, "Since I have been here, I have not had my children with me. They have been in my country for all the three years." Another referred to the fact that during his one year's stay, he had not written even a single letter to his wife and family.

There has undoubtedly been some improvement in

regard to recruitment since the Tea Districts Emigrant Labour Act* was brought into force in October 1933. This measure provides for the appointment of a Controller of emigrant labour and invests him with certain powers to safeguard the interests of the workers. Under circumstances which are set forth in the Act, a worker and his family are entitled to repatriation at the expense of the planter. The period of service which entitles a worker to this privilege (normally after three years of service in Assam) may be curtailed for ill-health or some other special cause. Certain areas from which labour is normally recruited are notified under the Act as "controlled emigration areas"—Bengal, Bihar, Orissa, the Central Provinces, Madras, and the United Provinces. In 1936, 21,000 persons were recruited by the Tea Districts Labour Association through their depots in these areas and another 2,000 by local forwarding agencies at Ranchi in Chota Nagpur. Licences are granted to local forwarding agents for recruitment in the controlled emigration areas which are liable to forfeiture if abuse of the law can be proved against them.

The recruitment of seamen is similarly beset with difficulties of a peculiarly formidable nature, for in this field the workers have always been the victims of a system from which

* It is interesting to note that the latest report on the working of the Act makes a reference to a bad harvest and scarcity in the recruiting areas, the consequence of which was that the number of workers offering themselves for recruitment was many times the required number. This enables the planters to make a choice from amongst the would-be recruits. It is stated that planters show a preference for recruitment of only married couples; but a number of cases have come to the notice of managers of tea gardens of deception practised in this respect, couples confessing later that they were not really husbands and wives. But even now the system of recruitment through *Sirdars* is prevalent, though the Controller of Emigrant Labour exercises a measure of control over their methods. During 1937 only fifty-two cases were reported of breaches of the law, resulting in thirty-three convictions. It is difficult to believe that the number of infringements of the law can be really as low as indicated in the report, and that none occurred in Madras and the United Provinces —not to speak of Bombay, which is an uncontrolled emigration area. Efforts are no doubt made by the Controller of Emigrants and his assistants to prevent hardships to emigrants travelling from the depots to the tea gardens. Among the 26,000 persons forwarded to Assam during the year, there were only nine deaths, six of them being children below the age of four. The Controller, by means of surprise visits to the transit depots at meal times, satisfies himself that the workers are neither ill-fed nor unduly fatigued.

there seems to be little relief. Shipping in India is, except for an insignificant proportion, practically a monopoly of European companies who have objected to any interference with the system of recruitment, controlled as it has been for long years by shipping brokers with Government licences. Hopes of relief came to the workers somewhat unexpectedly through the International Labour Conference at Genoa in 1920, and the Government of India appointed shortly after a committee of enquiry to enquire into the system of recruitment of seamen.

The committee reported that the system of recruitment had led to grave abuses and recommended the setting up of employment bureaux under officers with practical marine experience to obtain for the workers continuity of employment and relief from bribery which was found to be widespread and serious. But so strong was the opposition from the shipowners to action being taken on the committee's report that it was not till 1929 that the Government of India issued their orders. Licensed brokers and other intermediaries for recruitment have not been abolished, though in theory their powers have been curtailed. But seamen's representatives, who appeared before the Royal Commission, declared that no appreciable improvement in their conditions had taken place in spite of the action of the Government of India, bribery being as prevalent then as when the committee made its report. At present the large volume of unemployment among seamen complicates the situation, and until Indian ships come into existence in large numbers, there does not seem to be much scope for the solution of the problem of unemployment. According to the Indian Seamen's Union in Bombay, there is employment at any time there for only a third of the total number. Seamen are found in the neighbourhood of the shipping office in Bombay who have been out of employment for periods varying from one to four years. In Calcutta, the position is not in any essential respects different, only about a fourth of the number seeking employment being successful.

There is hardly any type of labour in India which is so exploited and low-paid as contract labour. In every province of India, there is a public works department, with an irrigation and a road-building branch under the Provincial Government employing labour on a large scale. Almost invariably public works undertaken by the Government are entrusted to contractors under the general supervision of the department. Employers of labour in constructional work do not deal directly with their workers, but through middlemen or contractors. The statement applies to public works, building and road work, irrigation and bridge construction, to the loading and unloading of ships and work of several kinds in docks, harbours, railways, etc. Payments of wages are made generally through the contractors, who are given lump sums out of which they pay a portion to the workers and retain the rest for themselves.

From the point of view of the Government, as of local bodies like district boards and municipalities who are also large employers of such labour, this arrangement is no doubt convenient, since no consideration need be given to the requirements of the many thousands of workers employed; and also it is more economical.* At the same time, as the Royal Commission pointed out, conditions of labour would be far better if employed by the department direct. Contractors, by the very nature of the work, are bound to offer to the workers the lowest possible rates of wages. The Commission, while not going so far as to lay down the inclusion of a fair wages clause, suggested a modified form for adoption in India, with the additional safeguards that contracts should lay down twelve years as the minimum for the employment of children, and some regulation in regard to housing and sanitation.

Then there is another class of labour which is classed as "temporary." How a worker who has been regularly at work for fifteen and twenty years and even more can be

* An example of economy was furnished in a memorandum prepared three years ago by the General Manager of the Iron and Steel Works at Jamshedpur. Quarrying of raw material, when undertaken by the company, cost 14 annas a ton. It was found economical to hand it over to private contractors, the cost being reduced almost to half; but the rates of wages were shockingly low, being in the case which came to the notice of the General Manager, one anna a day for an adult woman worker.

regarded as temporary, with none of the rights and privileges that go with permanence of occupation, seems incomprehensible to the lay mind. Often in one's experience the startling reply comes from the employer's side, "But he is only a temporary worker." It is futile to point out that perhaps he has been in regular employment for possibly twenty years. India is governed by rules and regulations which have a cast-iron rigidity about them. Workers in the workshops of a Government college in South India sought my advice some years ago, because they were sent home regularly at the beginning of April every year, when the institution was closed for a period of three months, and reinstated in July, and during these three months they were paid no wages. Argument in such cases is useless, because the authorities regard the fact that they are classed as temporary workers as conclusive.

Recruitment of labour for the mining areas presents more or less the same broad features, "the raising contractors," as the intermediaries are called in the collieries, being responsible for the supply of labour. The Royal Commission condemned in vigorous language this feature of the mining industry, and suggested direct relationship between the colliery managers and the workers. But the raising contractor still flourishes—whatever be the state of the industry. There are, of course, difficulties in regard to recruitment, seasonal difficulties, as at the time of sowing and harvesting when large numbers return to their villages and the output of coal diminishes; and those created by the recent enforcement of the law excluding women from working underground. These have led to a shortage of labour in the collieries, and special efforts have been necessary to obtain an adequate labour force for the collieries, especially as, after the disasters of the last three years involving the loss of several hundred lives, workers have not been anxious to work underground.

But a significant side-light on the methods of recruitment for the collieries is thrown by the figures of the excise department of the Bihar Government. The aboriginal tribes who supply the bulk of colliery labour have been known for their addiction to drink. In 1929, in the Jherria coalfields alone,

55,000 workers spent Rs.700,000 on drink and drugs. Six years later, 50,000 workers, earning about half the rates of wages paid in 1929, spent Rs.1,200,000 on country liquor. The explanation is to be found in the altered excise policy of the Bihar Government. Finding its revenues from other sources shrinking during the depression period and hard pressed for funds, a system was devised of auctioning out liquor shops and converting distilleries into outstills, with the result that the price of liquor dropped from 8 to 10 annas a bottle to about 2 annas (an anna is just over a penny) and the sale of liquor went up enormously in consequence. Precise statistics are somewhat difficult to obtain, but colliery managers and others in intimate touch with the workers believe that about half their wages are spent on drink. Drunkenness is a common feature in the collieries, especially during the week-ends, but the facilities afforded for obtaining liquor (which, it must be said to the credit of the present Government of Bihar, is being actively discouraged) have not only increased the revenue from excise, but served as an attraction for aboriginal labour.

It would be possible to add further details regarding the evils of the existing system of recruitment; but having regard to the main purposes of the volume, it may be sufficient to say that corruption and exploitation are rife in every type of industry. Indeed, in what are known as "unprotected industries"—carpet manufacture, *beedi* (indigenous cigarette) making, etc.—the practice has been widespread of pledging child labour against advances of money to the parents; and even the law penalizing the practice remains largely a dead letter.

In analyzing the problem and tracing it to its roots, one comes up every time against the basic difficulties—the scarcity of employment in the rural areas, the pressure of population, social causes, such as untouchability and the appalling illiteracy and ignorance of the workers. Until the social conscience has been roused to the terrible exploitation that is going on all the time, and employers realize that drastic action is necessary if industrial efficiency is to be raised by the recruitment of better types of labour through methods which will attract such types, piece-meal reform will not be effective. Some employers, who see further than the rest, have started technical and other schools for their half-timers and the children of their workers, and restrict recruitment as far as possible to these. The experiment wherever it has been tried has yielded uniformly good results; but such employers are an uncommon exception. The Industrial Commission, conscious of this grave defect in India's industrial structure, had suggested twenty years ago a broadening of the basis of secondary education in the country and the building up of vocational and technical schools to turn out men of the skilled foreman type for absorption in industry. But that recommendation is only now receiving serious attention at the hands of the new Provincial Governments. The evils of recruitment being left to the jobber class have also been taken up by these authorities, and it is possible that employment bureaux may be set up in some industrial centres on an experimental basis in the near future.

CHAPTER X

HOUSING

THE problem of housing is, unquestionably, one of the most important for the industrial worker. Suitable living accommodation at rents which are within the resources of the average workers would at once remove some of the gravest defects in India's industrial system. Because of the acute congestion in the cities and the high rents which the workers are compelled to pay for tenements that are really unfit for human habitation, they cannot in a large number of cases afford to have their families with them. The sex disparity in industrial areas, with its consequence of a high incidence of venereal disease, has already been described. There is all-round testimony to the direct connection between congestion in the cities and the rapid spread of tuberculosis in recent years. In the interests of the better efficiency of the worker and of safeguarding not only his health but of the population as a whole, house-building on a large scale in the cities should be regarded as an urgent necessity.

Some employers in almost every industrial centre have recognized, however inadequately, their obligations in this respect and built quarters which are rented out to the workers. But not even in regard to these can it be said that a substantial minority of the workers has been provided with housing accommodation. Apart from this consideration, the general rule laid down by employers and sometimes put into practice is that workers living in their quarters are liable to be turned out at twenty-four hours' notice on the declaration of a strike or a lock-out; and their movements, even during normal times, are carefully watched, particularly if they should show undesirable leanings towards a trade union.

One can best understand the conditions of the housing problem by detailed reference to a few of the important industrial centres in the country. Bombay is of exceptional interest in this respect, for a housing scheme was attempted on a fairly large scale shortly after the termination of the war when the textile industry entered on a boom period. A special cess was levied at the rate of a rupee per bale of cotton imported into Bombay, the proceeds of which were utilized for providing housing accommodation for the workers. The full programme was for 50,000 tenements; but actually only about a third of that number were built, most of them single-roomed, while the Bombay Improvement Trust built, in addition, about 9,000.

The majority of the workers live, however, in quarters which are known as *chawls* (blocks of flats erected for the accommodation of large numbers of families). Many of these *chawls* have tall narrow frontages and extreme depths, with the consequence that the rooms, especially those in the middle and on the ground floors, are denied both sunshine and air. Lavatory arrangements are frequently inadequate and crude, and the air is filled with an indescribable stench. As though this were not sufficient to poison the atmosphere, there is the common practice of throwing all the household rubbish and filth into the gullies. Much of this stagnates, and with the liquid sinking into the soil when the drains are in a bad condition, the net result is better imagined than described. It is to such a life that the worker and his family (if he has one) are condemned. To minimize discomfort the windows of the room opening on the gullies—the only outlets to the open—are kept practically always shut. Where the lavatories are not detached from the main building, of course nothing can keep out the stench.

A lady doctor appointed by the Government of Bombay some years ago to investigate the conditions of women workers in the City recorded her experiences in a document of vivid but depressing interest. One typical instance may be quoted: "In one room on the second floor of a *chawl*, measuring 15 feet by 12 feet, I found six families living. Six separate ovens on the floor proved this statement. On enquiry, I ascertained that the actual number of adults and children living in this room was thirty. Bamboos hung from the ceiling, over which at night clothes and sacking were flung, to partition each family allotment. Three out of six women were shortly expecting to be delivered. All the three said they would have the deliveries in Bombay. When I questioned the nurse who accompanied me as to how she would arrange for privacy in this room, I was shown a small space 4 feet by 3 feet which was usually screened off for the purpose. The atmosphere of that room at night, filled with smoke from the six ovens and other impurities, would certainly physically handicap any woman with an infant both before and after delivery. This was one of the many such rooms I saw."

Conditions in Bombay have not appreciably improved since this was written. The number of residential buildings containing one to ten tenements was about 28,000 in 1921, but had fallen to 23,000 in 1931. The average number of occupants per room in one-roomed tenements, which form 81 per cent of the total number, was just over four. Thirty-three per cent of the population was found at the time of the last census to live in rooms occupied by more than five persons at a time and 1 per cent in rooms occupied by more than twenty, the actual number in the last category being nearly 16,000. 256,000 persons lived in rooms containing six to nine persons and 80,000 in rooms occupied by ten to nineteen persons. In some wards of the city where the working classes preponderate, conditions were, of course, considerably worse.

Many of the streets in Bombay are used during nights for sleeping purposes, as, indeed, in many other cities like Madras and Calcutta, because the average floor space available for each occupant of a single-room tenement cannot be more than what could be covered by a small mat. With better housing, the night population on the pavements of Indian cities may decrease; but at present the pavement sleepers remain a practical proof of their failure to solve in a satisfactory way the problem of house accommodation for a large proportion of their population.*

* The general conclusions drawn by the Census Report are: (1) That if an average of more than two and a half persons per room were taken as an indication of overcrowding in Bombay, 96 per cent of the city's population would be considered to be overcrowded and housed so inadequately that the streets have to be used to supplement the sleeping accommodation which the

In Ahmedabad, which is rapidly developing into a formidable rival to Bombay as a centre of the textile industry, according to an enquiry conducted by the Bombay Labour Office, it was found that nearly three-fourths of working-class families live in one-roomed tenements. In Sholapur, another big textile centre in the Bombay Presidency, 33 per cent live in single rooms and 48 per cent in two rooms, though in these cases a closed-in verandah was counted as a room.

Madras is another good example of the squalor and filth in which the workers have to live. There are nearly two hundred slums in the city, in which, as the investigations of the Madras Sanitary Welfare League have shown, over 40,000 families or about a third of the city's total population live. The seriousness of the problem is accentuated by the steady and somewhat rapid growth of the population—from 527,000 in 1921 to 647,000 in 1931; and since then, of course, there has been a further increase. The Health Officer of Madras has observed regularly in his reports that the average death-rate for the city is highest in divisions inhabited by the labouring classes, and reduction could be expected only with improvement of housing conditions. Slum improvement, he declared not long ago, "has now become a most vital issue in Madras, transcending other civic problems. Unless it is tackled completely and comprehensively, the health of the city as a whole may be imperilled."

The report on the slums of Madras drawn by the Sanitary Welfare League is a document of extreme interest. At the time of investigation there were 181 slums, but new ones were springing up wherever space was available. Untouchables lived in a majority of these, the sites of which were

houses cannot provide; (2) 96 per cent of the population do not know what having a room to themselves means; (3) and only 4 per cent live in conditions which ensure reasonable privacy and domestic seclusion. The sections of the city where overcrowding in the worst forms is to be seen are Byculla with 99 per cent living in one-roomed tenements, Sewri 89 per cent, Mazagaon and Parel with 88 per cent, and Second Nagpada with 87 per cent. Out of the 32 sections of Bombay City, 13 show percentages of 80 and more of the population living in one-roomed tenements. The Census Report records two sections of Bombay in which there were 27 one-roomed tenements occupied by eight families and over in each, and in Mazagaon there were 36 such tenements.

owned in 26 cases by the Government, 25 by the Corporation of Madras, 103 by private individuals, and 27 by trusts. In slums of the first two kinds, the owner—the Government or the Corporation—is bound to provide water-taps, public latrines, and good roads. But in those owned by private individuals or trusts—and these formed the large majority—the tenant pays rent for the site and erects his own mud hut or thatched dwelling. The Corporation can neither insist on the owners providing these amenities at their cost nor afford to do so at its own.

The "*cheries*" (as the slums are called) are characterized by certain definite features. The first of these is the hopeless state of the dwelling. The huts, which are generally made of mud and thatch, or of old kerosene tins, are low hovels without any aperture for light or air, except a small doorway. The average size is 9 feet by 8 feet, though many are smaller. In some *cheries* the huts are built back to back, or are separated only by the narrowest alleys, with the result that there is overcrowding of the worst kind. In most cases the houses are so flimsy that they afford no effective shelter either in the rains or in the hot weather. A second feature is the insufficiency of the water supply; where the supply is inadequate, cleanliness is practically impossible. A third characteristic is the filthy condition of the precincts of the *cheries*. In many cases there is little or no conservancy, so that the streets are foul and unfit to walk in. Taking into account only water-taps actually within the *cheries*, or on public roads within a distance of thirty yards, one of the most startling facts the League discovered was that in 35 *cheries* of Madras, housing about 15,000 people, no municipal water supply whatever was available. Of the remaining 146, only 12 were adequately provided with water-taps. The rest, 134 in number, housing 183,000 persons, had only 460 water-taps; in other words, a third of the population obtained less than a twentieth of the Corporation's water supply. In these, there were, of course, no facilities for bathing, and the women frequently washed themselves and their clothes at the public taps, thus adding to the general untidiness and filth of the area.

In regard to latrine accommodation, 72 slums had none at all, while the other 109 had 121 latrines with about 1,200 seats. On the standard prescribed by the Factories Act it may be said that the slums should have had at least 500 latrines of 20 seats each. Some years ago a committee appointed to inquire into the causes of the high mortality in Madras wrote in the following terms:

"The lack of a sanitary conscience is not the sole cause for the indiscriminate deposition of excrement. No self-respecting person, be he *cooly* (a worker) or municipal councillor, could be blamed for refusing to use some of the latrines we saw during our inspection. It was obvious to us that the existing number of public latrines is totally inadequate, as they were being used to such an extent that it was almost impossible for the sweepers to keep them clean. Large numbers of flush-out latrines are required, and we are convinced that those would be used if they were made available."

Women residing in the slum areas have to get out of their houses an hour or two before sunrise and go to some coconut plantation or an open drain or some vacant space, because of the lack of latrine accommodation.

The drainage problem of the slums is an immense one, nearly 90 per cent of the *cheries* being on low-lying land without proper drainage. Those situated on the outskirts of the city are two or three feet below the road level, so that the drainage water can never flow away, and in the rainy season water from the roads actually flows into the slums.

In fact, after a heavy downpour water rushes from the road into many of the *cheries*, so that whole areas become swampy and the water stands knee deep. The houses themselves are so flimsy that many of them collapse, rendering homeless a number of families.

There is no street cleaning done in the slums owned by private individuals and trusts, and the lanes are covered with rotting kitchen refuse. In a majority of the slums there are no arrangements at all for lighting, while the rest are very inadequately lit. There are "markets" for provisions, and people squat in the dust with trays of cooked food and vegetables or meat exposed to dirt and flies; fruit not fit to be sold elsewhere is brought to these poor quarters and sold.*

Housing conditions in the other industrial centres are practically of the same kind. Next to Madras, in the same province, is Madura, the second city both in population and industrial importance. Mr. Gandhi, in a reply to an address from the Municipality, said:

You tell me that so far as Harijans (the untouchables) are concerned you give them equal opportunity in the matter of education and other civic amenities and privileges. I am sure, at least I hope, that you do not mean all that you have said in this paragraph. For if you really believe what you say, it means Harijans who are already labouring under a heavy handicap must eternally labour under that handicap because they are to get no more than equal opportunities. You will succeed in giving them equal opportunity only when you have removed the handicap under which they are labouring. I have come after having visited three *cheries*, and as I claim to have an eye for sanitation, I had had no difficulty in discovering that, if you will pardon me for saying so, the Municipality has done very little for its most useful servants. You will admit that it will be ludicrous to suggest that the inmates of the *cheries* have equal opportunities to live as they like with the citizens of Madura who may be living in palaces. One *cheri* I visited is surrounded by water and drains on all sides. In the rainy season, it must be a place unfit for

* The Sanitary Welfare League's conclusions are worth recording:

"There are numbers of huts harbouring more than one married couple. In the congested parts of the city some rooms accommodating whole families have no access to the outside air, except through the next room, also occupied by a family. In one such place investigators found two married couples with their children in the outer room and two in the inner room. There was no window to either room and all the cooking had to be done indoors.

"Rents are high—so high indeed that by comparison with the value of the property let out, the percentage return on the investment is the highest of any in Madras. One property in a *cheri* containing some 100 families was sold a few years back for Rs. 6,000 and was subsequently never repaired in any way. The rent collector, after deducting his pay, hands to his master in twelve months never less than Rs. 2,100, a return of 35 per cent on the investment. Small exploiters are even more extortionate. One property of 12 huts investigated, for example, cost Rs. 120 to build. It was let out to 12 families and brought in an annual rent of Rs. 216 after payment of ground rent—or more than the value of the property."

human habitation. Another thing is, it is below the road-level and all those places are flooded during rains. The cottages in all the three *cheries* are built anyhow. There is no lay-out of the streets or lanes and cottages in many places have no vents worth the name. In all cases without exception they are so low that you cannot enter in and get out without bending double. And in all cases, the upkeep of the place is certainly not even to the minimum sanitary standard. It gives me comfort that you have resolved to construct model *cheries* with lighting and water facilities. May I suggest to you that in all such matters time is of essence? I wish that in giving effect to this resolution of yours you have a rigid fixed time limit within which you would demolish the present cottages and get these poor people a chance of living somewhat like you and me.

In Cawnpore, which is to-day the most important centre of industry in Northern India with a population which has risen from 219,000 to nearly 300,000 in the last six years, conditions are not different. A small number of the workers have quarters provided for them by the employers. But the rest live in slums called *ahatas* belonging to private land-holders; there are about two hundred of these in the city with huts most of which are unfit for human habitation. A room at the back, with a verandah which can be screened off to serve as an extra room, is the usual accommodation. The size of the room generally is 10 feet by 8 feet (height 10 feet) and of the verandah 8 feet by 6 feet. The only outlet for light and ventilation is the main door. In the quarters built by the employers, which are mostly one-roomed tenements, the standard size is 12 feet by 10 feet; the rents vary from Rs.1–2–0 to Rs.1–12–0 for small quarters, and Rs.3 to Rs.3–8–0 for the large ones. The conditions of the *ahatas* are shocking, with the floor below the ground level and a bad odour permeating the entire area; and they become pronouncedly worse after the rainy season. Infant mortality in Cawnpore, especially in the working-class areas, often exceeds 400 per 1,000 births. Tuberculosis is widely prevalent in the *ahatas* because, owing to paucity of living quarters, it is common for two, three, or even four families to share a single room, and also to shelter adult relations

A typical workers' "lines," anywhere in India. The roofs are of corrugated iron sheets

The inside of a worker's quarters

One way of solving the housing problem in the industrial areas

family belongings

of either sex.* The trouble in Cawnpore, as in many other municipalities in India, is that slum-owners who get a very handsome return from their properties (15 to 25 per cent being a common rate) dominate the municipality and make it extremely difficult, if not impossible, for any programme of reform to be put through. There is an Improvement Trust in the city which has done good work in its own way. So far as the slums are concerned, it has not, as yet, had the authority to declare them unfit for human habitation, though it claims that with £7,500 a year (half of which it will contribute) it "can change the face of the city."

In Calcutta and Howrah, the evils of the problem are aggravated by the fact that the factories in these two cities employ over 80 per cent of the factory population of Bengal. In the jute mills area round Calcutta, and across the Hooghly in Howrah, there are colonies built either by the employers or by the *sirdars* called *bustees*. Rents for workers' quarters vary from 12 annas to Rs.1–8–0 a month. Going through a *bustee* is without doubt one of the most unpleasant experiences one can have in an industrial centre. Slums have grown up round mills and factories in most parts of India; but nothing can equal, for squalor and filth and stench, the *bustees* in Howrah and the suburbs north of Calcutta. The mills have built, no doubt, a certain number of "lines" as they are called for their employees—over 40,000 to accommodate about three times that number of workers. These quarters, which are usually 10 feet by 8 feet, are far better than the private *bustees*. They are all of the familiar type, a single room with a verandah in front for cooking and washing. Between many of these rows of quarters the intervening space is bricked and there are proper drains. In some of the improved types there are even windows and also roof ventilation, with septic tank latrines to solve the problem of conservancy and a fairly good supply of water.

But the great majority of the workers in the jute mills are condemned to live in private *bustees*. Under the Bengal Municipalities Act the duty of improving the slum areas is

* According to the Census Report, 62 per cent of the families in Cawnpore and 50 per cent in Lucknow live in one-room tenements.

cast on the owners who make very handsome incomes from the poor occupants. But vested interests see to it that these powers under the Act are never brought into operation. It would be impossible to describe the conditions of these *bustees*—"filthy, disease-ridden hovels," as they have been called, with no windows, chimneys, or fireplaces, and the doorways so low that one has to bend almost on one's knees in order to enter. There is neither light nor water supply and, of course, no sanitary arrangements. Access to groups of *bustees* is usually along a narrow tunnel of filth, breeding almost throughout the year, but particularly during the rains, myriads of mosquitoes and flies. At one time, in fact for several years after the war, the jute mills industry was in a condition of extraordinary prosperity and 200 per cent dividends were not uncommon in some years. During the depression output had to be restricted by voluntary schemes which have, however, failed to prove effective. The dividends, therefore, are no longer there—at any rate not on that colossal scale—but otherwise the *bustees* are precisely as they were ten or fifteen years ago.

Conditions in certain parts of Howrah, which is the second biggest municipality in Bengal, are even worse than in the northern suburbs of Calcutta. Land being extremely valuable has been built on to the last available foot. The lanes on either side of which these *bustees* have been built are not more than 3 feet wide, but right through them, as in the other mill areas, run the open drains. In a small room 8 feet by 6 feet, I found nine people living; in the next, which was hardly bigger, were eleven people and two goats on the tiny mud-floored verandah. Temperance reformers are in the habit of preaching strict control over the consumption of drugs and drinks, and there is no doubt that the industrial areas in India lead in the matter of consumption. Less expenditure on these and more on essentials like food and children's education is, of course, desirable. But it is a question for the industrial psychologist whether the worker who finds himself the helpless victim of terrible environments like these, without any of the joys and the restraints of family life in the village, can stand the strain of factory work and of these vile housing conditions without the aid of artificial stimulants.

When one turns from the urban industrial centres to those of special types of labour, such as on the railways and the plantations, or in the mines, the problem, though different in its setting in respect of each type, is essentially the same. Railway administrations can acquire land for house-building schemes and have done so, to an appreciable extent, spending about £4,000,000 by 1931. Varying proportions of railway workers on the different systems are provided with quarters for which rent is charged; but there is always a complaint from the workers that the interests of the least paid (and therefore the most in need) are not properly looked after. The Labour Commission recognized that there was still a dearth of quarters on most railways and recommended increased provision as rapidly as possible. The drop in earnings, however, has had the effect of slowing down the programme very considerably. But even where some housing has been provided, little attention is paid to lighting and proper ventilation, while as the Commission observed, there is a "depressingly foreign appearance" about many of the blocks built for the subordinate staff. The fact is that such schemes are often initiated by higher officials who bring little imagination to bear upon the working out of the details. There is hardly a union of railway workers in India which has not serious complaints to make about the inadequacy or unsatisfactory nature of housing accommodation.

In the plantations, where special attention is necessary for the adequate housing of the workers since they are recruited from considerable distances and unaccustomed to the heights (plantations of tea, which is the predominant crop, ranging from 2,000 to 6,000 feet above sea-level), though improvements have been reported, conditions are not what they should be. Housing, from the very circumstances of the industry, is an obligation on the part of the employer. The single-room tenement seems to be the rule, and there is the usual complaint of inadequate space, little light and ventilation, no plinths, and hardly any facilities for bathing and washing. It is difficult for the average person to verify statements concerning housing or any other aspect of the lives of the plantation workers because of their inaccessibility. The Labour Commission was impressed with the fact and observed that it was not right that the workers should be thus isolated from the outside world. The plea that unfair use might be made of facilities to visit them by "unscrupulous agitators"—a phrase so dear to the employers in India—it met by the suggestion that such a risk would have to be faced some day or other, and recommended that steps should be taken to secure public contact with workers' dwellings on all plantations.

Housing conditions are substantially the same in the mining areas as in urban industries. In the coal fields of Bengal and Bihar, there are three classes of workers: the agriculturists who belong to villages five miles and even more from the mines in which they work, but prefer to live in their houses; the second class, consisting of workers who come from much greater distances for a portion of the year and return home for the cultivating and harvesting seasons; and the third, who are permanently settled labourers in the collieries. In the colliery areas the workers live in single-room tenements called *Dhowrahs*, generally 10 feet by 10 feet. Everything is done in these quarters, including cooking and sleeping, though cooking is done on the verandahs or in the open in the dry season. The walls are naturally black with soot. Many of the roofs, I was told by the workers, are leaky during the rains, and it is difficult in a large number of these *Dhowrahs* to find a dry spot during a heavy downpour. Electric power is easily available in many of the collieries; but it has not struck any one in authority that adequate lighting of the workers' quarters might prove a welcome feature. Moreover, there is a scarcity of accommodation in the coalfields in the busy season, and in certain collieries there is overcrowding all the year round.

At Kolar, in Mysore State, where the gold mines are situated (the deepest one being over 7,000 feet below sea-level), I saw a few years ago workers, representing more than four-fifths of the population, accommodated in huts made of bamboo matting walls with corrugated sheet roofing. The large majority of the huts were 9 feet by 9 feet; most of the huts had no arrangements for drainage, and the water soaked or stagnated in the crude, improvised drains in front. The average number of persons in a hut was about four. The discomfort, especially in the heat of the summer, under the low corrugated sheet roofs, must be acute. Through the crevices of the bamboo mat walls dust blows in from the large dumps of cyanide near the workers' quarters and settles on the floor, the clothing, the vessels, and the food of the workers and, of course, is inhaled by them. And, as is the rule elsewhere in India, a hut must be vacated by a worker as soon as his job is terminated.

An experiment in housing which deserved greater encouragement and support than it has had was conducted shortly after the termination of the war at Nagpur, an important textile centre in the Central Provinces. Overcrowding in Nagpur does not differ from that at other centres. The experiment in regard to house building, which had shown great possibilities, was made possible by the joint efforts of one of the mills, the Y.M.C.A., and the Government of the Central Provinces. A plot of land of about 200 acres in extent at a distance of two miles from the mills was selected about fifteen years ago for the purpose on a long-term lease with the Provincial Government, and the entire cost of the scheme when completed was estimated at about £200,000.

The main points in the scheme for the erection of a model village were that each house would stand on its own ground with its own latrine and water-tap, and not more than a third of the space would be built upon. The scheme was worked on the basis of advancing money to the workers to be paid back in monthly instalments spread over seven years. The rate of interest charged was extremely low, about 3 per cent for those paying instalments regularly; but this rate was liable to be increased to 4½ per cent if even one monthly payment was missed, and 6 per cent for those who were more irregular. The scheme, when fully developed, would have comprised 1,500 houses, and the village would have had its own playgrounds, market-place and public gardens, a hospital, and a workers' institute. But, unfortunately, it was abandoned at an early stage, though a few quarters still remain as a reminder of a praiseworthy effort.

That such terrible housing conditions as have been described in the preceding pages are not inevitable is proved by the artificially built industrial centre of Jamshedpur, the home of the iron and steel industry in India. Few municipalities in India can boast of such good roads, a filtered water supply, a well-equipped hospital with dispensaries conveniently situated in different parts of the city, a number of schools for boys and girls, playgrounds and parks, an up-to-date dairy farm, and electric supply at an extremely low cost to the consumer. There is a town administration responsible to the Tata Iron and Steel Company which owns the entire land on which Jamshedpur is built. The municipal services, such as education, medical relief, water supply, drainage, and lighting, are maintained by the company, and it is claimed by those in charge of the administration of the town that expenditure on these services is the highest in India in proportion to the population.

No account of Jamshedpur would be complete without a reference to the housing scheme for the workers. The company has built about 5,500 quarters, with a little garden round each house and simple but satisfactorily working lavatories. The workers are encouraged to build houses for themselves, through loans which are advanced at 3 per cent and repayable in monthly instalments. For the simplest houses a loan up to four months' salary is given, and for houses of a better type up to half or even two-thirds of the total cost of the structures. The simpler houses are, it need hardly be said, much cheaper than the other type, and in many cases the labour is supplied by the families of the workers themselves, thus reducing further the cost of erection. There are about 7,000 of these in twenty-six different sections of the city.

Another scheme which deserves mention is that for which the Labour Association of Ahmedabad is responsible.

Through its efforts a number of two-roomed tenements have been built during the last five or six years (out of the funds of the Association) and rented out to members for reasonable rents. Employers have not been slow to copy the type of quarters which have the approval of the Labour Association, with the result that the single-room tenement is gradually giving way to the improved model. The Association, because of its strength and influence, has also been successful in enlisting the support of the municipality for a town-planning scheme, with particular attention directed towards the provision of suitable housing accommodation for the large numbers of workers in the city.

The difficulty so far has been that an extremely small number of the workers have enjoyed the franchise for even municipal elections, and though there is much enthusiasm and an occasional success for a workers' candidate, the expenses of an election are heavy and often prohibitive. Moreover, the franchise is such that property-holders monopolize power in the municipal corporations, and a really democratic candidate has had little chance of getting in. As an instance of how the workers are deprived of their legitimate dues, it may be pointed out that in several municipal corporations a fairly low rent is prescribed for a vote. A very large number of workers do, in fact, pay more than the minimum; but the qualification is added that only tenants of entire houses and not sub-tenants would be allowed to vote, with the inevitable result that a great majority are thrown out of the voters' lists.

What is wanted is a vigorous Ministry of Health embarking on a bold programme of house building. Money is cheap, and such schemes would prove directly remunerative. There would be, even without this, an enormous gain to industry through the attraction of better and more stable labour; efficiency and regularity of attendance would both show marked improvement. From the time of the Industrial Commission's Report in 1918 stress has been laid on the necessity of local bodies undertaking the development and lay-out of industrial areas for housing workers. But even after the lapse of twenty years, town planning has made little headway except in one or two cities like Madras—though even there, the Act has not been utilized in any appreciable manner for housing schemes for the benefit of the workers. In some of the bigger cities, like Bombay, Calcutta, Cawnpore, there are improvement trusts, but there has been no effective co-operation between the municipalities and these trusts. Provincial Governments have had the power, under the Land Acquisition Act, to acquire land for the construction of some work likely to be of public benefit. But who could satisfy these Governments that building houses for the workers came under this definition? Slum-owners are generally men of influence. The employers, as a rule, do not take the initiative in this matter, even if they are disposed to interest themselves in the welfare of their workers. And, it must be added, any suggestion emanating from a trade unionist, however good in itself, is suspect. Whether it is for house building or the opening of a school or a dispensary, the employer is apt to think of only one aspect of the matter: how far will it strengthen the hold of the union on the workers? The greater the success of the scheme, the stronger, naturally, will be the influence of the union responsible for its progress. Therefore, they think, it must be opposed, not outwardly often, but almost always in practice.

There are, however, welcome indications that under the new Provincial Governments which came into existence in 1937, a liberal policy in regard to housing is being inaugurated in several provinces. In South India employers have agreed in centres like Madura to advance considerable sums of money to their workers free of interest, for building houses, and the proposal is before the Government to utilize the co-operative movement for the same purpose. In Cawnpore, which frequently returns the highest rate of mortality in India (a substantial number of deaths being due to "respiratory diseases"), the Provincial Government has accepted the main responsibility for solving the housing problem. These examples will doubtless be copied by other provincial authorities and leading municipal corporations in the country.

CHAPTER XI

WAGES

ANOTHER important problem worthy of consideration is the earnings of the worker. In regard to wages in India, generalizations are impossible because of the wide variations in the rates and methods of payment in different parts of the country and in the various industries. In fact, the rates vary not only between one province and another and one industry and another, but even in concerns of the same type in one industrial centre and sometimes under one management.

In the various textile mills at Coimbatore in South India, for example, where the industry has made phenomenal progress during the last decade, wages revealed variations before a Court of Inquiry in 1938 of 100 per cent in many cases. The monthly wages of blow-room scutchers ranged between Rs.9–12–0 and Rs.14 a month; of strippers between Rs.6–8–0 and Rs.15; of grinders between Rs.6–8–0 and Rs.16; of drawing tenters between Rs.7 and Rs.17; and of reelers between Rs.7 and Rs.14. These rates, it may be added, are among the lowest in the textile industry in India. In Madura, about a hundred miles away from Coimbatore, the average monthly wages for blow-room scutchers are Rs.16–7–0, for strippers Rs.21–10–0. In Madras wages, it has been ascertained, are on the whole higher than either at Coimbatore or at Madura. The reason for the low wages in Coimbatore* and Madura is practically the same as elsewhere: in the first place wages for agricultural labour have reached levels unknown before (2 annas a day in several parts of India for adult labour), and with an unlimited supply of such labour, the employers find that rates which are slightly higher than those obtaining in agriculture are sufficient to attract the workers in large numbers.

* According to the Court of Enquiry the cost of living of a working-class family in Coimbatore, as stated by the workers, ranges between Rs. 15 and 25 a month. (A rupee, which is 16 annas, is about 1s. 6d. in English money.)

In fact, in the cotton textile industry which has spread through several provinces and States wages exhibit extraordinary variations. Weavers are paid in the Central Provinces Rs.15 to Rs.18 on one loom and Rs.30 on two looms. In Cawnpore, further north, weavers get Rs.35 to Rs.40 on two looms, and where the four-looms system is being attempted, over Rs.50 a month. At Ahmedabad, where the workers are the highest paid in all India, a weaver on two looms makes Rs.45 to Rs.50 a month, if not a little more. In Bombay, wages at one time used to be higher than in Ahmedabad. But so disastrous have been the effects of the several long-drawn disputes in the textile mills during the last ten years that wages have come down very considerably. In Coimbatore, in South India, a weaver on two looms does not earn half the wages of an Ahmedabad weaver, while still further south a weaver on four looms gets no more than Rs.25 to Rs.30 a month.

The problem is not only that wage rates differ in such striking fashion as have just been indicated in the different centres of the industry: but even in places like Bombay and Ahmedabad, where the millowners have their own organizations, they have not introduced standardized rates in all the mills in order to avert unfair competition among themselves and discontent among the workers.

The weavers are the best paid workers in the industry. In other sections, spinning, for example, wages are much lower, ranging from Rs.10 or Rs.14 a month in South India to Rs.25 or Rs.30 for the same kind of work in Ahmedabad. There are differences also in regard to wage rates: payment in Ahmedabad is fortnightly, whereas in the rest of India it is by the month. In some mills, again, wages are reckoned for some kinds of work by the month or on a daily basis, while in others the same work is remunerated according to piece-rates.

On the question of wages, a point which deserves special mention is that though wages in Ahmedabad are on an average much higher than in Bombay, in many cases by as much as 25 per cent, the cost of production, whether in weaving or spinning, is lower in Ahmedabad despite the higher wage rates, than in Bombay—thus proving that low wages do not necessarily mean economy in cost of production.

The problem of standardization of wage rates, at any rate in the same industrial centre, has been discussed during the last fifteen years without much progress being achieved. It was considered by the Bombay Industrial Disputes Committee in 1922 and again by the textile Tariff Board in 1927. Much of the discontent in Bombay (as in all industries in India) is directly traceable to the absence of standard scales of wages, and the Tariff Board made a strong recommendation in favour of the adoption of such a system. Unfortunately, there is no all-India millowners' association; there is one for Bombay, another for Ahmedabad, a third in Coimbatore, etc. But it is a well-known fact that even members of the same association are divided on racial and political lines, and the element of personal jealousy is surprisingly large. Common action is thus extremely difficult, even where it is in the general interests of the industry to adopt it. The Bombay Millowners' Association prepared in 1928 a standardization scheme, but little further progress has been made with it.

The manufacture of jute is another of India's major industries, giving employment even now to nearly 300,000 workers (actually 289,000). Indeed, just before the depression set in, the industry was in an exceptionally flourishing condition and found employment for another 100,000 workers. There is one peculiarity about the jute industry in India; namely that within a distance of about sixty miles along the banks of the Hooghly, both north and south of Calcutta, are to be found practically all the jute mills in India.

This concentration in a compact area is in strong contrast to the cotton textile industry which is spread over several provinces and States, though Bombay and Ahmedabad continue to be the major centres of production, being responsible for about 60 per cent of the total production in India. The textile industry has, however, in recent years spread somewhat rapidly in South India at centres like Coimbatore and Madura, while, in the north, Cawnpore and Delhi have forged ahead and new textile mills are being erected both in the Panjab and Bengal. It is significant that several textile mills in Bombay City have had to close down during a period when new mills were being erected in other parts of India. A notable instance is that of Cawnpore where, since 1929, the increase in the production of woven cotton goods has been 140 per cent, as against an all-India increase of 47 per cent during the same period.

Another feature of the jute industry which is worthy of note is that its control and management are almost entirely European, though within the last ten or fifteen years a number of Indian mills have also come into being. Because of these two peculiarities, location in a small area round about Calcutta and control being mainly in European hands, organization among the employers has been, on the whole, easier than in other industries. The Indian Jute Mills' Association is about half a century old and counts among its numbers most of the jute mills in Bengal. This Association has attempted in the past voluntary agreements on certain points, such as short-time work and the restriction of output during periods of slackened demand. But there has been evidence of an indisputable character that these agreements have not always been kept, some mills breaking by surreptitious means agreements to which they were a party and those outside the combine refusing to accept the obligations in regard to restriction.

So far as the workers are concerned, even these inadequate efforts at common action have not been made. To take a point which would have involved little or no sacrifice, standardization of wage rates, especially among mills belonging to a single organization, should have been a simple matter.* The necessity for such reform has, indeed, been pressed upon the mills on more than one occasion. So much bitterness and strife might have been avoided in this and in other industries if the employers had seen the wisdom of resorting

* "The latest report of the Chief Inspector of Factories, Bengal, for 1936 observes that while there were no alterations of an appreciable character in the basic rates in the jute mills, adjustments of wages in a number of mills were in the direction of standardization."

to prompt collective action. But consideration of the human aspect of industry has never been a strong point in India. The weavers, who are the best paid men in the jute, as in the cotton industry, make about Rs.6 to Rs.8 a week, though in other departments wages are much lower, and a great number do not earn even Rs.3 a week. But the enormous variations in rates render any general statement impossible.

There are approximately about a quarter of a million mine workers in India, about two-thirds of whom are engaged in the coal industry. If the term were to be applied strictly to those working underground, this proportion would exceed four-fifths. Most of India's coal comes from that narrow strip of land running westwards from Raniganj, on the outskirts of Western Bengal, for almost a hundred miles, and includes the Jharia fields, though there are coalfields also in the Central Provinces and in Hyderabad State. There are, of course, other types of mining in India;* manganese, chiefly in the Central Provinces, north-east of Nagpur; mica in Hazaribagh and Gaya districts in Bihar and north of Madras; rock salt mines in the Panjab, worked by the Government of India, and the famous gold mines in Kolar district in Mysore State.

A coal committee appointed by the Government of India came to the conclusion in 1937 that though there were other causes for the deterioration of the industry, such as the general economic depression, the indifference of landlords (owning the lands leased to the collieries) to their own interests and the apathy of the Government, the industry itself was mainly responsible for its general infirmity. Prices in the Raniganj collieries, which were just over Rs.12 in 1923 per ton, stood at Rs.3–4–0 per ton in 1935, while in Jharia the prices had dropped from about Rs.9–4–0 to Rs.2–12–0 in the same period. This drop in prices the committee ascribed to the inability of the colliery owners to agree on restriction of output and minimum prices. The

* On an average the total annual output of coal in India is in the neighbourhood of 22 million tons, of iron ore 1·4 million tons, of manganese ore 0·6 million tons, of copper ore 0·4 million tons, of mica 82,000 cwt., of rock salt 152,000 tons, and of limestone a million tons.

result was (the committee observed) that production costs were reduced to a subsistence or survival level, while repairs and renewals of plants were limited to the lowest point compatible with safety and efficiency, with no adequate provision for depreciation or new development. The temptation to raise the best quality coal as cheaply as possible by risky and wasteful methods proved generally irresistible, leading to the rapid exhaustion of the limited reserves of good coal.

Not all miners work underground, nor at those tremendous depths to which gold takes them. In some of the coal mines it is still the open quarry system, though several seams of coal now being worked in the Raniganj area lie as deep as 1,500 feet underground. There are seams of coal 60 feet thick and more running for 10 or 15 miles, and several seams one underneath the other. But vast as are India's supplies of coal, they are not inexhaustible. Apart from indiscriminate methods of working the coal mines, there is the serious damage that perennial fires are inflicting on coal deposits. It is a weird sight in the colliery areas; long tongues of brilliant copper-coloured flames shoot up into the sky and light the landscape at night. They are not temporary flare-ups but have been there for years and will possibly continue for a few decades. These perennial fires constitute a real problem, for not only do they consume the coal that is our mineral wealth, but working on neighbouring seams or those underneath the one that is on fire is a matter attendant with some risk to life. There have been very big disasters in the Indian collieries during the last two years with enormous loss of life. "Risks have been taken," observed the committee, "which would not have been possible with less ignorant labour."

Mining labour in India is liable to seasonal fluctuations, and both during the cultivation and the harvesting season there is a tendency towards labour scarcity which in some instances leads to an increase of wages. In 1936 the daily wages for miners ranged between Rs.0–7–3 in Raniganj to Rs.1 in Assam; for loaders, Rs.0–6–3 in Jharia to Rs.0–15–9 in Assam; for skilled labour, Rs.0–8–9 in Raniganj to

Rs.1–1–3 in Assam; for unskilled labour, Rs.0–6–0 in Raniganj to Rs.0–13–9 in Assam. In the mica mines the daily wages were Rs.0–4–9 for miners, Rs.0–4–6 for skilled labour, and Rs.0–3–9 for unskilled labour. For women in the mica mines the lowest daily wages were Rs.0–2–9 in Madras, while on the surface it was Rs.0–2–6. In the collieries women got Rs.0–2–9 in the Panjab coalfields, and Rs.0–3–9 in Raniganj.*

In the collieries wages have gone down enormously within the last ten years. The President of the National Association of Colliery Managers spoke (in February 1937) of the "ridiculously low wages of the workers"; but since that observation was made, women workers have been prohibited from working underground, and thousands of them thrown out of work. In the old days, families worked together in the mines and managed to earn a wage sufficient to keep them above the bare subsistence-level. But the new rule which has just come into operation has seriously curtailed family earnings. The Bihar Government (within whose territory the Jherria mines are situated) is evolving a scheme for finding other employment for these women, such as handloom-weaving, rice-pounding, basket-making, etc. Some of the collieries themselves have undertaken this task with the assistance of raising contractors. But the wages paid are extremely low, 2 to 4 annas a day in many cases.

Wage-rates for the colliery workers tend to fluctuate with the prices of coal. Since 1923 prices have dropped almost to a fourth of the rates then prevalent, and wages in India are generally the first to be affected by adverse circumstances as they are the last to rise in times of prosperity. The drop in prices might have been checked, as the committee pointed out, by an agreement among the colliery owners as to output and minimum wages. But there are such sharp divisions among them that common action even in self-interest has been impossible. Moreover, much of the labour

* It may be of interest to compare the average output of coal of a miner in India with that in other countries. In 1937 it was 131 tons above and below ground as against 298 in the United Kingdom, 207 in Japan, 210 in France. 311 in Germany, and 671 in the United States of America. (Report of the Chief Inspector of Mines in India for 1937, p. 4.)

is aboriginal, from a tribe known as the *Santhals*; in some areas, land is owned by the collieries and the tenants are compelled to work in the coal mines, an undertaking to render service in the mine being a condition of holding land. What chance is there, in these circumstances, of the workers combining to assert their rights? The greater part of the coal obtained is through labour working under raising contractors who receive a fixed payment per ton, in return for which they recruit the workers for mining the coal.

The question of wages in the plantations is a complicated problem. The system is different in the different areas; there are, besides, various concessions, such as free grazing, free fuel, the supply of rice and other necessities, blankets, housing, etc., which are regarded as supplementary payments in kind. In quite a number of instances land has also been allotted to the workers for private cultivation. But there are no fixed standards either for the calculation or for the payment of wages. And the existence of the recruiting agent, who is still the main instrument of exploitation, despite legislative checks, adds greatly to the handicaps of the workers.

In the South Indian plantations wage-rates were reported some years ago to be 7 annas a day for men, 5 annas for women, and 2 annas for boys and girls. But since the onset of the economic depression and the lack of normal demand for Indian labour in Ceylon, the Malay States and Burma, these have been reduced very considerably—to 4 or 5 annas for men and less than 3 annas for women. There have been complaints that in the calculation of the weight of the plucked leaf deductions are made for the amount of moisture in the leaf on an arbitrary basis; and that these deductions are in some cases sufficient to cover the cost of transport of tea from the estates to the ports. How much scope there is for fraud in such a system may well be imagined.

In the Assam valley tea gardens (Assam and Bengal produce by far the greater bulk of the tea in India) the average monthly earnings of men workers settled in the gardens are about Rs.7–13–0 a month, of women and children about Rs.5–14–0 and Rs.4–4–0 respectively. In the Surma valley the monthly rates are lower, being Rs.5–11–0, Rs.4–2–0, and Rs.2–13–0 respectively for men, women, and children. But the average monthly earnings of other kinds of labourers on the tea gardens are Rs.4–10–0, Rs.4–5–0, and Rs.3–1–0 for men, women, and children respectively. There are, of course, the usual concessions of free housing, medical treatment, maternity benefits; and in many cases free grazing and firewood, and land for cultivation, sometimes free of rent and sometimes at concession rates. Drinking water is supplied from tanks and tube wells and substantial sums have been spent in recent years in improving the sanitary conditions of the tea gardens. Many gardens have their own hospitals and doctors and qualified visiting medical officers. But conditions in a great many are still far from being satisfactory.

If very rough generalizations may be made, on the basis of figures collected some years ago, it would be true to say that wages, on the whole, are higher in Bombay and the Panjab and seem to be lowest in Madras. From an enquiry into the wage-levels in different provinces some years ago, it was found that the proportion of those earning monthly wages of less than Rs.13 was highest in the United Provinces, Madras coming next, followed by Bihar and the Central Provinces. In the next category of those earning more than Rs.13 but less than Rs.17–8–0 per month, the Central Provinces was first, followed by the United Provinces, Madras, and Bihar. As the scales of wages increase, the Panjab and Bombay emerge more into the picture. In the highest scale, of those earning more than Rs.32–8–0 per month, Bombay was first and the Panjab second.

Accurate details regarding the wages of workers in the different industries are extremely difficult to obtain, partly because of natural difficulties, but mainly as a result of the past indifference of the Provincial Governments. It is significant that though the Royal Commission on Labour had suggested to these provincial authorities in 1930 to supplement the information given in their memoranda with enquiries into the wages prevalent in the textile and other industries, the request was largely ignored. The most notable exception is Bombay, where the Labour Office makes and publishes systematic and detailed enquiries into the wages, housing, and working conditions of the workers. It is only within the last year or two that other Provincial Governments seem to have realized the necessity of compiling statistics, and one or two (like the United Provinces and Madras Governments) are working out schemes for the establishment of statistical bureaux like the Bombay Labour Office.

With regard to the compilation of figures in India, one observation seems necessary. Statisticians may work out in theory the courses of price levels and produce on paper an admirable thesis on whether real or actual wages have risen or not. But a great deal of allowance has to be made in assessing these factors in view of the fact that the ordinary worker does not buy his requirements at wholesale or even at retail rates. Very often he buys on credit, and the prices are different when ready cash is not available; also, generally, such minute quantities are purchased that the worker gains very little by a fall in price which may seem appreciable when applied to larger quantities. Enquiring into the price of cloth purchased by women workers in a mill in Madras, we found to our surprise that in practice they were paying almost double the market rates. The reason was that without ready cash they were compelled to pay in instalments every month, and the total exceeded by far the normal selling price. Therefore, when enquiry committees make a point of the heavy fall in prices as being an argument for a cut in wages, they forget that from the standpoint of the workers the difference in price-levels manifests itself but very little in the purchase of their requirements.

CHAPTER XII

EXPENDITURE

How does a worker spend his earnings? (which no one pretends is anywhere near a living wage) is the next question which is asked of those connected with the trade union movement in India. A certain amount is of course spent on his necessities—food, clothing, and house-rent. Then there is the demand of the money-lender, which must be met under any circumstances. Drink and drugs are a big item in the budget of a great majority of the workers, and it is interesting to note that the consumption of these is largest in the industrial areas. Amusements take the form of occasional visits to cinema houses or to festivals, but comparatively few can afford them; and still fewer set aside any portion of their earnings for such things as children's education.

It is impossible for any one who has not seen the problem for himself to realize how ruthless is the money-lender's exploitation of the worker. The root of all the trouble, as explained in the chapter on recruitment, lies in the village and the precarious conditions under which the peasant ekes out his living.

It is the superfluous population in the village, economically the most backward, that migrates as a rule to the urban areas in search of work. When the villager first arrives in a city, his resources are even more limited than those of the rural cultivator. He has no inherent objection to borrowing money, if he can obtain it—on any terms—for the initial bribe and the expenses of the first six weeks or more during which he will be paid no wages by the employer. Being (in most cases) a man without anything which can be mortgaged, he signs a document the contents of which are often not known to him in return for a sum which he could probably never obtain in the village. Speaking generally, the rate of interest in a village is lower than in the industrial areas because, from the money-lender's point of view, there is comparatively greater security; whereas in the city it is often of dubious value and often completely absent.

The money-lender in the town (a Marwari or a Pathan*) has a small shop close to the industrial areas. Often, he starts life with no money of his own; but caste rules so strong in many parts of India that I was told by a Marwari money-lender in South India that he started business with borrowed capital from one of the richer members of his caste at a rate of interest which would be considered reasonable under the circumstances—not exceeding, in this case, 12 per cent per annum. He settled in an industrial area where he was a complete stranger. But a Marwari does not need to advertise the fact of his presence; his coloured turban is sufficient for the workers to realize that a pawnshop is near at hand. In the instance I am relating, the young man was able to return the full amount of his loan in three years' time and was, when I spoke to him, the owner of several houses and had built up quite a considerable amount of money-lending business on rates which went up as high as 150 per cent. Inside the shop was an extraordinary and varied collection—brass vessels, silver jewels, ear-rings, finger-rings, nose-rings, old clothes, pots, shoes, umbrellas, etc., while in the corner of the room stood an iron safe containing, presumably, articles of gold and silver. Interest is low (in a comparative sense) when jewels are mortgaged (15 to 36 per cent). The rates rise for newcomers, for persons without any property to mortgage, and generally where the risk of non-payment is great. I asked this money-lender how much he realized from his debtors. On an average he thought he would get an interest of roughly 25 per cent.

The Marwari money-lender (called the *sowcar* in many parts of India) lends very often without security, relying only on the thumb impression of the borrower and the personal security of two of his fellow-workers. The thumb impression is affixed to a pronote in a printed book and the rates of interest are from 75 to 150 per cent. In many cases these *sowcars* get ignorant borrowers, hard pressed for cash, to

* The Marwaris are Rajputs, though they have spread all over India, while the Pathan is from the North-West Frontier.

sign or affix thumb-marks to bonds for much larger amounts than are actually lent: it is a convenient and well-known device for getting round the law against usury. The books of the *sowcar* are written in his own language which the ignorant worker cannot read, and the possibilities of fraud are very great.

More recently (in the winter of 1936) I spent an interesting afternoon in the jute mills area, about twenty miles north of Calcutta, talking to a Pathan money-lender. Outside the gates of almost every mill in Northern India and Bombay one can see on wages day groups of these men, tall, formidable-looking, and armed with *lathis* (big sticks). Physical resistance is useless, for the ill-fed worker is no match for the stalwart Pathan; and failing gentler methods of persuasion, there is, of course, the *lathi* as a last resort. Two annas per rupee per month on small sums of 5 or 10 rupees and one anna on bigger amounts like Rs.50 or Rs.100 are the usual rates of interest—which mean 150 and 75 per cent in each case. It is a remarkable fact, as this money-lender said with forty years' experience of the business, how few workers evade or repudiate their obligations. Public opinion among them is effective, though a man may sometimes run away to his village or to another centre and thus escape the embarrassing attentions of his creditor. On the whole, I was told, not more than a fourth of his dues were thus lost. But against it must be reckoned the heavy rates of interest charged.

An interesting case came to my notice in a Madras mill some years ago. A worker, who had borrowed Rs.110 at the rate of 75 per cent interest, was in terrible distress. He had paid, we calculated, over Rs.500 as interest alone, without repaying any portion of the debt. Officials of the union and his fellow-workers combined to raise a substantial portion of the debt, and obtained relief for him from the money-lender on the condition that the amount was repaid by the worker to the union funds without interest at the rate of Rs.2 per month. The man (who was paying formerly about Rs.6 per month as interest alone, with no hope of redemption) gratefully accepted the proposal. All went well for two years; but suddenly one month the payment stopped, and on inquiry it was found that he had celebrated a ceremony—the coming of age of his youngest daughter—which meant feasting his relations and an expenditure of roughly Rs.50. He had got involved, in consequence, in a fresh loan, and the same old unhappy experience was to be gone through. If cases of indebtedness were investigated, it would be found that this is in many ways typical of the manner in which the workers get into debt.

In the industrial areas, apart from the Marwari and the Pathan, very frequently the *maistri* or the jobber also follows money-lending almost as a profession. In a number of instances employers and contractors are known to have lent out money to their own workers; but this is no longer possible under the Payment of Wages Act. There is also lending in kind, as when shopkeepers supply food or drink on credit; and, of course, in each instance much higher rates are charged than for cash transactions and deception is not uncommon. In fact, anyone with a little superfluous cash thinks of lending it at incredibly high rates: it may be petty clerks, the widows of deceased workers or prostitutes who add to their income by lending out small sums at rates which commonly are 150 per cent, but may rise to even 300 per cent.

Marriages, ceremonies, and funerals are responsible for a large proportion of the debts. Attempts have been made in some unions to prescribe a maximum for such expenditure, and organizers have laid stress on limiting it to ten or fifteen rupees. But again and again in the course of work one comes across instances of amazingly reckless improvidence. In a compensation case in a textile mill in Madras arising out of a fatal accident, after obtaining with considerable difficulty (which involved legal proceedings) the full amount due, Rs.450, I suggested to the widow that the money should be invested in the Post Office Savings Bank. But she pointed out that Rs.200 had already been spent, in anticipation of compensation being paid, in connection with the funeral. And this was by no means an isolated or an exceptional case.

It would be no exaggeration to say that the overwhelming majority of the workers in India are hopelessly in debt. An enquiry into the economic conditions of about eight hundred workers in the textile mills in Madras revealed the fact that all but thirteen were in debt to the extent, on an average, of about six months' wages and were paying interest at rates ranging from 18 to 150 per cent. Sickness in the family, unemployment, marriages, funerals, and lastly—a very important item—drink and drugs were all contributory factors.

So serious is the problem that in Bombay after a riot in 1929, which had all the outward appearance of being based on Hindu-Moslem differences, the Enquiry Committee found that at the bottom of much of the bitterness among the Hindu workers was undoubtedly the feeling that they were being cruelly exploited by the Pathan money-lenders. The Committee called the attention of the Bombay Provincial Banking Enquiry Committee to the problem of the Pathan money-lenders, and thus the subject of money-lending came under the scrutiny of the latter. A number of districts were visited by its members and in most of them the evidence received on the transactions of the Pathans was alarming. Information collected from the various District Magistrates and the Commissioner of Police in Bombay regarding the extent of business carried on by these people, the terms on which loans were advanced, and the methods adopted for their recovery proved that, with the exception of some areas, the Pathans were to be found in small or large numbers practically in all parts of the Bombay Presidency. Poor wage-earners such as factory workers, domestic servants, peons, low-paid clerks, aboriginal tribes, the depressed and backward classes formed their main clientele. Agriculturists as a rule did not approach this particular class of money-lender, except in a few tracts (such as parts of Gujerat).

The Pathans, it was found, advanced any amount from Re.1 to Rs.500, though Rs.5 to Rs.50 were their usual limits. The rates of interest were extremely high, 2 annas per rupee per month being very common (150 per cent), though in some cases the rate rose even to 360 per cent. Default in payment led to a levy of penal interest; but recoveries were made, on the whole, regularly and punctually. Resort to the law courts was seldom found necessary as abuse, intimidation, and other questionable means of recovery were common and very effective.

In recent years both the Central and the Provincial Governments have adopted a series of measures to deal with the problems of indebtedness. Rural indebtedness, which naturally constitutes the main problem in India, has called for legislation in practically every province, and since 1934 more than thirty measures have been placed on the statute book by the different Provincial Governments.

So far as industrial labour is concerned, the Royal Commission dealt with its particular needs from more than one point of view. In regard to the attachment of salaries and wages, the Commission recommended that the salary and wages of every workman receiving less than Rs.100 a month should be exempted entirely from the possibility of attachment. Support for this was to be found in the conclusion of the Government of India that by increasing facilities of persons for obtaining credit, indebtedness had increased among certain classes of Government and railway employees, because creditors were assured of the full authority of the Government in collecting debts from its servants. In fact, the railway administration and the post and telegraph departments definitely favoured an amendment of the existing law, under which it was possible for creditors to obtain decrees for the attachment in advance of half or less of the salaries of the debtor workers. After consulting Provincial Governments, the Government of India amended the law in 1937, exempting altogether the salaries of workers getting not more than Rs.100 a month, and in the case of servants of Governments, local bodies, and railway administrations getting more than Rs.100 a month, from any attachment of the first Rs.100 and only half of the remainder. The first provision of the new law has probably made little practical difference to ordinary workers, because their wages were never subject to attachment in advance; but the second one has certainly minimized to some extent the hardships caused by the continuous attachment of wages.

Another problem which has been before the Government of India was imprisonment for debt. It has a history going back almost by half a century; in 1886 a Debtors Bill was introduced in the old Imperial Legislative Council with the support of the Government of India for abolishing imprisonment for debt where no fraud was proved. But there was such opposition to the measure that the Bill was amended, giving, however, discretion to Courts to release debtors genuinely unable to pay. Acting on the recommendation of the Royal Commission on Labour in 1930 that relief was necessary at least in the case of industrial workers receiving wages of less than Rs.100 a month, the Government of India sought an amendment of the law, but widening its scope to the community as a whole. Under the new law, which came into force towards the end of 1936, the imprisonment of debtors is not permissible except in cases of obstructing or delaying the execution of a decree by leaving the jurisdiction of the Court, or of a dishonest transfer of property, or of proved capacity to pay from assets which are liable to attachment.

With regard to the liquidation of debts, the Commission, not satisfied with the measures proposed to protect debtors, suggested that the law should be amended as to prevent a worker from entering into a contract with a money-lender which he could not possibly fulfil except through severe and prolonged hardship. The proposal of the Commission was that a worker, on presenting an application containing a statement of his debts and assets and creditors, should be entitled to the protection of the Court, which would issue a notice to the creditors and make its award after an enquiry into the worker's assets, his probable earnings, and reasonable expenditure for his own maintenance and that of his family for a period of two years. Though no action was taken by the Government of India on these lines, at least one Provincial Government, that of the Central Provinces, passed an Act in 1936, known as the "Adjustment and Liquidation of Industrial Workers' Debt Act." This measure is applicable to workers whose wages do not exceed Rs.50 a month. Under this Act a worker whose debts exceed his assets by more than three months' wages is eligible to the protection of the law. It is open to the Court to determine the real extent of the debts after investigating the transactions and reducing usurious rates of interest. An upper limit may be set to the amount of interest payable by the provision that it shall not exceed the total amount of the debt itself; and, further, the Court may decide whether the debts so scaled down can be paid within a reasonable time. The amount of wages which a worker may be compelled to pay would vary from a third to a sixth, payments being spread over a maximum period of three years.

Another aspect of indebtedness to which reference has already been made, namely intimidation and molestation by the money-lenders, has also been dealt with so far by two provinces, Bengal and the Central Provinces. The Bengal Act is applicable to Calcutta and three districts in its neighbourhood, which practically constitute the entire industrial area of the province. According to this measure, loitering near any factory, mine, dock, or railway station for the purpose of recovering any debt from a worker is punishable with imprisonment up to a maximum of six months. The Central Provinces law is of the same character but much wider in scope, in that it penalizes not only loitering but intimidation, molestation, obstruction, and even the persistent following of a debtor to his residence or place of work. It is possible that other Provincial Governments may follow the example of these. In fact, the United Provinces Government has already committed itself to the principle of a measure embodying the provisions of the one in force in the Central Provinces.

There have been other suggestions for dealing with this evil which is so widespread in the country. The special officer appointed to enquire into the problems of the workers in the gold fields of Kolar (in Mysore) suggested that the services of the Marwari money-lender should be utilized, but that his powers should be curtailed by the issue of a licence for money-lending on certain conditions: such as limitation of the rate of interest to 30 per cent, regularizing the accounts in a language with which the worker was familiar and the registration of all bonds and promissory notes before an officer. And in return, it was suggested, the recovery of amounts should be by deductions from wages or salaries.

How much indebtedness saps the vitality of the worker only those in contact with the industrial system of India know in all its ghastliness. The vast majority are in debt; the estimate that not less than two-thirds of the workers in the industrial areas are in that unenviable condition is, one may be certain, an understatement of the case. Many, indeed, are born in debt, and it is pathetic to see how faithfully a worker will strive to discharge a parental obligation, notwithstanding fraud on the part of the creditor. Standardization of wages, weekly payments, the wide extension of the co-operative movement, and legislation on the lines endorsed by the Labour Commission—all these will go a long way in improving the economic position of the workers. The Commission was perfectly right in analysing the situation in the following terms:

> The fatal weakness in the present system is the comparative ease with which the worker can borrow sums which he has little prospect of being able to repay. His lack of education tends to prevent him from taking long views; and the offer of cash to the extent of a hundred or two hundred rupees in exchange of a thumb-print is almost irresistible.
>
> The worker's debts are due to a large extent to the fact that the lender finds in him a profitable investment and is ready and, indeed, eager to give the worker money which is contrary to the latter's interest to accept. After weighing carefully the considerations on both sides, we are definitely of the opinion that it is in the worker's interest to reduce his attractiveness as a field for investment. In other words, efforts must be concentrated on diminishing his power of obtaining credit. We recognize the force of the argument against this conclusion. There are occasions when the worker is in grave need, and money-lenders often perform a useful function in assisting the worker in emergencies. But the widespread havoc produced by the present system of comparatively easy credit far exceeds the hardships that would

result from a reduction in the money-lender's readiness to lend. . . . Our proposals, then, are mainly directed towards making it unprofitable for the money-lender to advance to workers amounts which are beyond their power to repay.

But however much one may blame the money-lender, the terrible fact must be admitted that in existing circumstances he is, unfortunately, an indispensable institution. Legislation may render his path difficult, but it will not be beyond his resources to obtain his dues from the houses of the workers, especially when, as frequently is the case, the jobber inside the factory is also the money-lender. And whatever legislation may be adopted, so long as the worker cannot do without the assistance of the money-lender—because of the terribly low wages and the almost universal prevalence of bribery for recruitment and promotion—no real solution for the problem is possible. It is here that propaganda and education can play their part, supplemented by the growth of the co-operative movement.

Another big item in a worker's budget is expenditure on drink and drugs. After the war, Provincial Governments, because of the peculiar distribution of financial resources between the Provincial and the Central Governments under which those capable of expansion were retained by the latter, were more or less compelled to adopt a policy of encouraging the larger consumption of drink and drugs. In most provinces the revenue from excise is considerable, in Madras, Bombay, and Bihar being about a fourth of the total, and this is a most formidable obstacle in the way of the immediate enforcement of the prohibition policy of Congress Governments. Industrial centres are responsible for much of the consumption in the country, for most workers cannot do without their drink or drugs to forget the misery of city life and their terribly depressing housing conditions.

I sat in a drug shop one December afternoon two years ago in an industrial area north of Calcutta. During the mid-day interval the workers from the jute mills in the neighbourhood came in a steady stream. *Ganja* (a hemp drug) seemed more popular than opium. Little packets wrapped in paper went quickly, for 1, 2, even 4 annas —and all in cash. It seems there is a better demand for *bhang* (a mild intoxicant) in the hot weather. The trade seemed brisk, and as the vendor was friendly and willing to talk, I drew him into conversation after the customers had gone. Sixteen seers (a seer is roughly 2 lb.) of *ganja*, 6 seers of opium, and 3 seers of *bhang* were the quantities he had sold during the previous month. It struck me as a very profitable line of business, but I did not realize until I examined his accounts how much of the proceeds went to swell the revenues of the excise department of the Provincial Government. A seer of *ganja* costs just under Rs.5, but the duty is over Rs.42; a seer of opium is nearly Rs.19, on which the duty levied is Rs.72; *bhang* is very much cheaper, only 10 annas a seer, with a duty thereon of over Rs.3. But that is not all. On 16 seers of *ganja* he had paid, besides the duty, Rs.807 as licence fee; on 6 seers of opium Rs.275, and on 3 seers of *bhang* Rs.21, making a total licence fee of over Rs.1,100. Besides this, the duty on these drugs was Rs.1,120, while the actual cost was just under Rs.200. The worker thus pays really more than twelve times the actual cost price for his drugs. And while the shopkeeper's aggregate earnings amounted to something between 2,500 and 2,600 rupees in that month, his net profit was, he said, less than Rs.60. The Bengal Government gets most of the rest of the money. These are not the only drugs that the workers take, for some whom I saw were obvious addicts to cocaine; and there must be a certain number who prefer to drink.

Research into the problems of drink and drugs addiction in India, conducted by a special department of the School of Tropical Medicine in Calcutta, has revealed an extremely interesting problem, a notable feature of which is the admixture of religion with the prevalence of certain habits and practices. The use of *bhang*, for instance, is believed to have religious sanction, the drug being sacred to God; at marriages and on almost all social and ceremonial occasions in parts of northern India it is extensively used, and the consumption of the drug at religious centres like Benares and Allahabad reaches an exceptionally high level.

In large parts of India, and especially in the industrial areas of Bombay, Cawnpore, Calcutta, and Nagpur, the amount of opium consumed is serious enough to merit closer enquiry. In the Central Provinces about a fourth of the total opium consumed is given to children. The practice of giving opium to children, which is fairly widespread in some parts of the country, is, as a rule, to start with a dose of an eighth of a grain from the first month and continue it to the third or fourth year, the daily dose being gradually increased to half a grain. The main object is to lull the children to sleep while the mothers are away from home for work in the fields or in the factories. Opium is also administered to dull the pangs of hunger and as an antidote against many diseases in childhood. There has been a deep-rooted impression (now fortunately weakened by persistent propaganda) that opium is a preventive against many ailments peculiar to children. Medical investigations have shown that there is not the slightest doubt that children doped habitually with opium are stunted in their growth and have a look of emaciation, but show marked improvement as soon as the drugging is stopped. It is interesting to note that the opium habit was originally more common with the Moslems than with the Hindus, as the use of alcohol is strictly forbidden among the former. In recent years, owing to increasing economic distress and partly also because of educative propaganda, the consumption of opium has decreased appreciably, though in many industrial areas it is still regrettably high.

Opium, however, is not the only drug in common use. Mention has already been made of *bhang* and *ganja*; other drugs such as *charas* and cocaine are becoming increasingly popular. With greater investigation into the results of drug addiction, and proper treatment, there is bound to be considerable improvement in the conditions of the workers. Unfortunately, the importance of the subject is but little realized, and the valuable work of the School of Tropical Medicine at Calcutta is sadly restricted by lack of funds. Generally it may be said that the investigations of the Opium and Hemp Drug Commission, conducted at the close of the last century, have not been followed up by a detailed and systematic study of the effects of opium and hemp drugs on the masses. Regarding the latter, although the principal *ganja*-producing provinces are Bengal, Bombay, Madras, and the Central Provinces, consumption is highest in the United Provinces, Sindh, and the Panjab, due, it is believed, to climatic conditions and the existence of religious centres of pilgrimage. There is also a good deal of interesting information on the cocaine habit. But a systematic study of drug addiction is still required.

Several Provincial Governments have inaugurated within the last twelve months campaigns for prohibition in limited areas. Ahmedabad, in the Bombay Presidency, which is one of the biggest textile centres in India, is committed to total prohibition, the injunction applying even to medicated wines. In Salem District, in South India, where the campaign has been in operation since October 1937, physical exercises and amusements have been introduced in all the main subdivisions of the district. There is a movement to brighten village life by the organization of open-air dramas, songs, rural sports, and games; rural co-operative societies for promoting thrift and for the manufacture and sale of coarse sugar from the unfermented juice of the coconut palm have also been included in the programme of general uplift.

The movement is spreading to other provinces. In Assam, for example, a subdivision has been selected for experimenting with a scheme of total prohibition of drugs as well as liquors, both indigenous and foreign, particular attention being paid to opium, the consumption of which is particularly large in Assam, within the next year or two. In Orissa, a district has been selected for the closing down of all opium shops from 1939 and to prevent its smuggling into the district. Similarly in Bihar and the United Provinces certain areas have been selected for working out schemes of prohibition.

But apart from other factors, the financial limitations of the Provincial Governments are so serious that under existing conditions it would be impracticable to undertake prohibition on any large scale. For instance, Bihar, which has a population of about 32 million, has an annual revenue of less than Rs.5 crores (a crore being £750,000); and excise alone is responsible for more than a fifth of the total amount. In Bombay* the total revenue of the Government is about Rs.12 crores, of which nearly Rs.3 crores are derived from excise—the cost of introducing universal and free primary education in all parts of the province.

In the cases of the majority of the lower-paid workers, the conclusion is difficult to resist that the bulk of the income goes to the creditor as interest, to the drink or drug shop, and for ceremonies like marriages or funerals. Most of what remains of the wages is spent on food, fuel, clothes, and rent. Investigations have been made from time to time on family budgets, both officially in provinces like Bombay and by workers' organizations. While the results are certainly of interest, a word of caution is necessary in basing conclusions on them. Quite often a worker would give answers to questions relating to his family budget, not strictly in relation to facts, but rather on considerations of what would be proper. I have come across instances of workers who have given false returns even to their union. On closer examination they would admit in private: "But how can I say that I have only one meal a day?" Lurking underneath their pride is undoubtedly the feeling that a statement of the truth would be followed by embarrassing further examination. Occasionally, one gets a frank explanation from a worker as to how much he spends on drink. I asked one (a drainage worker in a municipality) who had a wage of Rs.18 a month about his consumption of liquor. He said: "I cannot do without drink, but on those rare days when I resist the temptation, my wife drags me to the toddy-shop, and between the two of us we consume 5 to 6 annas' worth a day"—or more than half his wages. Of course he borrowed

* The Premier of Bombay observed a few months ago, "The financial resources allowed to Bombay are inelastic and therefore incapable of yielding more revenue. All our schemes of rural development depend on fresh revenue being available. We have no more than two and three-quarters crores per year available for the beneficent departments of the Government—which is less than a fourth of our total budget for the year. We are committed to the policy of prohibition and therefore must expect to lose these three crores as prohibition is introduced throughout the province of Bombay in the course of the next three years."

freely, but how much he could not quite say. He paid interest, sometimes at 75 per cent, sometimes at 150 per cent; he also paid 8 annas a month as house rent. What he lived on after all these deductions he could not explain. The Madras Labour Union (a textile workers' organization) held an inquiry some years ago and examined about eight hundred family budgets. The column for drink and drugs was absolutely blank (as was the one for milk and *ghee*, except in 2 per cent of the cases), though in the vicinity of the mills there were numerous toddy, opium, and *ganja* shops, all in a prosperous condition. Unwillingness to make admissions of a certain kind is one obstacle to the collection of precise data. But often it is also incapacity, due to illiteracy and ignorance.

Subject to a margin of error which, in the circumstances, must be made on a liberal scale, investigations into the food of the workers reveal a terrible lack of both quality and quantity of food. The Bombay Labour Office, after an enquiry in 1923, came to the conclusion that in general it could be said that while industrial workers consumed the maximum amount of cereals prescribed by the Famine Code, it was less than the diet prescribed by the Bombay Prison Manual. From a report on the physique of mill-workers, in connection with certain investigations into the humidification of Indian cotton textile mills, it was found that the average weight of mill-workers was much less than of prisoners. During the big strike in the Bombay mills in 1928 the Joint Strike Committee put in the forefront of its demands a minimum wage, and urged that the wages of workers receiving less than Rs.30 a month should be brought up at least to that figure, accepting the daily diet of a prisoner as the standard. It is perhaps needless to add that the suggestion was rejected: and this was in a province where wages are comparatively high.

It is a common complaint that Indian labour is far less efficient than that in Europe, America, or Japan. I can recall the look of astonishment on the faces of the members of the International Textile Delegation which visited Madras in 1926 when a weaver from one of the mills asked in the course of discussion: "Do you regard working on two looms in Lancashire as too strenuous an occupation?" The answer was significant: "What do you eat?" said one of the delegation; and after we had gone into the question of food, he added: "You cannot expect more stamina on a diet of rice and lentils." It should not be assumed, however, that there is inherently less capacity in the Indian worker. Several managers have spoken to me appreciatively of the quickness of their workers in picking up difficult work involving the use of complicated machinery. The General Manager of the Tata Iron and Steel Works at Jamshedpur told the Industrial Commission that the substitution of Indian for European workers had not led to any deterioration in the quality of the manufacture. But, of course, it is impossible to expect the same standards for sustained work so long as housing conditions, wages, food, working conditions, and educational attainments remain what they are in India.

PART 4

WORKERS' ORGANIZATIONS

CHAPTER XIII

GROWTH OF THE MOVEMENT

SINCE 1918, when the first union was started in Madras, workers' organizations have sprung up all over India, and though it is difficult to be precise in regard to numbers, an estimate of 350,000 as the total membership of the movement would probably not be wide of the mark. In the first few years employers, confronted with a sudden growth of the movement and unable to get a measure of its strength, found it more prudent to yield to demands which were, on the whole, just—especially as resistance would have meant heavy loss at a time when industry seemed to be in an exceptionally prosperous condition. The task of organization was, naturally, easier in the big industrial centres and particularly where the workers were drawn from the same part of the country and spoke a common language. It has been almost impossible to influence the tea plantation workers because of their inaccessibility—the only effort in this direction being the propaganda among the Assam workers in 1921 which led to a disastrous strike; even among the miners the difficulties of building up unions have been extremely great. Unions have grown chiefly in the jute and textile industries, on the railways, and among transport workers in general.

Federations of unions also began fairly early to come into existence. In 1920, in Madras, which led the way, a Central Labour Board was inaugurated, committed to the definite objects of the establishment of new unions in the province, the creation of harmonious relations between employers and workers, the enhancement of wages, and the improvement of the status of the workers. The all-India Trades Union Congress came into existence later in this year, one of the main factors which hastened the birth of the all-India body being the requirement of the International Labour Conference at Geneva that the workers' delegation should be representative of the largest organization in the country. The Congress (which is not to be confused with the Indian National Congress) evolved, after a few years of a somewhat nebulous existence, a definite constitution for itself in Bombay in 1924. In general, it may be said that the constitution followed that of the British Trades Union Congress. It laid down for itself as its objects the co-ordination of activities of all labour organizations in all the trades and in all the provinces in India and the furtherance of the interests of Indian labour in matters economic, social, and political. The Congress also expressed its willingness to co-operate and federate with organizations of labour with similar objects in other parts of the world. An Executive Council, consisting of a chairman and other office-bearers and ten other members, was elected at the annual session. Affiliation of unions was conditional upon the acceptance of the rules and constitution of the Congress and payment of annual fees varying from Rs.10 in the case of small unions to Rs.50 in the case of the bigger unions. Autonomy to individual unions affiliated to the all-India Congress was, of course, conceded, but financial support from the Congress in a strike was contingent upon previous permission for its declaration from the Executive Council. It should be added, however, that this proviso was not strictly enforced in a number of cases. Provincial committees of the Congress were to be established in some of the provinces to work under the general guidance of the Executive Council and, in fact, four such committees were established to carry out the objects of the all-India movement.

A source of weakness in the constitution and the work of the Congress was that its executive consisted, as was inevitable in the circumstances, practically entirely of outsiders. Also, there was no possibility of scrutinizing the claims put forward by individual unions as to their strength, with the consequence that any organization which was willing to pay the largest amount of the affiliation fee, whatever its actual strength and membership, was in a position of greater advantage in influencing the decisions of the Congress than others who were either unwilling or unable to advance exaggerated claims. On the whole, however, it must be observed that the Congress did a great deal to focus attention on some of the real needs and problems of labour. In 1924 it sent its representatives before the Reforms Committee of the Government of India to urge greater representation of labour in the legislatures of the country through a process of election. At every annual session it passed resolutions drawing the attention of the Government to urgent reforms, the defects in the administration of existing legislation or the necessity for the introduction of new measures and, in some instances—such as the Workmen's Breach of Contract Act, the Madras Planters' Labour Act, and other reactionary measures—their abolition.

Besides the all-India Trades Union Congress, the railway unions federated themselves separately a little later into the all-India Railwaymen's Federation. It was ushered into existence in 1925 and practically all the railway unions in India were for a time affiliated to it. There is no doubt that the Railwaymen's Federation is still one of the strongest organizations in the country at present, though in recent years, as a result of prolonged strikes and a policy of large-scale retrenchment, the movement has lost much of its original strength and vitality. In recognition of its position as the most representative organization of the railway workers, the Railway Board has arranged during the last few years a meeting, at intervals of six months, with its chief representatives to discuss and, if possible, to settle outstanding questions in regard to the conditions of service of railway workers, especially on the State-managed lines.

There can be little doubt as to the gradual growth from 1924 of militant tendencies in the movement and the introduction of Communist propaganda, especially during strikes and lock-outs prolonged for weeks and months and characterized by the use of harsh and even brutal methods on the one side and consequent bitterness on the other. The first official notice taken of the Communist movement in India was at Cawnpore in 1924, when some of the Left-wing trade union workers were arrested, tried, and sentenced to various terms of imprisonment for forming a conspiracy. This, however, proved only a temporary setback to the Left wing. The fact that employers like the Bombay millowners and the agents of certain railways refused to countenance ordinary trade union organizations and methods, but showed a disposition to yield only when Communist influences had gained considerable ground among the workers, was a powerful stimulus to the growth of such tendencies.

After 1925 there were certain visitors from abroad who created contacts in some of the industrial centres with likely adherents to the creed. Owing to the extreme vigour with which some of the Provincial Governments pursued their campaign against the preaching of Communism, its champions found it expedient to seek the shelter of the trade union movement and carry on their work through the affiliated unions. They did not hesitate to get the unions over which they obtained control, especially in Bombay, registered under the Trades Union Act and sometimes to carry on negotiations with the employers. Early in 1927 they organized the Workers' and Peasants' Party in order to promote the organization of new unions and to wrest the existing ones from "reformist" control. A union known as the "Girni Kamgar Union" was started in Bombay with a membership which at one time was estimated at 54,000. At this stage it is unquestionable that they had secured a great hold on the minds of the workers in Bombay. A large sum of money was collected (about £15,000) and a strike was maintained for nearly six months in 1928.

Encouraged by this success, they extended their activities to Bengal and established a propaganda centre at Calcutta. Their influence was growing and, from their standpoint, there was reason for satisfaction in the prolonged strikes which had occurred in several parts of India during the year. They made determined attempts to capture the all-India Trades Union Congress. Beginning with the appearance of the late Mr. Saklatvala at the annual session of the Congress at Delhi in March 1927, they emerged as a distinct group, with their own tactics, programme, and ideology at the annual session of the Trades Union Congress at Cawnpore in December 1927 and at Jherria a year later.

This was also a period of intense agitation in India of a political character, brought about by the boycott of the

Simon Commission. An All Parties' Conference was held, under the chairmanship of the late Pandit Motilal Nehru, to evolve a constitution more or less acceptable to all political parties. The Communist elements secured representation in the conference and resorted to the usual tactics of lengthy speeches, sketching out the ideals and programme of their movement. Pandit Jawaharlal Nehru was at this time not only General Secretary of the National Congress, but a member of the Executive of the League against Imperialism. He had returned to India a year previously and was rapidly gaining influence as the leader of the movement in the National Congress which stood for the severance of the British connection with India.

In December 1928, at the session of the all-India Trades Union Congress at Jherria, very little work of a constructive nature was done. At the meetings of the Executive of the Congress lengthy resolutions were moved by the Communist leaders seeking to commit the Congress definitely to their programme. In the open session, which was a brief one, most of the time was taken up by rhetorical addresses and the adoption of a few characteristic resolutions. Pandit Jawaharlal Nehru, who attended the session for a few hours as a visitor, and whose connection with any union was not particularly obvious, was elected President of the Trades Union Congress for the forthcoming year.

1928 was, undoubtedly, a year of great outward manifestation on the part of the Communist group. The Government felt compelled to take note of their rising influence and adopted the usual dual policy: of repression, through what will be regarded as one of the biggest and most expensive State trials in the world, the famous "Meerut trial," and the promise, on the other hand, of reform through the appointment of the Royal Commission on Labour.

In 1929 Bombay again witnessed fresh disturbances, and an official Riots Enquiry Committee reported that conditions had been made favourable for the break-out of disorder by the inflammatory speeches delivered by some of the leaders of the Girni Kamgar Union. The strike was not so general as in the previous year, and the workers had already begun to feel disheartened by the continued absence of success. At Nagpur, at the end of the year, the all-India Trades Union Congress met under the presidentship of Pandit Jawaharlal Nehru. It was known beforehand that there would be a final trial of strength between them and the leaders of the unions working on constitutional lines. A series of resolutions was placed before the Executive Committee for adoption in the open session. These resolutions related to the boycott of the Royal Commission on Labour,* and of the annual International Labour Conference at Geneva, affiliation of the Congress to the Pan-Pacific Secretariat at San Francisco and to the Third International at Moscow, refusal to associate the Congress with the International Federation of Trade Unions, and several other resolutions the underlying implications of which were similar in character. When these resolutions were adopted by a majority in the Executive and their ratification in the open session was a foregone conclusion, the minority decided to withdraw themselves from the Congress and start a new organization under the name of the All-India Trades Union Federation.

This split, which, from the point of view of the Communists was perhaps premature—since they were anxious to claim the protection of the Trades Union Congress and did not wish to expose themselves to the full blast of the Government's repressive policy by assuming undivided control over the movement—led to interesting developments. The railway unions through their Federation decided to keep aloof both from the Congress and the new organization, while continuing their activities as a distinct group. The Trades Union Congress, with its newly elected Chairman, Mr. Subas Chandra Bose (who succeeded Pandit Nehru), did not find its work smooth or easy. There were dissensions of a personal character among its office-bearers, further aggravated by differences in views. One section was plainly for the methods recommended by the Third International at Moscow, while the other favoured the adoption of tactics dictated by Mr.

* It is interesting to note that the same suggestion was made by one or two leading Indian capitalists also.

M. N. Roy, who at that time was in India without his presence being known to the authorities. But Mr. Roy's conviction and long term of sentence in the course of the year deprived his followers of his services from behind the scenes. Moreover, during 1930 Mr. Gandhi's Civil Disobedience Movement dislocated all organized activities. And when the Trades Union Congress met in the spring of 1931 in Calcutta, it split into two sections amidst scenes of wild disorder.

In the meanwhile, efforts were being made by the office-bearers of the Railwaymen's Federation to bring about unity in the workers' movement. A draft programme was drawn up, bearing obvious marks of inspiration from Mr. Roy's creed, and placed before a Unity Conference which met in Bombay in May 1931. To this Conference representatives of the Trades Union Congress were also invited. Some of them took part and utilized the occasion for condemning the move for unity and indulged in violent denunciation, not only of those described as "reformists," but also their erstwhile colleagues who belonged to Mr. Roy's group. A sub-committee was appointed in spite of these obstructionist tactics, and the work was carried on of producing "a unity platform" acceptable to the different groups. After various efforts which modified the original draft considerably, a session was called in Madras in the late summer of 1932 at which only representatives of the Trades Union Federation and the Railwaymen's Federation were present, with a handful of those who affected certain leanings towards Communism, but who had neither the knowledge nor the general equipment for carrying on the propagandist work of the more experienced advocates of the cause who were either in prison or undergoing their trial at Meerut. The Federation provisionally formed at Nagpur was then dissolved, and a new body was brought into existence under the name of the National Trades Union Federation, claiming the adherences of the body first dissolved and of some, at any rate, of the railway unions.

A position of practical stalemate continued for some years in regard to the search for unity made by well-meaning members on both sides. The difficulty was not so much of evolving a common programme of work as of bringing the two sections into a single organic movement. The proposal was, therefore, made of constituting a Joint Labour Board representative of both wings, in order to press for certain reforms beyond the range of controversy and to facilitate common action during strikes and lock-outs. Such a Board was, in fact, constituted but failed to function. At last, after years of little appreciable progress, the National Trades Union Federation at its session in Calcutta in December 1937 decided to go forward with the proposal for amalgamation, while retaining its identity as a unit within the combined movement. The merger, which is provisional, took place at Nagpur (where, it is of interest to note, the split had occurred in December 1929) in April 1938.

The all-India Trades Union Congress, as reconstituted, represents once again all the workers' organizations in the country, with the exception of the Ahmedabad Labour Association which has always stood aloof from the all-India movement. The conditions of amalgamation are that the Trades Union Congress will not seek affiliation to any foreign organization, though affiliated unions are permitted this liberty on the condition that there is similarity of objects and methods. With regard to political questions and the declaration of strikes, it has been laid down that decisions will be conditional upon the support of a three-fourths majority, though here again individual unions are absolved from being restricted in their actions by a mandate of that character.

The Joint General Council of the new Trades Union Congress will have an equal number of representatives (44) from each section, and the Constitution of the Congress will be that of the National Trades Union Federation. The official flag of the new Trades Union Congress will continue to be red, but—the significance of the change is perhaps fully appreciated by the extreme Left-wing elements who have expressed their dissatisfaction—without the hammer and sickle.

Interesting as throwing light on the present conditions

and requirements of the Indian workers are the resolutions adopted by the National Trades Union Federation at its last annual session in 1937. One referred to "the deplorable plight of the workers on account of their extremely low wages, long hours of work, bad housing conditions, and lack of provision for sickness, old age, unemployment, and invalidity." The efforts of the Central and Provincial Governments to "improve the conditions and raise the standards of life of the workers" were described as being "negligible." Another resolution, affirming the conviction that "social ownership and control of the means of production" provide the only lasting solution for the problems of the workers, asked the Governments and Legislatures in India, nevertheless, to undertake a programme in the immediate future to include the following items:

(i) A scheme of social insurance for the workers against the risks of sickness, unemployment, invalidity and old age, and entirely under the control of public authorities; (ii) reduction of the hours of work to 48 per week, leading eventually to a 40 hours' week without reduction of wages; (iii) legislation for fixing a minimum living wage for all industries, regulated and unregulated; (iv) legislation for the protection and general improvement of the conditions of work and life of workers; (v) abolition of child labour under the age of fifteen.

In view of "the grave menace to human life in the coal-mines and the wastage of national resources, as disclosed by the report of the Coal Mining Committee," the Government of India was asked in a separate resolution to carry out the recommendations of the Committee regarding safety and prevention of wastage without any loss of time.

Regarding housing and slum clearance, the Federation referred to "the existence of repulsive slum areas in most of the industrial towns of India and their appalling conditions of overcrowding." The attention of Governments and local bodies was drawn to "the urgent necessity for liberal subsidies for the solution of the housing problem in an adequate manner." Referring to the hostility of employers, including the Government, towards the formation and growth of trade unions, the Federation expressed the view that a healthy growth of trade unionism was a primary condition for the maintenance of industrial peace and urged the Governments, both Central and Provincial, to adopt measures for the recognition of unions.

Among the other resolutions passed by the Federation, one was "a strong protest against the aggressive policy adopted by Japanese Imperialism in its wanton invasion of Chinese territory," while another demanded the full restoration of civil liberties to the people of India by the removal of restrictions on organizations and newspapers and of arbitrary bans imposed upon individuals engaged in public activities.

Special mention must be made of the Textile Labour Association at Ahmedabad, in some ways the strongest single organization of the workers in India. While most unions in India are company unions, in the sense that membership is confined to concerns under individual employers, the structure of the Labour Association is different. Within the framework of the Association, which is really a federation of unions, there are seven organizations, namely of throstle workers, frame-card-blow workers, weavers, engine mechanic operatives, jobbers and *mukadams*, winders and warpers. Each union has its own Executive Committee, while there is a Central Executive as well as an Advisory Committee; also permanent committees of representatives to supervise the different activities of the Association and a Joint Board of representatives to look after the interests of all the workers in the entire industry in Ahmedabad. Until the Payment of Wages Act came into force, the Labour Association had an arrangement with the various millowners for the deduction of the subscriptions of the members from their wages. The present membership of the Association, which is drawn from sixty mills in Ahmedabad, is in the neighbourhood of 24,000—a little over half the potential strength of the occupations in the day shift for which unions have been started.

In many respects conditions in Ahmedabad are abnormal, for though Mr. Gandhi left Ahmedabad some years ago and shifted his headquarters to a village near Wardha in the Central Provinces, his influence is still alive among both workers and employers. But it is significant that despite this factor the fear of victimization, even in Ahmedabad, is a real one. The Association, which has prominently among its benefits payment for victimization by the employers, has paid out no less than Rs.45,000 as "victimization benefits" alone during the last ten years, of which about Rs.3,400 were paid in 1936 to 95 members. The latest report of the Association observes that "not a step can be taken in the direction of extending union membership without provoking mass dismissals and large-scale victimization." Another unfavourable factor is held to be the large influx of workers into the city from outside who form a potential source of supply of blacklegs during strikes. Communist influences have also been at work in recent years in Ahmedabad, and though their hold on the workers is not appreciable, their propaganda has certainly discouraged the growth of the Association.

It is interesting to note the methods of the Association in protecting the interests of the workers. It took up during 1936 nearly 3,800 individual complaints, of which roughly half were settled satisfactorily in favour of the workers. The great majority of the complaints related to unjust penalties and unfair treatment, while a large number of the remainder arose out of an improper refusal to engage workers on their return after leave of sickness. There were, also, a certain number of cases of assaults on the workers. Though the Association makes special efforts to put down bribery, only thirty-seven cases were brought to its notice; but, as the report says, "they are only a few surface indications of the large volume of corruption which is rampant in the industry and which means to a worker terrible harassment and a heavy tax on his paltry income." Of wrongful dismissals, which is everywhere a potent cause of friction and misunderstanding, there were 570 cases during the year. Among other complaints were reductions of wage rates in contravention of agreements and difficulties in connection with the payment of maternity benefits. The Association provides legal aid to members, and there were 25 suits filed against employers for the recovery of unpaid wages. Nearly 200 cases of workmen's compensation were filed on behalf of the members, the total amount of compensation awarded being nearly Rs.30,000. In the hospital which (with a special maternity ward attached to it) is maintained out of the funds of the Association, over 700 patients were admitted for indoor treatment and about 50,000 as ordinary cases, while in the special maternity ward 56 cases were treated during the year. The Association spent on educational work Rs.41,000 on 32 schools imparting education to over 1,600 boys and girls. It runs (also from its own funds) four social centres in the city, maintains reading-rooms and libraries and physical culture centres, and has under contemplation the extension of its benefit scheme to cover unemployment.

Admirable as all this work is—a record unequalled by any other union in India—there has been a suspicion among the workers elsewhere that the Labour Association was not a genuine organization of the workers, but really a vigorous welfare centre. Mr. Gandhi has always been strong in his emphasis on arbitration and conciliation for the settlement of differences and, on the whole, Ahmedabad has been comparatively free from major strikes (excepting the general strike in 1924). The suspicion which had gathered round the Labour Association is, I am convinced, wholly unjust, based as it was on many grounds: its aloofness from unions and organizations in other parts of India, the collection of subscriptions through the employers, the deprecation of strikes except as a last resort, and the insistence on peace and non-violence. There are indications that some of Mr. Gandhi's immediate followers who accept him not only as their political leader but as a spiritual guide, valuing his moral teachings even more than his political judgment, will endeavour to start a workers' movement in other parts of India on the lines of the Ahmedabad Labour Association and pursuing the same methods and principles.

A feature of trade unionism in India which deserves mention has been the development of international contacts. Indian labour has undoubtedly gained considerably during the last fifteen years from the visits paid, first by an International Textile Delegation in the winter of 1926, followed next year by two representatives of the British Trades Union Congress. Both these delegations, after going round India, produced detailed and instructive reports on the conditions of the workers. There is no doubt that the visits of these delegations have done much to rouse the intelligent and active interest of workers' organizations in Europe in the terrible conditions of the Indian workers. Apart from these visits, it must also be stated that during strikes and industrial disputes, the British Trades Union Congress, the International Federation of Trades Unions, and sometimes also the Third International at Moscow have sent monetary contributions for the relief of the workers. In fact, it would be accurate to say that Indian workers, when involved in strikes, more readily look abroad for assistance than to fellow workers in the country. There is nothing surprising in this, because unions in India, even those which have been in existence for some years and claim large membership, have very small reserve funds, which would barely suffice even for a few days' relief to workers involved in a dispute.

But it is not only with European workers that Indian trade unionists have established contacts. For at least ten years delegates to the International Labour Conferences at Geneva have been demanding an Asiatic Labour Conference, in an Eastern setting, to deal with the problems peculiar mainly to Asiatic workers. Despite all that Indian workers owe to Geneva—and it is a great deal—the feeling has grown that both in the choice of problems for the agenda of the conferences at Geneva and in the methods of approach, the outlook is predominantly European. An Asiatic Labour Conference under the auspices of Geneva has yet to take place. But the workers of India, Ceylon, and Japan have made a modest beginning with such a conference of their own. Two sessions have been held, one in Colombo in 1935 and the second at Tokio in 1937. India will be the venue of the next session, and though attendance at these sessions has been small, the importance of bringing representatives of workers from different Asiatic countries must grow with each session.

CHAPTER XIV

DIFFICULTIES OF FORMING UNIONS

It may be of interest to refer in some detail to the manner and circumstances in which a trade union is generally formed in India. The decision to form a union is frequently taken before or even during a strike. Outside assistance of someone who is known to have had experience of trade unionism is sought by telegram. Rules and constitutions offer little difficulty, because they are copied practically wholesale from an older union. Since the passage of the Trades Union Act in 1926, registration is possible and, generally speaking, regarded as a desirable feature by the workers. The rules for registration are that seven members should sign a form and submit it with a copy of the constitution of the union to the Registrar of Trade Unions in the province, with a small fee. Inquiries are then held (often through the police) as to the bona fides of the application and, provided the rules and constitution of the union are such as to be in accordance with the Act, a certificate is issued. Half the Executive Committee may consist of outsiders, though in practice the proportion in most unions is much less. The Royal Commission had recommended its reduction to a third, so as to encourage a larger number of actual workers to gain experience of administering union affairs and ultimately of assuming responsibility. It does not, however, follow that employers would deal with even registered unions, and even the less unsympathetic among them impose further restrictions before granting recognition to a union.

It is wrong to say that outsiders do not encourage workers to take an active part in the union affairs. The difficulties are, in the first place, that it is rare to find, except on the railways, a worker who has had sufficient general education to enable him to guide the union with tact, prudence, and wisdom. Apart from this difficulty, it is demanding too much of human nature to expect that a mill manager in India or the head of a factory would tolerate for long one of his own workers being the secretary or some other responsible official in a trade union, listen to his representations, conduct negotiations with him, not only in normal times but even during strikes or lock-outs. One of two things is bound to happen under such circumstances sooner or later: if the worker be a conscientious and able individual, he finds himself discharged—for insolence, insubordination, inefficiency, or some other alleged cause. If, however, he is accommodating by temperament, he gradually loses the confidence of his fellow workers and resigns his position in the union—to improve his prospects inside the factory. Both these experiences are common in trade unions in practically every part of India.

A union will levy a subscription, as a rule, of one or two annas a month or a day's wage per year. The money is collected either in the office of the union or through specially selected members. The work of collection involves difficulties and risks; sometimes a worker who is collecting the subscriptions may not be prompt in handing over the amount to the union, and perhaps not all of it will reach the treasurer. Sometimes, if the subscription is collected near the mill gates or even occasionally inside the factory, employers are not slow to take disciplinary action in the hope that workers will be discouraged from joining the unions. In one or two notable instances, however, as at Ahmedabad and among the iron and steel workers at Jamshedpur, the practice was (until the enforcement of the Payment of Wages Act about a year ago) for the employer himself to deduct the amount of subscription from the wages of the workers and hand over the amount, sometimes a fairly large sum of money, to the officials of the union. But, as a rule, this method of collection is not acceptable either to the employers or to the unions. The employer regards it as outside his legitimate activities and sees no reason why he should encourage the growth of unions by offering such facilities. On the side of the union it is felt that to leave the collection of subscriptions to the employer is to place itself in a position of utter dependence on him and therefore to lose its freedom of action. A registered union has to keep careful accounts, have them audited annually, and explain any irregularities to the satisfaction of the Registrar. Recently, however, effect was given to a proposal for the free auditing of union funds. The consequence of this is that the unions are spared the expense of an auditor's fee; but on the other hand it enables an independent and official authority to assess the real strength of a union by a scrutiny of the subscriptions paid to it.

Some unions—not a large number—have adopted benefits such as death benefits, maternity relief, etc., for members who regularly pay their subscriptions. Death benefits amount to Rs.20—a greatly appreciated form of assistance for expenses of the funeral. Women members obtain in such unions (in provinces which have not adopted legislation on this subject) maternity relief to the extent of half the normal wages for some weeks before and after confinement. Apart from these activities, there are unions, especially registered unions, which undertake workmen's compensation cases free or practically free of charge, and also give free legal assistance in cases arising out of the unemployment of their members.

But the difficulties in building up a union are enormous. To inculcate the principles of trade unionism into the workers, the vast majority of whom are illiterate, is by no means an easy task, though their capacity to appreciate the advantages of collective bargaining and action is surprisingly great. Most employers are frankly hostile even to this day to unions, whether registered under the Act or not. I can recall to my mind an instance—though not the only one—in which every member of the Executive Committee of a union was dismissed; indeed, in another, every member was sent out and as membership included an overwhelming majority of the workers in the factory, it meant practically the wholesale dismissal of the entire staff and the recruitment of a new one. The Provincial Government was, of course, informed, but took no action. Other employers are more diplomatic. They will deal, they declare, only with a registered union and only through their own workers and not outsiders. Then further restrictions follow: So and so—perhaps an ex-employee or a Congressman, or one who has associated himself actively in the past with the workers—must be excluded from the Executive. Again, if the union is to be recognized, it would be laid down, there should not be more than perhaps two or three outsiders; also, there should be no public criticism of the employers at the meetings of the unions, and while negotiations are in progress no public mention of any of the workers' difficulties. There will probably be other local variations of these conditions for recognition. When all have been satisfied, it is the bare truth to say that a union, in forsaking much of its freedom of action, achieves little positive result for the members.

There are also other difficulties. I have had personal experience of more than one employer offering fairly substantial sums of money to leaders of trade unions in the hope of winning them over to his side. Where these methods have failed to corrupt them, rival unions are encouraged under men with few scruples either as to money or to principles of work. Not every one of those who affects the language of Communism in India necessarily draws his inspiration or his funds from Moscow. Quite a number of them are, of course, ardent believers in the creed and worthy of respect, even if the wisdom of their methods be open to question, for their earnestness and self-sacrificing zeal. But denunciation of the capitalist system and British Imperialism is the stock-in-trade of a great many besides the Communist. Some are good "baits" put forward by the police to trap genuine votaries of the revolutionary movement and can be distinguished by the almost wild terms in which they condemn the established order and yet seem to enjoy a strange immunity from prosecution. Others again are subsidized by the employers, who think it is good policy to prevent sound trade unions from being built up. For years I was kept out of an important textile centre by men who treated my "moderation" and "reformism" with contempt, but never themselves made any efforts to improve the wages or living conditions of the workers.

It is not surprising, in view of the formidable obstacles in the way of the movement, that there are so few unions in

India. According to the latest available figures, in 1935–36 there were only 205 registered unions in British India with a total membership of 268,000. The average annual income of a union was roughly Rs.2,600, or Rs.2 per member. Bengal had 59 unions with 81,000 members, Bombay was second with 50 unions, having a membership of 52,000, Madras third with 25 unions and 22,000 members, while only 22 unions in the Panjab had a membership of 64,000; but of these, two unions had a membership of 59,000, but an annual income of less than Rs.6,000. Several unions had either deficits or no balances to show in their audited accounts. From the standpoint of industries, the railway unions, which numbered 50, had an aggregate membership of 150,000, 26 textile unions had a membership of 27,000, and 8 seamen's unions had practically the same strength as the textile unions.

According to the latest report of the National Trades Union Federation there were 63 affiliated unions with a total membership of 151,000 at the time of its last session in 1937. Including the figures of membership of the Ahmedabad Labour Association and of the all-India Trades Union Congress, and making allowance for unregistered unions, it is doubtful if the total number of workers organized under the different movements would exceed 350,000. There are a few unions in some of the Indian States like Travancore, Cochin, Baroda, Mysore, and Hyderabad. Railway workers in the two last-named States have their own unions affiliated to the all-India Railwaymen's Federation, but the difficulties of organization in the States are on the whole even greater than in British India. If trade unions have been suspect in British India, they are not more respectable in the States. Mysore, for instance, "a model State," as it has been called, for its comparatively enlightened administration, has very stringent regulations to prevent "agitators," as organizers of unions are often described in India, from making contacts with the workers in the Kolar gold fields.

With the inauguration of the new Constitution, on account of the extended franchise and the comparatively larger number of seats in the various Legislatures for labour (some of which are open to contest by representatives of registered trade unions), quite a number of individuals who were not noted in the past for any active interest in the welfare of the workers have suddenly become keen partisans. There are even employers who are exploring possibilities in this direction.

So far, whatever other difficulties there might have been in the path of the trade unions, it could be said that the movement was on the whole free from dissensions based on caste, creed, and religion. No doubt there have been occasions on which employers, anxious to break up the solidarity of the workers, have introduced such complications. In order to smash a strike an employer may recruit untouchable labour. At least in one instance I know that by these means it was possible to create difficulties between the Hindu workers and the untouchable blacklegs. Sometimes the fact that money-lenders round a factory happen to be Moslems has led to Hindu-Moslem friction, blazing out into a communal riot. Nevertheless, in normal times unions have kept singularly free from these artificial distinctions.

One cannot be sure, however, that in the future that healthy tone will continue to prevail. The extension of the franchise, based on the recommendations of Lord Lothian's Committee, has one supreme drawback, namely that it divides such workers as have been granted the vote, not on an economic basis but on grounds of caste, religion, and creed. Hindu, Moslem, Christian, and untouchable workers must vote in their several water-tight compartments, not for the candidates of their own choice but for those who share with them the accident of a common religion or faith. There can be no more mischievous device than this for the aggravation of an evil which has already wrought considerable havoc in Indian public life.

Spying, of course, is a common practice in India. The police keep a vigilant system of espionage in order to watch all trade union activities.* Their representatives are in-

* It must be said to the credit of the Provincial Governments under the control of the Indian National Congress that since they assumed office in July 1937 they have discouraged this practice.

variably present at workers' meetings, and somehow manage to get detailed accounts, not only of their public gatherings but even of committee meetings. The correspondence of the active leaders of the movement is subjected to censorship, though this would be vigorously denied by the authorities. Their movements are watched and reported with minute care, especially during periods of political or industrial unrest. I was astonished, during a big textile workers' strike in South India some years ago, to be told by the Chief of the Police of the district: "I am more concerned with what you say to the men in your small private meetings than with your public utterances"; and I discovered that he knew, within less than an hour or two, practically everything that had transpired at gatherings at which not more than five or six "trusted" men were present. It is impossible to describe the strength and influence of the police, especially in the smaller towns of India. In the big cities, on account of the existence of a daily Press and a fairly active public opinion, the police are, on the whole, careful to act with restraint—at any rate in normal times. But in a small and out-of-the-way place, where perhaps there is a single factory in an area of hundreds of square miles and the workers are more backward in their outlook than in the city, I have known at union meetings the Inspector of Police, the sub-Inspector, and a few constables, all in their uniforms, making their presence felt by occupying prominent places on the platform. The employer would on occasions be obliging enough to allow the use of the firm's motor car or van for the purpose of conveying the police to and from the police station.

For an ordinary individual to offer hospitality to an organizer of unions in such a place is to take considerable risks. A hint to desist is the first symptom of police displeasure. If it is ignored, there is always the danger of arrest on some pretext or other, especially in times when political feeling runs high and special measures have to be taken. These are not mere possibilities. I write from personal experience. At one small place whither I had gone on the invitation of the workers (then on strike) the owner of a dilapidated cottage in which I had been accommodated whispered to me within a few hours of my arrival that the sub-Inspector of Police did not appreciate his action and implored me to move out. The verandah of a Hindu temple was then converted into a temporary abode; but my difficulties did not cease. This time it was the turn of a person who gave me food to receive the warning. He had peremptory instructions to stop it—otherwise, he was told, there would be "trouble." That night I left the village.

Complaint in such cases, as I have discovered from experience, is worse than useless. After months of delay one gets from the higher authorities a pompous reply to any complaint somewhat on the following lines: "After careful inquiry into your allegations it has been proved to our satisfaction that there is no basis for your complaint that the police (of the place mentioned) had exceeded their powers. In fact, they have now in their possession a document, signed by the very persons you mention in your complaint, that there was no threat of any sort conveyed to them, or any pressure put upon them to act in the manner you suggest. In these circumstances the Government feels that no further action is called for."

One learns after a time to regard these constant pinpricks as part of the game. It has seldom struck the officials in the districts, whether British or Indian, to regard the needs of the workers as human problems. After all, when they are on tour it is on occasions convenient to accept the hospitality of the manager of a mill. Especially in a small town, camping in a tent, with all the worries of obtaining supplies, is far from pleasant. It is much easier to stay with the manager of the local mill in his neat electrically-lit villa, and to use his car. From the point of view of the manager it is certainly useful to enlist the friendly sympathy of the local officials. Should trouble arise with the workers, there is little difficulty in having a report sent to the headquarters of the province on familiar lines: how good the wages are in comparison with those in the neighbourhood (especially in the fields), how considerate the manager is, and how all the "mischief" is due to the misplaced zeal of a certain agitator. The settlement of a trade dispute is generally left to the police to handle, and on their reports, obtained through their plain-clothes agents, decisions are taken.

Spying, however, is not the monopoly of the police. Many employers have their own arrangements for obtaining information regularly as well as through special informers; and some are enterprising enough to have their stenotypist sit with the representatives of the police at workers' meetings to take down speeches. In a very large number of instances it is the *maistri*, *sirdar*, or jobber who supplies the information. Conditions are, of course, changing rapidly in India, but for several years the workers were afraid to hold their meetings until after sunset so as to avoid being seen by the employers' agents.

It may be useful, as illustrative of the difficulties in India, to refer in some detail to the efforts made in recent years towards the organization of the workers in a big textile centre in South India, whither the industry has shown definite signs of shifting on account of certain favourable factors, such as the abundance of exceptionally cheap labour and proximity to the cotton-growing areas.

There was, during the period of unrest following the close of the war, a strike among these workers which led to the imprisonment of its chief office-bearer and the complete extinction of the union. Efforts were made several years later (at the end of 1929) to revive the union and spread the movement to other mills in the neighbouring districts. Wages in many departments were less than half of those prevalent in Bombay and some of the bigger centres. Early in 1930 the workers in what is now perhaps one of the biggest spinning mills in India struck work after a meeting of theirs had been addressed by a colleague of mine. No definite steps had been taken to start a union, but a comparison of the rates of wages in the different mills in India proved sufficient incentive for the declaration of a strike which lasted ten weeks and finally ended in the unconditional return of the workers. At a very early stage of the dispute they requested an official known as the Labour Commissioner to visit the area, intervene in the dispute, and bring about, if possible, a settlement. But he declined the invitation on the ground that the employers had not sought his help, nor had he instructions to intervene unless the invitation came from both sides. At a later stage the strikers applied to the Government for the appointment of a Court of Enquiry under the Trades Disputes Act which had been passed in the previous year. It was then found that, although the Act had been on the statute book for nearly nine months, the rules under which action could be taken were not ready! But the Government had no hesitation in rejecting the application as not being technically correct. The official reply, however, considerately added that even if no objection were possible for a technical reason, there was no intention of taking any action in the manner suggested by the workers. About a week later, when the Royal Commission visited Madras, the representative of the Government, faced with his own reply, pleaded that another application was likely to be considered on its merits. This was, of course, intended merely to tide over the embarrassment of further questioning on the part of the Commission—since no action was ever taken and the workers were starved into submission.

A sub-committee of the Royal Commission had previously visited the place* and found that a prohibitory order under Section 144 of the Criminal Procedure Code (a weapon whose use is familiar to all workers in India) had been passed on the secretary of the newly started textile union preventing him from holding any meeting on the ground that it was likely to create discontent. An assurance from

* So panic-stricken were the local officials that members of the Commission were warned immediately on arrival that they were "sitting on the edge of a volcano"—in fact, that a large mob of some thousands was outside the railway station—and police escort would be necessary during their stay in the town. I went out to gauge the situation and found a large and friendly crowd who had come with garlands and music to welcome the Commission. "Do you intend to go on strike?" I asked them. "Not unless you want it," came the reply. I explained the position to them in a two minutes' speech, obtained the assurance that there would be no strike, and conveyed it to the members who were waiting for me to return. There was, of course, no strike, and the Commission dispensed with police protection, much to the disgust and annoyance of the officials.

him that the meeting was solely for the purpose of translating the questionnaire of the Commission and eliciting information from the workers to be placed before the Commission had no effect. The District Magistrate, a European official, made the admission in the course of his evidence that no action had been taken, either by the Government or by himself, to bring to the notice of the workers the fact that members of the Commission were visiting the town for their enquiry.

The union was registered under the Trades Union Act in the summer of that year. In November the secretary drew the attention of the Labour Commissioner to certain difficulties in the mills, some of which, if true, implied violation of the provisions of the Factories and the Workmen's Compensation Acts. There were other complaints also in regard to housing, low wages, absence of a tiffin shed, and heavy bribes. Payment of wages was delayed in many cases to the 20th of the following month. Some of these complaints, after inquiry, were set right. But the leading employers, a British firm of long standing (though many of these complaints did not refer to their mills), apparently determined that the union should not be allowed to function.

Trouble began in the early months of 1931. There was a short-lived strike which was settled by the intervention of some public men who had no connection with the union. The employers seemed to have decided that the union, registered though it was under the Trades Union Act, should be dissolved. A printed notice to that effect was put up and time was given to the members of the union within which to make up their minds. We found that the union had made considerable progress during the fifteen months of its existence despite opposition, and the workers seemed in no mood to yield. They had, in fact, accepted the ultimatum of the employers even before our arrival on the scene, and a lock-out had been declared involving about 9,000 workers, a substantial proportion of whom were women. Finding that there was no possibility of an immediate settlement with the employers on any just and equitable basis, we sought Government assistance. Four days after the commencement of the lock-out the Government, we were seriously told, had no official information regarding the dispute or its causes! There were, of course, two obvious ways open: one was to depute the Labour Commissioner to effect a settlement, or at least to make a report. The second course was to appoint a Court of Enquiry or a Board of Conciliation under the Trades Disputes Act. The first would have been the simpler and more expeditious method, but the Government was not anxious to intervene in the dispute, except in so far as it affected the maintenance of law and order. Requests were repeatedly made to the Government in subsequent weeks, as the strain of the dispute became more acute, to take action under the Trades Disputes Act, but without any response; and all through the burning heat of April we sat, day after day in the office of the union, watching and observing. At one stage, after the lock-out had been in progress for about three weeks, the men seemed inclined to reconsider their position, but the women would not agree. When a mediator sent by the employers appeared on the scene to test the workers' morale, he received a striking answer from the women. To his query, "What has the union done for you?" they replied, "Before the union came into existence we were not treated as human beings; now we have found our self-respect. Before the union was started we paid not less than Rs.5 to the *maistri* to get a job, or when we wanted leave before confinement. Now we pay Rs.2 or sometimes nothing at all."

The deadlock seemed complete, and finding that the Government was immovable, we approached the local municipality. A special resolution was passed authorizing the Municipal Council to appoint a sub-committee of independent persons to enquire into the dispute and bring about a settlement of the dispute. It concluded a unanimous report in the following terms:

> There remains the most important question of all, the recognition of the union by the authorities. We have been assured by the Manager that there is no foundation for the allegation that membership of the union has been penalized in the past, or will be penalized in future, though he admits that men have been

dismissed for collection of subscriptions within the Mill. It appears that every member of the Executive Committee had been dismissed within recent months. There is, further, the notice put up on the notice board of the Mill which assumes the dissolution of the union. And, quite frankly, we are convinced that the Mill authorities regard the existence of the union with the deepest disapproval.

With regard to the recognition of the union, we feel compelled to make certain observations. It is registered under the Trades Union Act. It seems to exercise an extraordinary hold on the vast majority of the workers who are its members. There have been industrial disputes in the City in previous years; but none that we can recall in which there has been demonstrated such unity by the workers and such exemplary non-violent conduct as on the present occasion. We have no doubt that the union has created a new consciousness among its members, the effect of which has been to give them a new outlook on life. It is, if we may venture to express our opinion, not the path of prudence and wisdom for an employer to ignore—much less to oppose—a movement which is recognized throughout the world as a legitimate one. So long as the present relationships last, with the labourers determined to maintain the union and the employer challenging their right, there can be no lasting settlement. We would earnestly urge the Mill authorities to reconsider their attitude and revise it in accordance with the spirit of the times.

The lock-out ended shortly after the report was made with the withdrawal of the employers' notice, though their opposition to the union was unremitting for several years and the recognition of the union only followed another lock-out of about three months' duration in the early part of 1938.

It is, unfortunately, the fact, at least the impression has been created very strongly in the minds of the workers, that employers in India, whether it be the Government or a railway or a private individual or firm, can only be made to take notice of injustice when discontent reaches danger-point and a strike is imminent.

What is true of the general relations between employers and workers is equally true of the machinery of the Government responsible for the collection of information relating to labour disputes. Throughout India, perhaps more in some provinces than in others, the settlement of labour disputes was regarded, until the inauguration of provincial autonomy a year ago, as a matter of law and order. All information in regard to a dispute was collected and conveyed by officials belonging to the police department. It is a generally accepted fact that the police, except in big centres, do not take an impartial view, either because they are under an obligation to the employer or they fear being reported by him to the higher authorities. There are instances on record of employers openly rewarding the police for their services at the end of a strike. The first notice of a strike or a lock-out from a district is sent not to the Department of Labour at the provincial headquarters but to the department in charge of law and order. It is that aspect of the labour problem which has dominated the entire official outlook in India, whether it be in regard to a single dispute or the direction of policy from the centre.

But apart from the difficulties created by the unfriendly attitude of the employers, there are others which seem inevitable in the present stage of organization. The intelligent worker, after he has had a few years' experience of trade unionism, becomes surprisingly practical in dealing with some problems. Several times in the course of my work I have been told in answer to a suggestion that perhaps a strike under certain circumstances might be desirable: "The times are bad and a strike has no chance of success." There will be general agreement among those who have worked in the Indian trade union movement that the workers' shrewdness and practical sense are much beyond what one would expect of men with little education. This is true not only in abnormal times when decisions about strikes have to be taken, but in dealing with Bills on labour legislation. I can never forget the objection raised by members of the executive of a textile union in Madras to a proposal for the complete abolition of fines in factories—for fear of more drastic punishments taking their place. As a matter of fact, the soundness of their view has been established since the Payment of Wages Act has regulated the amounts of fines that may be levied and the conditions of such levy. Employers in some centres have practically stopped fining their workers: but they compel them to take leave, without wages of course, and the period may be extended to two or three weeks.

The ignorance of a worker comes up, however, in a curious way. He expects, for the one or two annas that he pays as subscription every month, far too much from the union. It is easy enough to deal with cases of workmen's compensation or matters in which legal remedy is available. But a worker thinks that membership of a union is (or should be) an insurance against any action by the employer. It will not do for the leader of a union to suggest, even in private, that absence without leave or on false grounds or some serious omission on the part of a worker may justify disciplinary action by the employer. Few unions in India will sift complaints with meticulous care and take up only those in which they are satisfied that the worker has a genuine case; it is safer, on the whole, to act on the presumption that every complaint is good. Otherwise, there is dissatisfaction and even suspicion as to the honesty of those in charge of the union's affairs.

Another difficulty is that the worker must have something tangible periodically for his membership: a rise in wages or shorter hours of work or some legislation to improve his conditions of work. He is not convinced by the argument that in a time of depression, he should be grateful that there has not been an attack on his standards of life. "I have been a member of the union for two or three years, but what has it done for me?" is a question which one often hears from a worker. Even if he has not thought of it himself, the suggestion is made by one of the employer's agents and sticks in his mind.

Moreover, the low subscriptions make it impossible (except in some of the railway unions) for an adequate staff to be maintained. The workers do not see why the clerical staff of their unions should be paid on a higher scale than they receive, but the quality of the work turned out by men on Rs.20 or Rs.25 a month is extremely poor. Organizers of unions, and those who respond to calls for help from strikers, cannot hope for even their actual expenses to be met out of the workers' meagre funds. The task becomes intolerably irksome and heavy after a few years unless those who undertake it have means of their own and can be independent of the unions. But such men are rare.

It is not surprising perhaps that the organization of the workers has made such little headway in India considering the formidable nature of the obstacles. At the same time, those who attend union meetings are several times the number of active members, and during strikes they all act together, members and non-members. The fact is that organization has been looked upon by employers and Provincial Governments with such hostility that though in theory there is a law permitting registration of unions, no steps have been taken to bring them into existence. The Registrar of Co-operative Societies is expected to facilitate the growth of the co-operative movement; but the Registrar of Trade Unions has not similar responsibilities cast on him in his own sphere.

PART 5

INDUSTRIAL DISPUTES

CHAPTER XV

SOME MAJOR STRIKES AND LOCK-OUTS

A BRIEF reference was made in the introductory chapter to the early days of the first trade union in India which was started in Madras during the war. With the conclusion of the Armistice in 1918, fresh trouble began to arise. The employers, who were now free to turn their undivided attention to the union, declared two lock-outs in the course of a few months—the second on the ground that the manager and two of his European assistants had been assaulted inside one of the mills. Since racial and political motives were attributed to those responsible for the organization of the workers, it is relevant to point out that among the resolutions passed by the union, one expressed deep regret at the assaults and appealed to the workers to assist the police in tracing the culprit. About three weeks after the declaration of the second lock-out, the employers made a public statement expressing their willingness to meet more than half-way "a properly constituted union" of their work-people; but they objected to one "started by men who knew absolutely nothing of labour conditions in Madras or over the rest of India," and whose activities caused "untold mischief, misunderstanding, and needless suffering." The lock-out did not end for almost four weeks in spite of negotiations, and the union was compelled to start relief measures, such as the sale of cheap rice and the opening of a bank for the benefit of members who could get loans at a rate of interest not exceeding 12 per cent.

These early struggles in Madras, brief in comparison with subsequent disputes, as trials of strength, had their immediate reactions on almost every industrial centre. Conditions after the war—the unprecedentedly high prices of foodstuffs and the failure of wages to rise in proportion to prices assumed an epidemic form—aggravated economic discontent, and from 1919, for two or three years, the strikes were mainly directed towards an increase of wages and the securing of a ten hours day. It was a favourable moment for industrial labour to assert its rights. Industry was in an exceptionally flourishing condition, making phenomenal profits, and dividends of 200 per cent in industries like jute and cotton seemed almost a common event.

A feature of these early strikes was their short duration and the success which attended them. Of ninety-seven strikes concluded in Bengal (the centre of the jute industry) in the second half of 1920, two-thirds were completely successful from the standpoint of the workers. It is significant of the temper of the movement at its commencement that in March 1919, during a strike of the Madras tramwaymen, a public meeting was held with public and influential support requesting the Madras Government to devise immediate measures for the prevention of industrial disputes, the specific proposal being for the establishment of an arbitration board for the settlement of all outstanding differences.

When the first epidemic of strikes broke out between the years 1919 and 1921, some of the Provincial Governments most affected appointed committees of enquiry. In Bombay, there was the Industrial Disputes Committee in 1921 to consider the practicability of creating machinery for the prevention and early settlement of industrial disputes. The committee made several important recommendations, the most important one being that whenever there were differences which seemed irreconcilable or were likely to assume serious proportions, a Court of Enquiry was to be appointed, to be followed if necessary by an industrial board of conciliation. It made other recommendations on such points as the attitude of employers towards trade unions, the establishment of works committees, the starting of co-operative societies, housing, and general welfare work.

On the recommendations of this committee, the Bombay Government in 1924 published the draft of a Bill to provide for enquiry into and the settlement of trade disputes. But for the intervention of the Government of India, which expressed a desire to introduce all-India legislation, the Bill would probably have become law in the course of the year and thus prevented much of the industrial strife which took place in the subsequent years. It is illustrative of the long delays associated with labour legislation in India, that the Government of India's Trades Disputes Act was not placed on the statute book until 1929.

In 1921, the Madras Government also proposed to appoint a committee of enquiry with an official chairman and invested with functions similar to the Bombay enquiry committee; but, unfortunately, the newly-constituted Madras Central Labour Board declined to co-operate with the committee for political reasons, and the proposal was dropped as a result.

In Bengal, where also there were numerous strikes, the Legislative Council urged and secured the appointment of an enquiry committee. Its main recommendations were the establishment of joint works committees in industrial concerns, the constitution by the Provincial Government of a conciliation panel to deal with disputes in public utility services and the appointment, also under official auspices, of special conciliation boards in the case of private industrial disputes if both parties desired such intervention.

The Government of India, too, showed some anxiety in those early years to demonstrate to the workers its interest in their welfare. The late Lord Chelmsford (who was Viceroy at the time) said in an address to the Central Legislative Assembly in 1920: "I would earnestly impress upon employers the necessity for sympathetic consideration of the claims of labour. It has too often proved the case that employers, after a long and ruinous struggle, have been forced to concede claims that they might have allowed with honour and with profit as soon as they were presented."

Mainly as a result of the legal action taken by Messrs. Binny & Co., in Madras, against Mr. Wadia and nine associates of his on the lock-out committee in the High Court in 1920, the Government of India took steps to introduce legislation for the registration of trade unions under a special law giving them certain rights and privileges and, in particular, immunity from the application of the law of conspiracy, though actually it did not come on the statute book until 1926. A more immediate manifestation of its sympathy with the workers was the new Factories Act reducing the hours of work from twelve to ten per day, increasing the rest interval from half an hour to one hour, extending the scope of the definition of factories from establishments employing fifty persons to those employing twenty persons and empowering the Provincial Governments to go further at their option by lowering the limit to ten persons.

There is no doubt that industrial and political unrest in India tended at this juncture to mingle in one stream. India was in the throes of almost frenzied political excitement after the Amritsar tragedy, symbolized in Mr. Gandhi's first non-co-operation movement in 1920. Under his leadership thousands of students abandoned their studies and numerous lawyers, who have always formed the backbone of the Nationalist movement in India, their professional careers. Many of these drifted into the newly started trade union movement which was spreading with remarkable rapidity to all the main industrial centres. Leadership and organizing capacity were thus available to the trade unions.

Trouble started again in two of the Madras mills towards the end of 1920 and again in the summer of the following year. These two stoppages, the first big disputes in India, covered in the aggregate over eight months, the loss of working days being well over a million. It was in the course of the first dispute that the employers obtained an interim injunction from the Madras High Court, restraining the leaders of the union from interfering with their business. The second dispute, which lasted over four months, had disastrous results, including more than one serious riot, incendiarism, and some loss of life. Funds were collected for relief purposes at centres like Bombay and Ahmedabad in a substantial amount, Mr. Gandhi alone being responsible for Rs. 30,000 (about £2,300), which he sent from Ahmedabad. During 1921 there were nearly four hundred strikes all over India (a number which has never been equalled since), involving 600,000 workers and an aggregate loss of nearly seven million working days. The largest number of strikes occurred in Bengal and Bombay, the two main industrial provinces in India, Madras and the United Provinces being the other areas affected by industrial unrest, and a disastrous one in some of the Assam tea plantations.

In the three subsequent years there was, on the whole, less industrial unrest. With the fall in prices of foodstuffs and concessions already granted to the workers, either in the shape of increased wages or allowances, there was not the same urge to the use of the strike as a weapon as in the year immediately following the cessation of the war. Its effectiveness was not always apparent to the workers, for in 1922, 79 per cent of the strikes were completely unsuccessful, as against 54 per cent in the preceding year. Another factor which undoubtedly exercised a stabilizing influence on the workers' minds was the abandonment of the non-co-operation movement and the return to fairly normal political conditions. The consequence was that the number of strikes declined to 278, involving a loss of four million working days.

In 1923 the cost of living fell further and a period began of efforts by employers in more than one centre to reduce wages and to withdraw or curtail concessions like dear food allowances made in earlier years. Also, the workers put forward other difficulties, mainly exploitation by their immediate superiors through extortion, bribery and corruption, and defects, some of which were serious ones, in working conditions. The total number of strikes during the year was 213, involving 300,000 workers and a loss of five million working days, Bombay Presidency contributing more disputes than all the other provinces put together, with 109 disputes involving a loss of three million working days.

The most serious strike was at Ahmedabad (almost the only one during the last twenty years of a major character) amongst the textile workers, affecting 56 out of 61 working mills, involving nearly 45,000 workers, and a loss in working days of nearly two and a half million. Though the workers were unable to prevent a wage-cut, the compromise effected was to limit the reduction to 15⅝ per cent, against the millowners' original proposal of 20 per cent.

In fact, Bombay continued to be the centre of industrial

unrest in 1924. The millowners' decision to withhold the payment of the bonus granted in previous years was answered by the declaration of a general textile strike in the city. The Bombay Government appointed a committee under the chairmanship of Sir Norman Macleod, Chief Justice of the High Court, to consider the nature and basis of the bonus, and to declare whether the workers had "any enforceable claim, customary, legal or equitable," to its payment. The committee came to the conclusion that the conditions of the industry did not justify its payment and that the workers had no such claim as was specified in the terms of reference to the continuance of the bonus.

In 1925 industrial discontent manifested itself in renewed activity, especially among the textile workers of Bombay and the railway and jute workers in Bengal.

Another attack by the Bombay millowners on wage rates followed on the ground that the industry was passing through a period of acute depression. The Millowners' Association decided on the reduction of the dearness allowance by 20 per cent from September 1925, which in effect would have meant an average wage reduction of about 10 per cent in their earnings. Not until the announcement by the Viceroy of the suspension of the excise duty did the employers agree to defer action.

Between 1921 and 1926 there were over 1,100 strikes in India, involving nearly two million workers and causing a loss of over thirty-seven million working days. Over 500 of these took place in the cotton textile industry and nearly 150 in the jute industry. There were 59 railway strikes during the same period, though the loss in working days was even more than in the jute industry, over three and a half million.

Undoubtedly, Communist influences were beginning to emerge into the open in India. But to explain the phenomenon of the large number of strikes which took place in this period solely on that ground is to ignore the facts of the situation. The attitude of several employers (such as the millowners of Bombay and agents of railway companies) was uncompromising and hostile towards organizations which sought progress among the lines of negotiation and friendly representation, though what they would not concede to the more moderate elements they were compelled to yield in response to threats from the extremer sections.

Nor can the Governments, both Provincial and Central, escape their share of the responsibility; once the pressure of outer circumstances lessened, they became leisurely and even dilatory in their attitude towards labour. As an instance, reference may be made to the reforms committee appointed by the first Labour Government in 1924, which had strongly recommended increased representation to workers through election by properly constituted unions in place of the utterly inadequate arrangements made in the Government of India Act of 1919. But all that the workers obtained was a paltry increase in the number of nominated seats in some provinces, the position in the Central Legislature being left untouched. The consequence was that labour legislation suffered greatly for want of effective representations in both Houses at the centre. Even Government legislation backed by official strength was considerably modified in the course of its passage under capitalist opposition. A notable instance was that of the Workmen's Compensation Act which was placed on the statute book in 1923. Mr. Joshi's Maternity Benefits Bill, a private measure, was thrown out three years later by a combination of the Government with the capitalist classes.

In fact, one of the most striking features of the old Constitution was that no labour legislation had the slightest chance of success unless it had the support of the Government, and even then only in attenuated form. And outside the legislatures, it was difficult not to be driven to the conclusion that only through widespread industrial unrest could the Government be induced to move forward. Even the appointment of the Royal Commission on labour, one felt, followed years of strife and bitterness.

The years 1926 and 1927 were comparatively quiet, partly because of a slight revival in trade and partly, also, because of a realization on the part of the workers that prolonged strikes were not always helpful to their interests.

By this time several new labour measures had been placed on the statue book—a revised Factories Act, a Mines Act, the Workmen's Compensation Act, and the Trades Unions Act. The hours of work had been reduced and working conditions had undergone definite improvement. Nevertheless, industry could not claim to be above anxiety. With the grant of protection to the textile industry were coupled, by the first Tariff Board, suggestions for the more efficient management of mills and a reduction in production costs. Perhaps for the first time in India the term "rationalization" came into use in connection with industrial development. Some of the more enterprising employers in Bombay attempted to work out schemes for increasing the number of spindles and of looms per operative; but these experiments, without, from the standpoint of the workers, compensating benefits to them, necessarily produced acute discontent which broke out into strikes.

In 1928 there was a fresh wave of industrial unrest sweeping over the country. The total number of disputes was only 200, or half the number in 1921; but the loss in working days reached the record figure of thirty-one and a half million or more than the total for all the previous five years. The textile workers in Bombay, who had recovered their morale after two years of comparative rest, declared a general strike as a protest against the decision of the employers to introduce schemes of rationalization of work.

Both the extreme and the moderate sections of textile labour in Bombay formed a joint strike committee to see the fight through. This committee formulated seventeen demands, which evoked from the employers a scheme of standardized wages for all mills in Bombay city, but on a basis of reduced wages for weavers—the highest-paid class in the industry. Relief measures were organized with appreciable success, the fund totalling nearly Rs.200,000 (£15,000). The strike, which commenced in April, continued until the beginning of October, when a committee of inquiry was appointed by the Bombay Government under the chairmanship of Sir Charles Fawcett, acting Chief Justice of the Bombay High Court. This strike alone, perhaps the most serious that has yet occurred in India, was responsible for a loss of over twenty-two million working days.

The Fawcett Committee made certain recommendations with regard to the standardization of wage-rates and the fixation of the number of workers to be employed on different types of machines, and urged co-operation between the Millowners' Association and the workers' organization in order to give practical effect to the scheme. With regard to the seventeen demands put forward by the general strike committee, a fact worth noting is that the committee held a majority of the demands to be fair and reasonable.

But industrial unrest was general during the year, resulting in strikes in the iron and steel works at Jamshedpur, the East Indian and South Indian Railways, and the textile mills at Sholapur (in Bombay) and Cawnpore (in the United Provinces). The dispute in the iron and steel works in Jamshedpur was also of a prolonged character, lasting over five months and resulting in a loss of nearly two and a half million working days. The duration of the strike in the workshops of the East Indian Railway at Lilloh, a suburb of Calcutta, exceeded four months and involved a loss of about a million and a half working days. Another important strike was in some of the jute mills near Calcutta, being spread over nearly four months.

After the hectic efforts of 1928 it is not surprising that there was a considerable decline, both in the number of disputes and of working days lost, though there were in the following year 141 disputes involving a loss of twelve million working days, Bombay continuing to be the chief centre of interest.

The general strike in the Bombay textile mills lasted from April to September 1929, a notable feature of the strike being that it was the first occasion on which the conciliation provisions of the Trades Disputes Act were utilized. The court of enquiry held that the prolongation of the strike, accompanied by riots and disturbances of a widespread and serious character, was due to the uncompromising attitude of the leaders of the extremist section of the union. Another important strike during the year was in the Bengal jute mills, resulting in a loss of nearly three million working days, the cause of the strike, which lasted eleven weeks, being the decision of the employers to increase the working hours from 55 to 60 a week.

But other forces now came into operation. The split in the ranks of the all-India movement at the end of 1929 and the formation of a separate organization by the more moderate elements was one factor responsible for the comparative peace which followed. The appointment of the Royal Commission on Labour, though it was denounced by the Left-wing elements, created hopes of reform through negotiation and friendly settlement. While the enquiry was in progress, many of the leaders of the Left-wing in the workers' movement were taken into detention at Meerut on charges of conspiracy, and the trial dragged on for over four years. After the secession of the moderate elements from the main body, the All-India Trade Union Congress split into two warring factions. There were also serious political complications in India with the revival of the non-co-operation movement under the name of civil disobedience. Several thousands of men and women went to prison in 1930 and 1932, and the movement, especially on the latter occasion, was met by vigorous repression of political activities and a suspension of the ordinary procedure for the maintenance of law and order. In some parts of India the executive was disposed to draw no fine distinctions between political and trade union activities, and so long as the police succeeded in putting down organized manifestations of discontent, their methods did not worry the authorities.

The cumulative effect of all these factors, accentuated by the severe shaking of India's economic system during the depression, was to be seen in a pronounced decline in the number of disputes. Between 1930 and 1936 the number remained fairly steady in the neighbourhood of 150 a year and the loss of working days ranged between two and two and a half million; 1934, however, was an exceptional year, the number of working days lost being nearly five million; and so was the following year, though in a different sense, the number of working days lost being less than a million.

The fact is that during these years the trade union movement suffered a severe set-back, and with the deepening of the depression in economic conditions came further attacks on the standards of the workers which they were powerless to resist. Jute mills in Bengal resorted to short time for restriction of output and a number of textile mills, particularly in Bombay, were compelled even to close down. Those which continued to work adopted measures for reducing wage-rates by cutting down further the dearness allowance. Another device was to close down completely for a few months, and then to re-open as though in response to the workers' appeal on reduced wage-rates. In 1933 more than 50,000 workers in Bombay city were thrown out of employment. In these circumstances, driven by the prospects of starvation, they accepted even reduced rates as better than no employment. Encouraged by this attitude of the workers, other mills followed the example of introducing further reductions in wage-rates, and by 1934 almost every mill in Bombay had brought down wages by a substantial proportion.

The millowners in Ahmedabad attempted to copy the example of Bombay but without much success, for Mr. Gandhi, as one of the members of the permanent arbitration board, refused to countenance any proposals for wage reduction without an exhaustive enquiry. Prolonged negotiations took place, culminating in a reduction of 6¼ per cent, subject to the condition that the minimum earnings of a two-loom weaver should not go below Rs.41–4–0 for twenty-six working days.

The focus of unrest seemed to be transferred from the textile and jute industries to the railways, which were faced with a large deficit in their revenues on account of the unprecedented drop in agricultural prices and the shrinkage in trade.

In 1930 there was a strike of a major character on the G.I.P. Railway in Bombay as a protest against the unsatisfactory conditions of service, such as low wages and absence of facilities for leave. The strike was a failure so far as the workers were concerned, and ended with the discharge of several thousands who had participated in it.

As has already been pointed out, since the passage of the Trades Disputes Act in 1929, very little use had been made of its provisions for the appointment of either a court of enquiry or a board of conciliation, unless the dispute was of such a character as to lead to embarrassment if left untackled before it assumed serious proportions. The most notable instance of such action on the part of the Government of India was the appointment, in 1931, of a court of enquiry, presided over by Justice Murphy, a judge of the Bombay High Court, to enquire into certain matters connected with the policy of retrenchment carried out on practically all the railways. The actual number of employees on all the railways in India at the end of March 1930 was nearly three-quarters of a million, of whom 40,000 had been discharged—75 per cent of them being permanent workers and the rest temporary. Before this retrenchment on the railways was effected, there had been in some of the railway workshops large-scale reductions of staff owing to the amalgamation of workshops and the introduction of up-to-date machinery.

It is doubtful if the Railway Board would have felt compelled to appoint a court of enquiry, but for the threatening attitude of the All-India Railwaymen's Federation, which might have led to stoppage of work on at least some of the most important railway systems in India. It was not until the Federation commenced taking a ballot as a preliminary to the declaration of a general strike that the Railway Board was induced to agree to this step. Full facilities were given both to the railway administrations and to the Railwaymen's Federation to present their cases. At least on one important railway, State-owned and managed (the East Indian Railway), the criticism of the workers that representatives of the union had been specially marked out for victimization was practically endorsed by the court. All the office-bearers of the unions and those who gave evidence before the Royal Commission had been retrenched—a fact admitted by the railway authorities, though they did not accept its implications.

What is of interest, also, is that the court unanimously held that the interpretations given to the Railway Board's general directions for the methods to be pursued in carrying out retrenchment were varied, because of lack of precision in the instructions to the agents of the several railways.

There had been from the side of the workers widespread complaint against officers entrusted with the task of recruitment on the score of corruption, favouritism based on communal and family bias; and in many cases there were allegations of official disapproval of active association with a trade union. The court, after investigations into the history of 650 individual cases from all over India (roughly a third of the total number of petitions received), held that in a considerable proportion of the cases examined there was room for the legitimate inference that they had been unjustly retrenched. The general attitude of the railway administrations was apparent even from the very restrained conclusions of the court. It drew attention to the fact that in important particulars the instructions of the Railway Board had not been followed by several administrations; that in regard to discharge of men with ten years of service and over, not a single railway administration had paid heed to the orders of the Railway Board and, in fact, only two had cared to consult the unions of the workers.

If this could be the history of a dispute to which the strongest workers' organization in India, with fifteen unions affiliated and a total membership of nearly 130,000, was a party, it can easily be imagined how less organized or even completely unorganized workers would fare in similar circumstances.

In another dispute on the B.B. & C.I. Railway, the board of conciliation appointed by the Government of India gave its findings largely in support of the claims put forward by the workers.

But unrest on the railways continued, and a strike followed, this time on the Madras and Southern Maharatta Railway, in 1932 which lasted ten weeks. But in industry in general there were on the whole few strikes comparable in magnitude with those of previous years. A certain amount of propaganda was conducted at textile centres in 1932 for the organization of a general strike of these workers throughout India to prevent further cuts in wages, but obtained little support, and the threat was never put into action except in Bombay, which was responsible for 92 out of a total of 159 for the whole of India, inflicting a loss in working days of nearly four million on the industry out of a total of less than five million working days for the whole of India. The strike in Bombay lasted two months, but had never any prospects of success and ended in complete failure.

The generally unsympathetic attitude of the old Provincial Governments towards labour was revealed in their proposals for the representation of labour under the new Constitution. Under the Montagu Act the total number of labour seats in the various provincial legislatures through nomination by the governors was only nine. Before Lord Lothian's committee in 1932 the recommendations placed by the Provincial Governments for labour representation in the new legislatures were two each in Madras, the United Provinces, and Bihar, three in Assam, and one each in the Panjab and the Central Provinces. The Bombay and Bengal Governments proposed no specific number. In comparison with these proposals the recommendations of Lord Lothian's committee (which were finally incorporated in the new Constitution) must be considered generous, 38 seats in the various provincial assemblies, all on an elective basis, some by trade union constituencies and the rest by special constituencies.

In regard to the settlement of industrial disputes, the Provincial Governments of this time could not be shaken out of their conviction that the policeman's *lathi* and the prohibitory sections of the Criminal Procedure Code were more effective methods of suppressing strikes than the use of the conciliation machinery provided in the Trades Disputes Act. Until the inauguration of provincial autonomy in 1937, labour was a "reserved" subject—that is to say, not under the control of ministers responsible to the legislatures—and in more than one province, the Government member in charge of labour held also the portfolio of law and order. In any event, the composition of the executive was such that it favoured at every stage the landlords and the capitalists.

Rare as were the occasions on which the Trades Disputes

Act was utilized for the settlement of industrial disputes, it is typical of the official mentality that in 1934 the Bombay Government should have launched a prosecution against eight leaders of the general strike in the textile mills by invoking the sections of the Trades Disputes Act relating to illegal strikes. The grounds alleged for the prosecution were that some of the demands of the strikers were not in furtherance of a trade dispute, and secondly that the strike was designed to inflict "severe, general, and prolonged hardships" upon the community. Fortunately for the workers, the prosecution failed, as also the Government's appeal against the original decision before the High Court of Bombay. It was held both by the court which originally heard the case as well as by the High Court that there was no proof for the allegation that "severe, general, and prolonged hardships" had been inflicted by the strike upon the community as a whole, and the Bombay Government's contention was rejected.

This judgment has had its effect on the Government of India, for the Bill amending the Trades Disputes Act seeks to alter the conditions prescribed in the Act necessary for the declaration of a strike as illegal. Instead of providing that a strike or lock-out satisfying certain conditions should be automatically illegal, the present proposal is that a strike involving or likely to involve serious and prolonged hardship should be illegal—but only on a declaration to that effect by the Provincial Government. Such a declaration, moreover, would have to be coupled with a reference of the dispute to a court of enquiry or a board of conciliation.

The judgment served also one good purpose, namely, of hastening in Bombay a provincial measure for facilitating conciliation. In 1934, an Act was passed applicable in the first instance only to the textile industry in the city and suburbs of Bombay. A Commissioner of Labour was appointed under the Act as chief conciliator, as also a Labour Officer, whose functions were defined as being "to watch the interests of workmen with a view to promote harmonious relations between employers and workmen and to take steps to represent the grievances of workmen to employers for the purpose of obtaining their redress." In fact, the Act went further and authorized the Labour Officer to be a delegate on behalf of the workers in a dispute if required to act in that capacity. Some of the new Provincial Governments (like the United Provinces) are likely to copy the chief features of the Bombay Act.

CHAPTER XVI

METHODS OF SETTLEMENT

It is interesting to note that there has been a sudden revival of industrial unrest since the inauguration of provincial autonomy in April 1937. During the year 1937 nearly ten million working days were lost as a result of 379 disputes—the highest number of disputes on record since 1921. The chief centre of unrest was Bengal, where over six million working days were lost because of a prolonged strike by the jute mill workers; Bombay was next, with a loss of nearly a million working days, closely followed by the United Provinces. Of the 379 strikes no less than 221 strikes were in the cotton textile and jute industries, the total number of days lost in disputes in these being about six and a half million. The majority of the strikes were due to demands for an increase in wages or the restoration of cuts effected during the period of the depression. Forty-six per cent of these (a much greater proportion than in previous years) resulted in some concessions or benefits to the workers involved in these disputes. It is almost certain that 1938 will surpass the record for the previous year, mainly because of the disputes in the textile industry. All over India, and particularly in Madras and the United Provinces, there have been big strikes or lock-outs following the awards of committees of enquiry appointed by the Provincial Governments.

It is easy to explain the recrudescence of industrial unrest in India since 1937. The advent of popular Governments in the provinces has had the undoubted effect of stimulating the hopes of the workers. In particular, the Congress Party, which has assumed office in eight provinces, is committed to a programme of far-reaching reform by a resolution adopted at its Karachi session in 1931, including such items as a living wage, minimum wages in each industry, adequate housing, relief of indebtedness, maternity and unemployment benefits, sickness insurance, old age pensions, free education for the workers' children, and certain fundamental rights like freedom of association and of speech.

It is fortunate for the workers that industry in general and the cotton textile industry in particular have shown since 1936 unmistakable signs of prosperity. The latter, in fact, has created a new record of production for itself by exceeding 4,000 million yards between April 1937 and March 1938, an increase of about 17 per cent over the previous year's total.

It is to the credit of the new Provincial Governments that within less than a year of their assumption of office they have appointed in the case of at least fifteen disputes committees of enquiry or boards of conciliation, most of them under the Trades Disputes Act. This record is in marked contrast to the almost complete indifference of the previous administrations, which during seven years between 1929 and 1936 seldom utilized the machinery provided in the Act.

The result of the recent efforts by independent tribunals in the different provinces has, on the whole, been to effect considerable improvements in the wages and working conditions of the workers. The right of the workers to form unions has not only been recognized by these tribunals, but in many cases conceded by the employers without any other conditions than that of registration under the Trades Union Act and previous notice of strikes. Wages have been increased, particularly for the textile workers, by proportions reaching up to a maximum of 25 per cent in some cases. Holidays with pay have been recommended and in some centres granted by the employers. Schemes of sickness insurance are being evolved in more than one province and will form the basis of legislation or voluntary agreements at several centres. There has also followed a tightening up of the administration of labour legislation like the Factories Act. It is significant that employers' organizations have expressed their apprehensions that the pace of labour legislation initiated in Congress-governed provinces may prove too much for industry to bear, and held out the warning that unless this policy is altered, industry may gradually shift into Indian States where labour conditions are far more favourable to the employers.* At the same time, it must be said in fairness to the Provincial Governments that while conceding to the workers rights which have so long been withheld from them, steps are also being taken, mainly by legislation, to discourage lightning and unauthorized strikes.

A reference to industrial disputes in India since 1921† affords abundant proof that the workers have at all times been willing to accept negotiation and arbitration as a method of settlement. Between 1921 and 1928 there were, as the records show, twenty-two disputes in which, as a result of informal negotiations by the Provincial Government concerned or one of its officials, boards of conciliation or arbitration or courts of enquiry were appointed, in most of which the award was accepted by both sides. In some cases, indeed, the termination of the dispute followed almost immediately on the appointment of such a tribunal. Between

* In fact, four new factories for which machinery had already arrived in, or was on its way to, Cawnpore, will be established in the State of Bhopal. Labour organization is more difficult in the States than in British India and there is less insistence on regular factory hours. Gwalior has still a ten hours day.

† It is interesting to note the number of industrial disputes that have occurred in each year since 1921 and the dimensions of each dispute.

Year	*No. of stoppages beginning during the year*	*No. of workers involved (in thousands)*	*No. of working days lost (in millions)*
1921	396	600	7·0
1922	278	435	4·0
1923	213	301	5·1
1924	133	312	8·7
1925	134	270	12·6
1926	128	187	1·1
1927	129	131	2·0
1928	203	507	31·6
1929	141	531	12·2
1930	148	196	2·3
1931	166	203	2·4
1932	118	128	1·9
1933	146	165	2·2
1934	159	221	4·8
1935	145	114	1·0
1936	157	169	2·4
1937	379	648	10·0
	3,173	5,118	111·3

1928 and 1936 there were eleven instances in which settlement was reached by conciliation or arbitration, only in three cases by action on the part of the Provincial Governments under the Trades Disputes Act. When it is remembered that the Provincial Governments which were in charge of the administration of labour in the different provinces until 1937 were strongly pro-capitalist in bias, the decisions of the various boards of conciliation and of the courts of enquiry—which could not inevitably in the circumstances be composed of men with labour leanings—must strike an impartial observer as of special significance. And in practically every strike within my knowledge the workers offered to resume work on an assurance from the Provincial Government of the appointment of an independent tribunal.

How fruitful, both for employers and workers, arbitration can prove is writ large across the industrial history of Ahmedabad, which to-day is only next to Bombay as the main centre of the textile industry in India. Indeed, at the present rate of expansion, Ahmedabad may outstrip Bombay in the course of the next ten years. Mr. Gandhi realized very early in his public life that peace in industry was possible only through the establishment of machinery for the prompt disposal of complaints from the workers. A strong point of the labour activities in Ahmedabad was an arbitration board consisting of a representative on behalf of the millowners and one for the workers to decide all points in dispute, particularly in regard to wages, with a right of appeal, in the event of disagreement, to an impartial umpire acceptable to both sides. To mention the latest instance, in September 1933 the Millowners' Association proposed a reduction of 25 per cent in the rates of wages. Discussions continued throughout the rest of the year and the whole of the following year. The dispute was settled, with the consent of both parties, in January 1935 on the basis of an agreement which provided for the standardization of the wages of piece-workers and the evolution of a scheme for automatic adjustments in wages. The settlement, however, failed to materialize; further discussions of the proposal of the millowners to effect a cut of 20 per cent in wages led ultimately to a reference to an umpire, who gave his award in January 1937 in favour of the workers.

The millowners at Ahmedabad are, according to the Labour Association, less keen now on continuing the practice initiated and fostered by Mr. Gandhi since the transfer of his headquarters to the Central Provinces. But the position achieved by Ahmedabad in the textile industry is largely due to the comparative absence of disputes which have been so disastrous in their effects on Bombay. On the side of the workers, too, it can be claimed with justice that in the matter of wages, Ahmedabad is ahead of every other centre of the textile industry in India, in some departments the rates being more than double those prevalent in South India for the same kind of work.

Nevertheless, the wise example of Ahmedabad has not been followed in other centres of industry, for the simple reason, so far as the employers are concerned, that they have not been willing to accept the basic condition of the workers' unqualified right to form a union. Over three thousand strikes took place in India between 1921 and 1937 in which well over five million workers participated, inflicting on industry a loss in working days of considerably over a hundred and ten million. But even this bitter experience has not sufficed, except in the case of a few employers who see further than the rest, to impress upon them the necessity of collective bargaining with workers' organizations.

How the workers maintain themselves during these strikes is a matter of considerable interest. There is hardly any union in India which can afford to give strike pay to its members, although some of the better organized unions undertake to provide a little temporary relief to individual members who have been victimized during a dispute, either by giving them a lump sum or some money every month until they can find employment elsewhere.

But there is an extraordinary sense of comradeship among the workers. In 1920, when the workers of the M. & S.M. Railway workshops at Perambur (a suburb of Madras) first organized themselves into a union, they made a collection amounting to Rs.8,000 (approximately £600) for starting a food-store and providing medical relief to its members. But just at that time the workers of the textile mills in the neighbourhood were involved in a prolonged dispute with the employers and stood badly in need of assistance. Without much hesitation, the railway workers handed over the entire amount for relief work with no hope of getting it back. Twelve years later, when it was the turn of these railway workers to seek assistance from outside during their ten weeks' strike, the textile union, remembering with gratitude the earlier episode, made a collection of Rs.3,000 (£230) on wages day as its contribution to the relief funds of the railwaymen.

It is during these long disputes, sometimes running into many months, that one realizes the dogged nature of the ordinarily placid and docile Indian worker. A certain amount of relief may come from outside: from other workers' organizations in India (though this is little) or abroad, or from employers in other centres—not altogether from an altruistic motive it need hardly be said! But all this is inadequate, even negligible, when the numbers involved and their families are taken into account. How the workers maintain themselves during these incredibly long periods of unemployment no one can quite tell, even after intimate contact with them. It is undoubtedly true that expenditure on drink and drugs is severly curtailed from even before the commencement of a dispute. Great economy in food is observed, a single meal sufficing in most cases. As many as possible return to their homes, thus partially solving the problem of relief and minimizing the chances of disorder. Some of them even find odd occupations in the neighbourhood and earn a precarious and scanty livelihood. But as against this, there is the invisible pressure of the police and of the employers, exerted in a variety of ways, particularly after the first week or two.

When a strike occurs, if the conditions of the industry are such that prolonged cessation of work would inflict heavy losses on the employers, there is, after an initial display of stubbornness and resentment, an inclination on their part to come to terms. In such cases, the dispute is comparatively short-lived, as is proved by the record of the early disputes immediately after the close of the war.

Since 1924 or 1925, when economic conditions have been less favourable to the employers, there has not been the same anxiety for the early settlement of disputes. In fact, there are some instances of employers themselves deliberately fomenting strikes through *agents provocateurs*, during periods of accumulated stocks of goods, in order to be spared the burden of the wages bill.

There is also an additional factor which has led employers to permit the prolongation of disputes even if they have not been responsible for their instigation. It was found at more than one centre that one of the inevitable reactions of a long strike, especially an unsuccessful one, is the practical disappearance of a union for a year or two once normal conditions are restored. There is something in the psychology of the Indian worker which, while it gives him patience and strength and courage to go through acute suffering for weeks and even months, seems nevertheless to produce a pronounced reaction from which he takes time to recover.

There is, generally, a complaint on the part of the employers in India that no notice is given of the workers' intention to go on strike and no written representations are made as to the nature of their difficulties. Such a statement is often only a half-truth, and an excuse for withholding wages for the period of the strike. Whether formal notice is given or not—though this is becoming the practice of registered unions—practically every employer has sufficient warning of brewing discontent among the workers and sufficient knowledge as to its causes. It seems somewhat absurd, in view of the fact that employers can summon and obtain police aid at very short notice, to demand formal notice from an unorganized body of workers—most of them illiterate—when anyone who has the courage and ability to come forward as the spokesman of his fellow-workers is instantly marked out as the ringleader, to be dismissed immediately after the dispute is settled.

I have watched and participated in several strikes and lock-outs in India, some of them spread over two, three or even four months. The first few days are comparatively easy to pass. The pressure of hunger has not yet made itself felt, and as there are no sanctioned legitimate holidays in India (except in a few isolated industrial concerns), a strike has not infrequently the air of a holiday—processions with music, and garlands for some "labour leader" who is summoned by telegram to lead the strike, and generally an excellent and buoyant spirit. The first signs of strain begin to manifest themselves after a fortnight. Daily meetings (sometimes both morning and evening) tend gradually to lose their interest, the attentions of the police are apt to become increasingly uncomfortable and the shopkeepers hesitate to supply foodstuffs on credit—one of the usual methods of the police to "induce" the workers to return to work. The amount of resourcefulness and lack of scruple exhibited on such occasions by the employers with the assistance of the police would be incredible to one unacquainted with Indian conditions. If the workers' morale shows signs of weakening, no particularly strong measures are called for. In the smaller towns, motor lorries, filled with agricultural workers picked from neighbouring villages and given a joy ride and a meal for going into the mills, create the impression that there is an adequate supply of blackleg labour. If among the strikers there are any members of a so-called criminal tribe under special regulations, the police bring pressure to bear on them to break away from the rest. Another device is to play upon caste or religious feelings, though they are seldom noticeable among the workers in ordinary times, in order to break the workers' solidarity. Every one of these observations is based on personal experience.

But when one recalls the number of strikes and lock-outs that have taken place in India, the terrible handicaps under which the workers have fought for their rights and the grave provocation offered to them on occasions to break out into violence, the number of instances in which the temptation has proved too strong must be regarded as remarkably small. I have myself undertaken, where the chief of the police was a strict and impartial man, to see a strike through without elaborate precautions, and accomplished the task without a stone being thrown or a glass pane smashed. Sometimes, of course, when the workers are driven to desperation, regrettable outbreaks do and have taken place. But even then they are not always to blame. In one big strike in the early years of the movement (the names and details are withheld as some of the participants may still be in service in India) there was arson and murder, and the Provincial Government came near declaration of martial law—so serious were the disorders. The official explanation at the time was that the workers had got out of hand because of the incapacity of their leaders to control them. The facts, as narrated to me several years later by one of the officials who had a great deal to do with this difficult situation, were that the blacklegs, who enjoyed special police protection, had themselves started the fires in order to throw the responsibility for what followed on the strikers.

Provincial Governments, with their law-and-order mentality, could never regard the growth of the workers' movement with approval and any scheme, however good, was viewed with deep suspicion, if it emanated from a labour leader. We wanted in Madras about ten years ago a maternity ward in the industrial area. Its need was not in question—a large number of the cases in the chief maternity hospital in the city being drawn from this area—and the minister in charge of medical relief was favourably inclined towards the proposal; but it was vetoed, because, as the employer was candid enough to tell me, he had warned one of the officials concerned that a maternity ward would have meant accession of strength to the union. Some years later, we made attempts to start a workers' club, whose main activities were to be temperance propaganda, experiments in improved diet, physical exercises and a reading-room. A certain amount of money was in fact promised for the club, but would not have been adequate without some financial help from the Government (a matter of about Rs.3,000, £230). The executive councillor in charge of labour promised support and money was available for the purpose. But one of the officials, with whom I had previously come into conflict in the course of my trade union work, decided that the scheme should not be allowed to materialize! Apart from personal antipathies, officials in India with rare exceptions have been obsessed with the fear that trade unions, if allowed to develop, would foster mass consciousness; and with the political struggle in India periodically flaring up into movements like non-co-operation and civil disobedience, they have felt presumably that no risks should be taken in regard to the organization of the workers.

There are no insuperable obstacles in the way of a healthy trade union movement growing in India—except the hostility of the employers and until last year also of the Provincial Governments. If it had been encouraged instead of being suppressed, and the practice built up of formulating agreements between workers' and employers' organizations, labour conditions would not have been so ghastly as they are to-day. The epidemic of strikes all over India, which shows no signs of abatement, is the result of acute industrial discontent pent up during the last seven years and bursting out under conditions which seem favourable to the workers.

There has been more recourse to the conciliation provisions of the Trades Disputes Act within a year of the inauguration of provincial autonomy than in all the previous eight years during which the Act was on the statute book. The recommendations of the various committees of enquiry in Bombay, Cawnpore, Nagpur, Madura, and Coimbatore go much further than those of similar committees under the old regimes, in granting to the workers amenities which have unquestionably been due to them. As employers get accustomed to collective bargaining with workers' organizations and drop their old-fashioned outlook of veiled but unqualified hostility to the formation of unions, the method of arbitration will once again replace resort to strikes. The workers have always preferred settlement by negotiations; but under the conditions which prevailed in India until popular Governments came into power in 1937, they have generally had no alternative to the weapon of the strike.

PART 6

LEGAL PROTECTION FOR THE WORKER

CHAPTER XVII

LABOUR LEGISLATION

THE contents of several labour measures, both Central and Provincial, have already been described in connection with some of the main problems of the workers. The additions to the statute book, particularly in the post-war period, constitute an impressive record of social progress—or would do so if a lengthening code of legislation and social progress were in Indian conditions the same thing.

But it is necessary to bear in mind one all-important point before passing on to a consideration of labour legislation in India. As remarked in an earlier chapter, the application of the Factories Act covers, on a generous estimate, not more than three or four million workers, while the total number of those engaged in industry cannot be less than thirty million. There are numerous seasonal factories which, though employing power, do not engage the minimum number required under the Factories Act and therefore escape all control; then there are the unregulated factories which may, and in many cases do, employ even hundreds of workers, but are outside the range of legislative regulation based on the use of power of some kind.

The total number of registered factories in 1936 in British India was 10,226, of which 9,323 were actually working, 5,581 perennial and 3,742 seasonal. The average number of workers employed in these factories was 1·65 million. The number of workers in the cotton textile industry was 438,000 and in the jute mills 289,000. Comparatively few women are employed in factories, their total number during the year being 234,000, and ever fewer children, only 12,000; in fact, there is evidence to show that the number of children employed in organized industry is rapidly declining.

The average number of persons working in and about the mines regulated by the Mines Act (which applies only to British India and not to the Indian States) was 270,000 in 1936, of whom 131,000 worked underground, 69,000 in open workings, and 70,000 on the surface. But it is significant that while there were during the year 214 fatal accidents in mines regulated by the Mines Act and 978 serious accidents involving injuries to 1,011 persons, altogether in all the mines there were 477 fatal accidents* and 1,032 serious ones.

In fact, taking all labour legislation into account, affecting factories, mines, plantations, docks, railways, harbours, etc., it is doubtful whether more than seven or eight million at the outside would come within its protective influence. The rest, who constitute by far the greater majority of the industrial workers, are engaged in small or what are known as unregulated industries.

The first Factories Act in India was passed in 1881, substantially amended ten years later, and again in 1911, following a report of the Factories Commission, when the Act was replaced by a more comprehensive measure. This was overhauled in several respects in 1922, and improved in respect of specific provisions in 1923, 1926, and 1931. The Government of India considered the numerous recommendations of the Royal Commission and introduced a new Factories Act in 1934, which came into force in January 1935. This measure, which consists of eighty-four sections, is undoubtedly an enormous improvement on its predecessors. The new Act has not only tightened up administration in several directions but broken new ground. Some Provincial Governments, taking advantage of the option given to them under the Act, have extended the application of several provisions, particularly those relating to health and safety, to factories employing more than ten persons. Seasonal factories enjoyed under the old law an amount of latitude not accorded to perennial factories. But it has now been laid down that only factories ordinarily not working for more than 180 days in a year can come under that category. The rules governing the grant of exemptions from certain provisions of the Act to seasonal factories—mainly ginning

* Two hundred and thirteen persons lost their lives on account of explosions or ignitions of fire-damp and coal dust; 67 by falls of roof; 74 by falls of sides; 7 in shafts; 35 by suffocation by gases; 12 by explosives; 25 by haulage; 19 by other accidents underground; 3 by electricity, and 22 on the surface.

factories, cotton and jute presses, and factories dealing with tea, coffee, sugar, rubber, and indigo—have been made more rigid than before.

The Commission had pointed out the inadequacy of the penalties imposed even when convictions were secured for breaches of the law. The scale of penalties in the new Act has been revised by the provision of higher maximum penalties for second and subsequent convictions.

In regard to the atmospheric conditions inside factories, there was need for protecting the worker from injury or serious discomfort, either through artificial humidification or a high temperature. Inspectors of factories have now been armed with authority to compel factory owners to adopt measures for the reduction of temperatures where conditions are such as to cause discomfort or danger to the workers and various other provisions. The provisions relating to the better ventilation of factories, particularly to protect workers from dust or other impurities and from danger against instability of factory buildings, follow in general the recommendations of the Commission.*

Another provision which is a welcome feature, from the standpoint of the workers, is the power given to Provincial Governments to insist on the establishment of crèches in factories employing a minimum of fifty women. In other directions, too, the powers of Provincial Governments to safeguard the health and safety of the workers have been extended under the Act.

With regard to hours of work in factories, a maximum working week of 60 hours and a daily limit of 11 hours was laid down in the Act of 1922. An interval of at least an

* How these provisions sometimes work in practice is pointed out in the report of the Chief Inspector of Factories, Bengal, for 1936. In a fitting room of a rubber factory, 124 feet by 24, 416 persons were employed. The room was so overcrowded with workers and work benches that the operatives were compelled to stand shoulder to shoulder and back to back whilst doing their work. In addition, the fumes from the benzine used in the process made one gasp when entering the room. As the maximum number of persons who could be employed in the room, including the space occupied by the benches and other fittings, was 90, prosecution proceedings were instituted for violation of the rule. Although a conviction was obtained, a fine of Rs.50 (£3 15s.) only was imposed.

hour (or two half-hours) a day was prescribed, as also a weekly holiday, and the prohibition of night work for women. Under the new Act the weekly hours of work have been reduced to 54. Various other changes, all for the better, have been introduced in regard to the daily limits for women workers, the conditions governing the grant of exemptions, the reduction of hours of work for children between the ages of twelve and fifteen (to five hours per day). The main Act has already been amended twice since its passage into law: once to prevent women from being employed even in a supervisory or official capacity at night, and again to give Provincial Governments extra powers to bring workshops not using power within the operation of the main Act.

There is no doubt that conditions inside factories are gradually improving as a result of the new law, though, as the latest report of the Government of India admits, there is still room for considerable improvement in regard to health and sanitation in several provinces, notably Assam, Bengal, Bihar, Bombay, Orissa, Sind, and the Central Provinces. A definite advance is reported with regard to ventilation and the introduction of cooling plant in the Bombay Presidency, whose Chief Inspector of Factories remarks that "air conditioning has become a business proposition."

But the complaint about the inadequacy of the factory inspection staff which was voiced before the Royal Commission, not only by the workers but even by the Government of India, is still valid. The number of factories has increased rapidly all over India, especially since the acceptance of a policy of protection, but Provincial Governments, who are responsible for the administration of labour legislation, have never been noted for their anxiety to observe a high standard; and in recent years, financial stringency has provided an excellent ground for not expanding the inspection staff. Of just over 9,300 inspections during 1936, 3,000 factories were inspected once, 2,350 twice, 1,000 three times, and 800 more than three times, while about 1,200 factories were not inspected at all. There were 940 convictions under the Factories Act during the year in all India, of which

15 were in the United Provinces, 99 in the Panjab, 25 in Bihar, 5 in Orissa, 61 in the Central Provinces, and 3 in Assam. There were no convictions at all in the Frontier Province, Baluchistan, Ajmer, and Delhi.

Convictions are not generally easy to obtain for breaches of the Act. The factory staff is utterly inadequate for effective supervision, and the chief inspector is burdened with office work of a routine character, with the inevitable consequence that he can give little time to his more important duties. In some provinces only the chief inspector can sanction prosecutions, and since he is bound down to his office for at least half the year, and prosecutions imply attendance in the courts, the tendency is to avoid recourse to law, except in unavoidable circumstances, for flagrant or repeated breaches of the Act. There was also a fear until last year (1937) that a sudden increase in the number of prosecutions might not meet with the approval of the Provincial Government, and considerations of prudence dictated a policy of keeping it down as low as possible.

No one who knows conditions in India needs to be told that the administration of the Factories Act could be much more effective. An inspection once or even twice a year does not ensure due observance, especially as an employer manages somehow to obtain previous notice of the inspector's visit and takes special measures for the occasion. Although in recent years administration has improved, and convictions recorded in the reports of the Provincial Governments are on the increase, punishments for breaches of the Act (even when convictions are secured) are generally not severe enough in some provinces to exercise a deterrent effect.*

* In the Panjab, according to the latest report on the working of the Factories Act, the number of factories which remained uninspected during 1936 was larger than in the previous year. The Government remarked on the fact that no improvement was reported in the case of small establishments, set up in buildings originally intended for other purposes, in regard to lighting, sanitation, ventilation, and humidity control. With regard to the increase in the number of accidents in the province from 912 to 1,145, the Government endorsed the remark of the Chief Inspector of Factories that factory owners and their staffs did not sufficiently realize the importance of proper fencing and guarding of machinery. Though convictions were obtained in practically every case of prosecution for breach of the provisions of the Act, fines con-

There was no Compensation Act for workers before 1923, when the first Act was placed on the statute book. It came into operation in the following year; some minor changes followed in the next three years in the light of experience. As a result of the investigations of the Royal Commission, the measure underwent an overhaul in several respects and the new Act came into force in 1934. Its scope was widened considerably, the Act as revised covering about six million workers as against four million under the original Act. Substantial changes also were made in the scales of compensation. Whereas formerly the compensation for a fatal accident ranged from Rs.240 (£18) to Rs.2,500 (a little less than £200) the scales were increased to Rs.500 (about £38) and Rs.4,000 (about £300) respectively; similarly, in the case of permanent total disablement the minimum compensation was raised from Rs.336 to Rs.700 (from £25 to £55 approximately) and the maximum from Rs.3,500 to Rs.5,600. Rates of compensation for temporary disablement were also enhanced, particularly for the lower-paid workers. The waiting period during which workers temporarily disabled received no compensation was reduced from ten days to seven, and the new Act added four occupational diseases to the schedule. Various other changes were also made, many of which had been recommended by the Commission.

At the same time, it is instructive to note how even when legislation is brought before the Central Legislature by the Government of India, owing to the pro-capitalist character

tinued, in the words of the Government's report, "almost ridiculously low," averaging in 1936 only Rs.28 (£2 2s.) per case. Only 99 prosecutions were instituted, but 55 of these were for working beyond the prescribed hours. As the Government pointed out in reviewing the report, "Overwork is a prolific cause of accidents and ill health. A factory can be inspected only once or twice in a season and it is at least probable that it overworks them on many other occasions (besides the one in which it is caught in the act) and a fine of the standard usually imposed makes deliberate disregard of one of the most important provisions of the Act a highly lucrative operation. The only remedy against deliberate violation of the Act is frequent inspection, followed in cases of violation by heavy penalty. More frequent inspection than is carried out at present is impossible; but that is no reason why a heavy penalty should not be exacted on the rare occasions when the offence is discovered." The plea usually made by offending occupiers of factories was that the times being bad, the offence should be overlooked or lightly punished.

of the legislature, modifications are introduced in the provisions to the detriment of the worker. For instance, in the case of death the amount payable under the Act was thirty times the monthly wages, ranging between a minimum sum of Rs.240 to Rs.2,500. The Royal Commission had recommended a substantial enhancement, the limits suggested being Rs.600 and Rs.4,500; but the select committee on the amending Bill reduced the figures to Rs.500 and Rs.4,000 respectively. Similarly, for total disablement, the original Act had prescribed sums representing forty-two times the monthly wage, with a minimum of Rs.336 and a maximum of Rs.3,500. The amending Bill introduced by the Government of India proposed an increase of the minimum to Rs. 840 and the maximum to Rs.6,300. But the select committee reduced these figures to Rs.770 and Rs.5,600 respectively. For minors, the amending Bill had proposed the same minimum and maximum as for adults, but the select committee introduced a flat rate of Rs.1,200 for all minors as the amount of compensation. In regard to temporary disablement also, the select committee reduced the figures of certain classes of wages. It is important to remember that the amending Bill of the Government was based on the recommendation of the Royal Commission, which included both officials and representatives of the employers. But the select committee maintained that the increases proposed in the Bill were too heavy, taking into account the drop in prices since the report of the Commission. A minority made strenuous efforts in the Legislative Assembly to restore the limits proposed in the amending Bill, but without success.

Under the new Constitution which came into operation in 1937, certain powers vested hitherto in the Government of India have been transferred to the Provincial Governments. These relate to the addition of new classes of workers, the extension of the schedule of industrial diseases and the framing of rules governing procedure.

It is interesting to note that since the Workmen's Compensation Act came into operation, both the number of cases in which compensation was paid and the total amount of compensation have increased greatly. In 1925 the number of cases was a little over 11,000 and the amount of compensation paid Rs.644,000. The numbers increased gradually up to 1930 when the number of cases was 23,600 and the amount of compensation paid Rs.1,247,000. In the subsequent years there was a considerable drop in both categories, the reason being that workers were afraid to insist on the payments legally due to them under the Act for fear of losing their employment, especially during a period of acute depression. In 1931 the number was 17,500 (almost a 25 per cent decline), while the amount of compensation paid was Rs.1,066,000. In 1932, there was a further drop in cases to 14,300 and in the amount paid to Rs.823,000. In 1936, the latest year for which figures are available, there were 28,500 cases and the amount of compensation paid aggregated Rs.1,464,000. The vast majority, 25,900, were for temporary disablement. The number of total accidents was over one thousand, though fully half the amount of compensation paid was for these.

An increasing number of employers are insuring with well-known insurance companies and cases are being now handled by claims agencies. Also, organized unions like the Labour Association at Ahmedabad (which was responsible for fighting about two hundred cases of compensation and obtained payments aggregating Rs.30,000, (£2,300 approximately, during the year) undertake this as one of their main activities. Soon after the Act came into force in 1924, some of the big unions in Madras initiated an educative campaign all over the province to explain the provisions of the Act and the procedure to be followed. A number of public-spirited lawyers came forward to take up compensation cases free of cost for the workers. Their out-of-pocket expenses and the cost of stamps were met out of a fund to which workers who obtained compensation from their employers contributed up to a maximum limit of 2½ per cent of the amount. The effect of these steps was seen immediately in the enormous increase in the number of compensation cases from all over South India.

Both employers and workers are getting accustomed to

the law of compensation, but even now there is no legal obligation on the part of an employer to pay compensation without an application from the worker. Unions are sometimes faced with the embarrassing alternative of deciding to fight a case on behalf of an injured worker, with the risk of his losing his employment afterwards, or of advising him to accept a much smaller amount than is legally due to him but with the assurance of continuing in service. I remember a case of one—in fact, of several similar ones—who had lost two fingers and was entitled to compensation amounting to Rs.84 (about £8). The employer offered him Rs.7 (10s. 6d.) but was willing to let him continue in employment. Insistence on Payment of the full amount might have involved, on the other hand, loss of service. After some deliberation, the worker decided to accept the employer's terms. This was in a registered union which was fairly stable and vigorous. But workers who are unorganized have not the vaguest notions, even if they have heard of the Compensation Act, of the procedure to be followed. Lawyers' fees are on a scale beyond their capacity to pay, and the assertion of a legal right may mean loss of employment and, at the best, a few months' wages as compensation. Under these circumstances, it is inevitable that the workers should be content with what the employers offer them, regardless of the scales prescribed in the Act. Well-intentioned inspectors of factories often intervene in cases of accidents (as reports of these must be submitted to them under the Factories Act) and obtain some compensation, though this is no part of their legitimate duties. The working of the Act illustrates a difficulty in the administration of all labour legislation which is general in character. Beyond a point, it does not pay a worker in India to demand fulfilment of a legal right.

The payment of wages has been placed on a statutory basis under the Payment of Wages Act which came into force in 1936. There were two questions in regard to this matter before the Government of India—the control of fines and the prevention of delays in payment; and secondly, the enforcement of a weekly payment of wages in industry in the place of the monthly system which is the present practice in many industries. The Royal Commission had suggested the adoption of certain measures, such as the regulation of fines and the deductions from wages, the regulation of recruiting advances, the prevention of delays in the payment of wages and the adoption of a weekly system of payment. At the same time the Commission had favoured, as a first step, the application to the textile industries, the railway and engineering workshops and the iron and steel works, of a maximum limitation of the wage period to sixteen days.

But opinion among the employers was, on the whole, adverse to the limitation of the wage period in the manner recommended by the Commission. And as the workers' organizations were unable to arrive at a unanimous view on the point, the Government of India decided not to include in the Payment of Wages Act any limitation of the wage period except the monthly one.

To prevent delays in the payment of wages which in certain factories extended as far as three weeks into the following month, the law has now laid down with regard to the workers in receipt of wages or salaries of less than Rs.200 a month a maximum interval of seven days after the conclusion of the wage period. This, however, is shortened to two days in the case of discharged workers, while on railways and in large establishments employing at least one thousand persons the normal interval may be extended to ten days. The attention of the Royal Commission had been drawn to the hardships caused by payment of wages on holidays, especially in the collieries. A provision was, therefore, inserted in the law compelling payment to be made on a week-day.

The power to levy fines has been curtailed in several ways under the Act. Thus, the fining of children is prohibited, while in the case of adult workers limitations have been imposed on the right of employers to levy fines, such as a maximum of sixty days from the date of imposition for its collection, and of the amount of fine to half an anna per rupee of a worker's earnings (which works out at $3\frac{1}{8}$ per cent). Moreover, an employer is required to specify on the notice board the grounds in respect of which fines may be imposed. Lastly, it is laid down that the amounts recovered in the shape of fines should be devoted to the support of some form of labour welfare approved by a recognized authority.

The effect of this measure has been a curious one. Most employers have given up fining their workers, and in fact the practice has gone out of use—only to make room for a more drastic punishment. Workers are now compelled in some industrial centres to take leave, the period of which may extend to two or three weeks—without wages. Employers admit that it is fining of a kind, but beyond the provisions of the Payment of Wages Act. A second device to get round the measure is to introduce differential rates of wages for good, bad and indifferent qualities of work, and calculate the wages of a worker on an arbitrary basis.

Another practice condemned by the Royal Commission was that of deductions from wages for damage or losses. It was ascertained by the Bombay Labour Office that this practice was in force particularly at Ahmedabad, where in one mill employing 420 weavers the value of spoilt cloth handed over in a single year exceeded Rs.18,000 (£1,350); while in another with 180 weavers the value of such cloth amounted to nearly Rs.16,000 (£1,200). The Act now prohibits deductions of this kind. In some other respects also the Act offers protection to the workers. Thus deductions on account of advances given to workers before the commencement of employment are prohibited, except from the first payment of wages; nor is an employer entitled to recover an advance given for travelling expenses.

It is perhaps remarkable that before the Mines Act of 1923, there was no statutory regulation of hours, the first Act remaining practically unchanged on the statute book for twenty years. The miner, his wife, and in many cases his children, went underground, worked and rested in the mine, perhaps staying for twenty-four hours or more at a stretch; after they had cut enough coal they left for their village for a few days and came back after an interval. Such spasmodic mining was carried on for some months, the workers camping in the huts provided by the owners. But the Mines Act of 1923, based on an international convention accepted at Washington, forbade children under thirteen years of age from going underground, limited the hours of work underground to 54 a week and above ground to 60, but without any daily limit. The Act was amended in 1928 prohibiting women from working underground, the prohibition take to effect gradually during a period of ten years (it became absolute only in 1938) and restricting the maximum number of daily hours of work to twelve. In the Legislative Assembly, there was considerable opinion at the time in favour of an eight hours day. The Royal Commission, two years later, recommended by a majority the reduction of above ground hours to 54, but leaving the daily limit at the existing point. It is needless to add that the colliery owners, both European and Indian, resented these amendments as interference. The draft convention of the International Labour Conference in 1931 prescribed the hours of work at 7¾ hours underground in coal mines. The Government of India promised to examine the possibility of reducing the statutory limits for hours of work in accordance with the draft convention; in forwarding it to those concerned, the Government expressed its tentative preference for a nine hours day, since with such a limit the miner would be given much better protection than at present and the industry also assured of greater regularity of work.

As a result of the recommendations of the Royal Commission important changes were made in an Act which came into force in 1935. The hours of work were limited above ground to 54 a week and 10 per day; while below ground the weekly limit was abolished and the daily limit fixed at 9 hours. The maximum spreadover was limited to 12 hours a day, with a statutory rest interval of at least an hour for work above ground in excess of 6 hours. In regard to the employment of children the minimum was fixed at fifteen years, with the proviso added that persons between the ages of fifteen and seventeen should not be employed below ground without a medical certificate of fitness. The constitution of mining boards was altered so as to provide for workers the same number of nominees as employers, and it was laid down that the miners' representatives were to be nominated by registered trade unions where these included a substantial proportion of the miners. There were further improvements, though of a minor character, in the Act of 1935.

A series of disastrous accidents in the collieries, however, led to another amendment of the Act in 1936 based on discussions with representatives of coalowners, mine managers, and the Government of India. The main change effected was in favour of giving the Government of India power to promulgate temporary regulations relating to safety without previous notice of publication. This change was necessitated by the fact that under the ordinary procedure changes in rules cannot be effected within a period of less than nine months and often take considerably longer. The alteration in the procedure now enables the Government of India to frame temporary regulations which are valid for two years but must be replaced by permanent regulations made in the ordinary way.

Two of the most serious mining accidents in 1936 were in the collieries, involving in one case, at Poidih, 209 deaths, and in the other 35. The accident at Poidih was, in fact, the most serious that has ever occurred in the history of coal mining in India. The disaster occurred in a colliery near Sitarampur in the Raniganj coalfields, due it is believed to an explosion of a highly explosive atmosphere of inflammable gases existing over a large part of the mine or to ignition afterwards propagated by coal dust. The cause of the ignition could not be definitely ascertained, but is presumed to have been a defect in a safety lamp or its misuse in the presence of gas or a light from a match or other apparatus for producing a light.

With regard to dock workers, the Government of India, taking advantage of a convention adopted by the International Labour Conference in 1932, introduced a measure in the following year in the Central Legislature in order to protect those engaged in the handling of cargo against the risk of accidents and ensuring some inspection by an independent authority to provide adequate protection for their safety and welfare. A code of regulations enforcing safety measures and the submission of reports of accidents was prepared by the Government of India. These regulations follow, though to a limited extent, those in force in Britain and include provision for the safe maintenance of approaches over wharves, docks and quays, and of the means of access to ships and also for first-aid being rendered in cases of accidents. The hours of work in docks have so far not been regulated by legislation, though in most ports they are limited to nine hours a day, with overtime permissible up to a maximum of three hours. The minimum age of employment in docks was fixed in 1922 at twelve years, though this provision applied only to the handling of goods at piers, jetties, landing-places, wharves, quays, docks, warehouses, and sheds. In 1931 the Indian Ports Act was amended in order to remove an ambiguity in the law under which it seemed possible to employ under-aged children in the work of coaling of ships. But the recommendation of the Royal Commission that the minimum age should be raised from twelve to fourteen years, though accepted in principle by the Government of India, has yet to be implemented.

Reference has already been made in earlier chapters to other measures on the statute book, such, for example, as the Trades Union Act, according to whose provisions unions can be registered provided they satisfy certain conditions in regard to subscriptions, the audit of accounts, etc., and accept certain duties and responsibilities in regard to their members. In view of the illiteracy and general ignorance of the workers the Act permits the presence of outsiders on the executive of a registered union to a maximum limit of one half of the total number. Under the new Government of India Act, political rights have been conferred on some registered unions, such as the right of electing a certain number of representatives to the various legislatures.

Labour representation in the various Provincial Legislative Councils under the Montagu Act (which came to an end in April 1937) consisted of three seats in Bombay, two in Bengal, and one each in the Panjab, Bihar, the Central Provinces, and Assam, in all cases representation being through nomination by the Governor. Under the new

Government of India Act thirty-eight seats have been allotted to labour in the provincial Assemblies—eight in Bengal, seven in Bombay, six in Madras, four in Assam, three each in the United Provinces, the Panjab and Bihar, two in the Central Provinces and Berar, and one each in Orissa and Sind. The Delimitation Committee, which was charged with the duty of framing the constituencies, decided in favour of allotting some seats to trade unions and the rest to special labour constituencies. Difficulties were felt particularly in the case of workers on the tea plantations in Assam residing in an area of more than 28,000 square miles, almost a million workers exhibiting different racial characteristics.

The Royal Commission, in dealing with the question, had expressed the view that if special representation was to be given to industrial labour, the method most likely to be effective in securing the return to the legislatures of the best representatives of labour was that of election by registered trade unions. The working of this method should also exercise, observed the Commission, an important influence on the healthy development of trade unionism in India.

The Delimitation Committee, however, could not be persuaded to accept this recommendation without considerable qualifications owing to certain difficulties brought to its notice, such as the existence of rival unions. While recognizing the advantages of labour representation through stable organizations, the committee felt that the limitations imposed by the Trade Unions Act, giving no power to the Government to inspect the registers of a union or to satisfy itself whether the union was functioning properly and its accounts regularly kept, were a serious obstacle.

Certain conditions were, therefore, laid down to ensure that only genuine unions were accorded the right of representation: such as the existence of a union for two years and registration for a year before the date fixed for the preparation of the electoral roll, a minimum membership of 250, facilities for the inspection of books by the Registrar of Trade Unions, and for professional audit.

With regard to candidates, the committee prescribed certain qualifications, such as a minimum age of twenty-one years, residence in the province for six months preceding the date to be fixed by the Provincial Government, membership of a union in the case of a trade union constituency, and continuous employment in a factory, a mine, a railway, a dockyard, a harbour or in any other industrial establishment for a period of not less than 180 days in the twelve months preceding the date of preparation for the electoral roll in the case of a special labour constituency.

Plantation labour in Assam and Bengal presented special difficulties of their own. There are over a thousand tea gardens in Assam alone, with a population of nearly a million, practically half of whom come from Bihar, other areas contributing labour in substantial numbers being the Central Provinces, the United Provinces, and Madras. The workers, as has already been pointed out, have no organization, being emigrants (mostly aboriginals) from different provinces, speaking different languages, illiteracy being almost universal and complete isolation from the general currents of life an outstanding feature. A further complication from the standpoint of building up an electorate, both in Assam and in Bengal, according to the committee, was that tea plantation workers are entitled to repatriation at the end of three years at the expense of the employers, and, therefore, the vast majority could only be termed temporary residents.

The Government of Assam had proposed that four different centres in the province should be selected and a primary and informal election in certain tea gardens held by a show of hands, one delegate being elected by fifty workers. These delegates would in due course elect at each centre, by means of coloured boxes and formal vote, a member for the Provincial Assembly. The Bengal Government had a somewhat different solution in view: the manager or assistant manager would be the presiding officer at the polling station in each tea garden and voting would be direct under his supervision, with no election of delegates and no electoral colleges. The committee was not satisfied with either of the solutions propounded by the two Provincial Governments, holding direct relations between the electorate and the candidate to be essential, as also independence of any control by the employer. The committee therefore proposed that candidature from a constituency should be open to a member of any tribe recognized in the provinces of Bengal, Bihar, Orissa, and Assam. Such candidates should be given free access to the tea gardens, allowed to form trade unions and encouraged to bring genuine grievances to the notice of the manager.

Other measures have already been described—the Trades Disputes Act, the Tea Districts Emigration Act and also a series of measures adopted in recent years to deal with the evils associated with the indebtedness of the workers.

The question of the regulation of workshops which do not employ powdr machinery was discussed by the Royal Commission, which recommended the adoption of a separate measure unconnected with the Factories Act. Its essential features were to be a limitation of hours for children between the ages of ten and fourteen, a weekly holiday for all workers and various provisions of a simple character to safeguard their health and welfare. The new Factories Act enables Provincial Governments to bring some workshops at any rate under regulation; but an all-India measure to give effect to the recommendations of the Commission has yet to be adopted. The Central Provinces' Unregulated Factories Act of 1937 is, however, based in important respects on the proposals of the Commission, though it has gone further in limiting the hours of work for adults. This measure is applicable in the first instance to workshops employing 50 persons or more and engaged in the manufacture of *beedis* (indigenous cigarettes), shellac, and leather tanning. But option is given to the executive to extend its application to other industries and to workshops employing a minimum of 25 persons.

But in another respect, the Government of India has taken legislative steps to protect child labour from exploitation. In several parts of India the practice is widespread of pledging the labour of children on nominal rates of wages and for indefinite periods in repayment of loans advanced to their guardians or parents. The Royal Commission condemned the system as worse than indentured labour, for the child not being a free agent was practically sold to his employer. A measure was adopted in 1933 declaring all bonds relating to the labour of children below fifteen to be void, and providing criminal penalties both for those entering into such bonds and those taking advantage of them. Its passage seems, however, to have made little difference in practice. It is no one's business to insist on its enforcement, and the Government of India has, significantly, not issued a single report on its working during the five years that it has been on the statute book.

Until about 1929 maternity benefits were unknown in India, except in a few individual concerns under benevolent employers. In 1926 a private member's Bill in the Central Legislative Assembly was opposed by the Government of India and its capitalist supporters and defeated. The Labour Commission had expressed the view that the time was ripe for the introduction of maternity benefit legislation throughout the country, at any rate for women permanently employed in industrial establishments on full-time processes. But Bombay led the way in this matter in 1929, thus anticipating the recommendation of the Royal Commission, and went further in 1934 by amending the Maternity Benefits Act in the light of experience. The maximum period for maternity benefits was extended from seven to eight weeks; but the period of employment necessary for qualifying for this payment was also raised from six to nine months. The Central Provinces, which had followed the example of Bombay in 1930, also carried out certain amendments in the original Act in 1935, practically copying the changes introduced in Bombay. In Madras a private Bill more or less on the lines of the original Bombay Act of 1929 became law in 1935. In 1938 the United Provinces Government adopted a measure somewhat more liberal than the Bombay Act, and it is expected that in the course of the next year or two other provinces will fall into line.* The Government of

* The Panjab Government, alone among the Provincial Governments so far, opposed even the introduction of a Bill in the Legislative Assembly in 1938 on the ground that the province, being industrially backward, could not afford to add to the burdens of its comparatively few industries.

India has also taken action in regard to the centrally administered areas of Ajmer-Merwara and the city of Delhi, the Bombay Act coming into force in Delhi from January 1937. In the Assam tea plantations maternity benefits have been in force on a scale more generous than the Acts passed by some of the Provincial Governments.

But with regard to maternity benefits, as in the case of many other measures intended to benefit the workers, their ignorance and economic helplessness, coupled with the absence of a vigilant public opinion which could compel the Provincial Governments to enforce proper observance, leave many loopholes for the unwilling or unscrupulous employer. The court of enquiry at Coimbatore (an important textile centre in South India) remarked in its report in 1938 on the very large number of maternity cases in which the employers had not fulfilled their obligations.

Apart from the unsatisfactory administration of labour legislation, there is the other aspect which is examined in the next chapter on "unprotected labour." India, for all the industrial development of the last twenty years, is still a land of small industries run without machinery or power and employing just a handful of workers. They constitute the vast majority of the industrial workers, but have remained, so far, outside the influence of legislation.

CHAPTER XVIII

UNPROTECTED LABOUR

If conditions in regulated factories liable to periodical inspection be as unsatisfactory as those just described, it seems needless to point out how much worse conditions must be in the small and seasonal factories which are less liable to inspection. Under the latter category come cotton ginning* and pressing, tea, jute pressing, etc.; the workers are primarily agriculturists, the great majority living in their village homes. The work requires as a rule little skill, and most of the factories are small in size. No one has ever made an attempt to organize these workers, despite their extremely low wages, three to four annas a day being quite a common rate. The employer may be the owner, or more often a contractor taking on workers for the day. In Madras, where seasonal factories are about a third of the total number of registered factories, the practice is to let them out on contracts. While there is no effort on the part of the workers to obtain better conditions, factory owners combine and, in the words of the factory inspector of the Panjab, "they sweat the workers."

Under the Factories Act, hours are limited to nine per day and fifty-four per week. But the seasonal factories can obtain certain exemptions from some of the provisions of the Act, though the conditions have been made, on the whole, more stringent than before the revision of the Act in 1934. The factory inspection staff in many provinces being utterly inadequate, there is little effective inspection and, as one of the chief inspectors of factories recently observed, seasonal factories show little regard for the suffering of their workers.

The question of dust is an important one, especially in

* The worst offenders in the Panjab were cotton ginning factories. It was frequently found, complained the Chief Inspector of Factories, that cotton ginning factories started the day's work at 5 a.m., while notices exhibited in the factory showed that the work should commence at 6.30 or 7 a.m.

cotton presses and gins, tea factories and rice mills. Many of the ginning sheds are very hot in the summer, being covered with corrugated iron sheets. Owing to the dust nuisance, asthma, bronchitis, tuberculosis, and other diseases of the respiratory system are common in centres of the cotton ginning industry. In the tea factories the atmosphere is impregnated with tea fluff, and the women and children work with a cloth tied round the mouth and nostrils. On the hills, where the plantations are situated, the windows have to be kept closed, as otherwise the mist and dampness might spoil the tea.

Then, of course, there are all kinds of small factories, which employ the majority of the workers in India. They do not come under the Factories Act, either because they do not employ power, or because the number of workers employed is less than ten or twenty. Some Provincial Governments have utilized the power conferred on them to bring smaller establishments employing a minimum of ten persons under the Factories Act; but, even so, a very large number do not come under the provision and carry on work in the most unsuitably cramped buildings, with little provision for light and air, ventilation, and sanitation.

There is also the problem of the unregulated industries, chiefly tanning, *beedi* (indigenous cigarettes) making, carpet manufacture, etc. With regard to the tanneries, the Labour Commission referred to "the lack of sanitary arrangements and drainage"; to "the earth space being littered with evil-smelling refuse and sodden with pools of filthy water"; to "the absence of washing arrangements and, in the majority of cases, also of latrine accommodation." The workers have to eat their food in the midst of such surroundings. Hours of work often exceed twelve, and in the Madras Presidency children from eight to twelve as well as older boys are found at work at night. Their hours sometimes exceed those of the adults, and for performing additional tasks such as water-carrying, etc., no additional cash wages are paid, but merely two cloths per year.

Tannery workers (practically all of whom are Harijans)

in some parts of India live in sheds constructed by the owners of the factories. One typical shed in Bombay, 23 feet by 20 feet, accommodated 30 men; another, also typical, which was 12 feet by 8 feet, accommodating six workers, was only 3½ feet in height. These sheds have no plinths and only in the case of a few is there a window. Some workers who have their families with them construct their own huts with broken planks, old jute bags, and sheets of discarded kerosene oil tins. There is neither ventilation nor sanitation in these quarters. Some of the factory owners in Bombay bring labour from the Madras Presidency by offering free dwelling-places to the workers, very few of whom can afford to bring their families.

The tanneries themselves are even more insanitary and unhealthy. Decomposing flesh, removed from the hides, is left on the floor in heaps. There is no proper drainage to wash off the dirt, and the stench is offensive, almost stifling to a visitor. The tanning of hides involves hard manual labour done under painful conditions. The removal of flesh from the hides necessitates the use of sharp instruments, and accidents are in consequence fairly frequent. But that is not all. Hides have to be soaked in water containing a strong solution and the workers have to stand in pits with bare hands and feet in such water to a depth of a foot or more. In practically every case that I saw in the tanneries I visited, the workers were suffering from cracked skins and sores all over the body. Boys from the age of nine are engaged in some of the processes, with reactions on their health which can be imagined. When the industry was in a prosperous condition they worked for more than twelve hours a day; but at present they work for ten to twelve hours a day, with a recess for meals which may extend to half an hour. Since the workers must finish a certain amount of work every day, they are naturally anxious to return as soon as possible after their mid-day meal. They get few holidays in the year (in some cases four), but even on those days they have sometimes to work for a couple of hours. Wages vary widely, from Rs.8 to Rs.10 per month for the great majority. But there is no date fixed for the payment of wages, and in some tanneries the workers have to wait until the 20th of the following month. It is needless, perhaps, to add that most of the workers are in debt, the rate of interest varying from 120 to 300 per cent.

Another unregulated industry employing several thousands of workers in different provinces is the manufacture of indigenous cigarettes known as the *beedi*. The industry has grown rapidly within the last ten years, particularly in Madras and the Central Provinces. Referring to the places where the industry is carried on, the Royal Commission observed: "Many of these places are small, airless boxes, without any windows, where the workers are crowded so thickly on the ground that there is barely room to squeeze between. Others are dark semi-basements with damp mud floors, unsuitable for manufacturing processes, particularly in an industry where workers sit or squat on the floor throughout the working day. Sanitary conveniences and adequate arrangements for the removal of refuse are generally absent. Payment is almost universally made by piece rates, the hours are frequently unregulated by the employer, and many smaller workshops are open day and night. Regular intervals for meals and weekly holidays are generally non-existent."

In these factories very young boys are employed for long hours, the smaller children being preferred for their supple fingers in rolling the dry leaves into cigarettes. It is the general practice for children to begin work at five or six years of age, and work without a weekly rest day for ten or twelve hours a day on a wage of about two annas. Many of the parents of these child workers are in debt to the employers and pledge their labour as a method of repayment of the loans.

The same is true of the carpet factories in the Panjab, where the Government admitted before the Royal Commission that in the carpet factories at Amritsar a considerable proportion of the workers were children between the ages of nine to fifteen. They were either the children of the older workers or of their relations or friends who, in return for a loan, had contracted out the labour of the children at so much a month. It goes without saying that these workers are unorganized, because of their illiteracy and helpless economic condition.

A large number of the workers are children employed in the mica factories, many of them being no more than six years of age. In the process of wool cleaning there are children of about eight years of age who sometimes rest with their mothers on piles of evil-smelling, dirty wool, their faces and clothes covered with dust.

More or less similar conditions obtain in the manufacture of shellac. Leaking roofs, earth floors, poor lighting and ventilation; an almost universal absence of washing and sanitary arrangements, bad smell, and a lack of drainage for drawing off the water in which the lac has been washed—these phrases are taken from the report of the Royal Commission. The Director of Public Health in the Central Provinces complained that the washing pits, reservoirs, and drains were not properly cleaned at regular intervals, and the same water was used for washing over and over again for a week or more and allowed to stagnate before being drained off. Terrible as these descriptions read, they are not appreciably worse than conditions in the ginning factories and presses thirty years ago when the Factories Commission went round India.

The workers in these non-regulated factories are correctly described as being the least protected of the industrial workers of India. Eight years have passed since the publication of the report of the Royal Commission, but it is only now that the Government of India is considering the question of taking action. Of course, there are difficulties in the way of enforcing a measure, however simple, because of the possibilities of evasion. It would involve the expansion of the factory inspection staff in the provinces on a considerable scale and strict supervision on their part. Many of these industries, especially *beedi* manufacture, are carried on without practically any machinery, and whatever may be the minimum of persons to be employed to bring an establishment under the law, it would be easy to split larger ones, so as to evade legal responsibility. While the scope for evasion must inevitably be large, even an unsatisfactory law has its own uses and tends quietly in the direction of improvement of working conditions.

CHAPTER XIX

WORKING CONDITIONS

In the two previous chapters the question has been discussed how far labour legislation, under the conditions prevalent in India, affords adequate protection to the worker. The answer, which any impartial study of the facts must furnish, is inevitable that in the first place only a minority of the workers come within its influence; and secondly, even for them, their poverty and ignorance and the power of the employers are factors which have minimized the effectiveness of such legislation to a considerable extent.

And, after all, how far has labour legislation in India touched the real problems of the workers? The resolutions of the National Trades Union Federation, quoted elsewhere in this volume, point out the big gaps that still exist. To take one of the most important, the question of sickness insurance was discussed by the Royal Commission, and it came up later before the Central Legislature in the form of a draft convention of the International Labour Conference relating to the subject. The Government of India would not ratify the convention, urging in defence of its position that it was impracticable in the existing circumstances.

The Commission itself, after dealing with both the advantages and the difficulties, had decided by a majority that it would not be possible to introduce a comprehensive sickness insurance scheme in India. Among the reasons given by the majority were the migratory character of industrial labour, the dearth of qualified medical practitioners and the inability of the workers, in view of their low wages, to participate in any scheme on a contributory basis. The Government of India has issued more than one circular on the subject to Provincial Governments, but beyond rousing interest in the subject nothing has been done.

There is, as everyone who knows India will admit, a terrible lack of medical relief. Expenditure on public health and medical relief, which at present is less than 5 per cent of the total revenue of the Government, needs to be raised very considerably if tangible results are to be obtained. It is, undoubtedly, a fact also that Indian workers, being poorly paid and the vast majority being in debt, would find contribution to a sickness insurance scheme a strain; but the use made of this as an argument against the introduction of such a scheme is only an excuse for not taking action.

A feature of welfare work carried on by some employers at present is the provision of sick leave and a "compassionate allowance" for those who are sick for more than a certain period. But great difficulty is frequently experienced in obtaining sick leave. Large mills have their own medical men as a rule, and in such establishments the grant of sick leave is sanctioned only by the mill doctor. The doctor, being a servant of the company, has to be extremely careful not to endorse more than a certain number of leave applications on any day. I have seen, even in such cases, recommendations for leave being finally signed (or cancelled) by the manager. The difficulty from the standpoint of the employer appears to be twofold: in the first place, if every worker who is ill were to be granted leave, it would be extremely hard to keep the mill running during epidemics of malaria; and, secondly, there are undoubtedly cases in which leave is sought on false pretexts. But the result is that very frequently workers who deserve leave do not get it. An extreme case came to my notice a few years ago. A weaver complained of chest pain while at work and applied for leave. The mill doctor, after examining him, refused to sanction it on the ground that he was not so ill as to need leave. The man struggled on at his looms for three more days and died, though he was actually at work a few hours before death. A protest to the management elicited the strange answer that the weaver, after consulting the doctor, took no further steps to acquaint him with the serious nature of the complaint. The episode illustrates the harshness of the system. The man worked, not because he was in a fit condition to do so; but to stop away, in spite of the mill doctor's refusal to grant leave, would probably have meant dismissal, the loss of gratuity, and of other concessions.

Of course, there are immense difficulties in the way of a proper sickness insurance scheme being worked in India. Apart from the very low wages of the average worker, there is the consideration of the general level of public health. In a country which has over a hundred million cases of malaria every year, not to mention tuberculosis, hookworm, venereal disease, and leprosy, any scheme of sickness insurance is likely to create difficulties in the unhealthy seasons of the year.

The complaint of many employers in India is that labour is irregular and inefficient. But the answer was furnished by the Royal Commission which stated quite truly that what is regarded as inefficiency is nothing more than self-defence on the part of the Indian worker against excessive work. And not only Indian employers: the late Mr. Tom Shaw (who visited India some years ago as the leader of the International Textile Delegation) observed that there were five times as many people in the carding room of a Madras mill as in Lancashire. The number of looms in charge of a man in the cotton mills in India is generally two, though experiments have been made in some centres to train men to work on three, four, and even six looms. The fact is that the low standard of living and the unhealthy surroundings levy a heavy toll from the working-class population, and its power of resistance, whether to disease or to temptation, is extremely low. At the same time the Indian worker does not compare unfavourably, for ability and intelligence, with one in other industrial countries, and he can adapt himself with commendable skill to new methods and conditions of work.

Schemes of rationalization are being rapidly introduced in India in the textile and other industries and, it may be added, the millowners are not alone in this respect. In several of the railway workshops most up-to-date machinery has been installed, and in some cases different workshops on the same system have been amalgamated, with the result that on all the railways taken together, several thousands of workers have been thrown out of employment. The

Court of Enquiry, set up by the Government of India in 1931, admitted in its report that there was much to be said for the point of view of the workers who claimed the right to be consulted as to the methods by which the hardships of large-scale unemployment could be obviated. On account of the comparative strength of the railway unions, these workers were, on the whole, in a more favourable position than workers in other industries. Some employers have been pleased to grant bonuses amounting to fifteen days' wages for every year of service at the time of discharge under such circumstances. But the general practice is still to send out workers with fifteen, twenty, or even twenty-five years of service without any compensation in the name of rationalization.

Much is made of "welfare work" in several industrial establishments in India, and no doubt fairly substantial sums of money are expended by some employers. But the delegation of the British Trades Union Congress which visited India at the end of 1927 came to the just conclusion that while "welfare work has its uses, provided always that it is completely controlled by the workers themselves, is made applicable to the whole of an industry, and does not impinge upon trade union organization and activities," as it is carried on in India "it is a delusion and a snare." In some cases, said their report, "welfare schemes have, for the time being, made the creation of trade unions impossible just where they are most needed, and in one case have led to the fostering of a "shop union" in rivalry to the properly established union struggling to organize the whole of the workers in the trade." Until employers in India abandon their hostility to unions, it is impossible to expect from the workers appreciation for welfare schemes conducted (so it is claimed) for their good, but in the running of which they have no voice.

The hours of work present another problem. At present, in many industries under the Factories Act, the 54 hours week is in force, which means in most cases a nine hours day. In the engineering and metal industries the normal week is 48 hours, based on an eight hours day. In the cotton mills, on account of the heavy demand for goods in the last two years, double shifts have become a common feature, though it has struck few employers that men on night shifts would appreciate a resting-place during the interval, which is as long as two hours in certain centres.* It must be remembered, in connection with the number of hours, that on account of the lack of housing facilities in the neighbourhood of the mills and the absence of cheap and quick methods of transport, workers are compelled, in a large number of cases, to live three, four, and even five miles away; and it is a common experience for a man to start from his home at four in the morning in order to be at the mill gates in time for work and to return long after dark.

No provision in the Factories Act is at present so much appreciated as the nine hours day, and the general demand from the workers is for a further reduction by an hour. The question whether a reduction in hours of work would lead to diminished production has been considered several times in India—in fact, on every occasion that such a reform was introduced. The first textile Tariff Board came to the conclusion about ten years ago that a reduction in working hours in some of the mills in Bombay had, in fact, resulted in a slight increase in the efficiency of the weavers, and a

* With regard to working hours in the Bengal jute mills, the report of the Chief Inspector of Factories for 1936 makes some interesting observations. Under the old Act, the eleven hours day and the sixty hours week allowed a sufficient margin between the hours actually worked and the limits laid down by the Act to deal with any abnormal work. But under the new Act this margin has disappeared, and therefore provision has to be made for additional groups of workers to deal with extra work at short notice. Though in theory the additional groups or shifts are supposed to be manned by entirely different sets of workers, the policy is so uneconomical as to make it impracticable and, therefore, when extra hours beyond the ten per day or fifty-four per week have to be worked, the same labour is undoubtedly employed. All that the Act requires in such cases is the posting of sets of working hours in the form of groups or shifts. These do not require to be notified to the Inspector and consequently the chances of detecting illegal employment or excessive hours are negligible. In the rare instances of proof of such irregularities being obtained, the courts in Bengal took the view that it was impossible to discover exactly what the provisions were in the Factories Act relating to overtime and, therefore, a conviction could not be sustained for a *mala fide* infringement of the provisions.

representative of an important group of mills admitted it to be a fact. Another employer said that while there was no great difference in the spinning department, on the weaving side, while a weaver working for twelve hours a day could only register about 70 per cent efficiency, by working for ten hours efficiency had been increased to between 75 to 80 per cent. The Tariff Board added in its report that the experience of mills in other centres was also that through increased efficiency and improved conditions, such as the installation of humidifiers, the drop in production caused by the reduction in working hours in the spinning department had been reduced to 10 per cent, while in the weaving department there had actually been an increase in the production.

This view has been confirmed afresh since the introduction of the nine hours day, evidence before the various committees of enquiry in 1938 proving that production has improved to such an extent as to make up 3 to 5 per cent of the loss caused by the shortening of the working day.

The problems of miners have already been described; but the coal industry illustrates somewhat poignantly the conditions under which all industrial work is carried on in India. After a series of major diasters in the colleries, the Government of India appointed an expert committee which submitted its report in 1937. The committee remarked that "risks have been taken in India which would not have been possible with less ignorant labour." Much interesting light was thrown in the report on the methods of industrial management in India by the fact, to which the committee drew attention, that while depreciation and interest charges had fallen, in regard to several collieries the dividends paid had improved, indicating that "whatever may happen to the property or the machinery or the labour force, the advisability of keeping shareholders satisfied was not lost sight of." In the case of several companies (the dividends ranging between 12 and 65 per cent) no efforts had been made either to pay adequate wages or to introduce improved methods to prevent avoidable waste.

The managing agency system flourishes in coal-mining as

in other industries in India. Companies are directed and controlled by business firms in Calcutta who describe themselves as managing agents receiving either a fixed percentage on the gross proceeds *plus* a percentage on other transactions or by a commission on raisings *plus* a fixed monthly sum for office expenses. "All these methods," observed the committee, "place a premium on high outputs, big sales, and large profits, and focus effort on immediate rather than future gain." Shareholders do not take sufficient interest or, rather, are ignorant of the technique of company management. No firm of managing agents has a technical expert on its Calcutta staff, though it is from Calcutta that the policy of every company is directed, even in regard to small details. Managers of collieries told the committee in confidence that they were on occasions faced with the alternative of either adopting unsound mining methods of or losing their livelihood. The court of enquiry which investigated a fatal subsidence in a colliery in 1928 reported that six mining experts were asked for their opinions as to whether under certain conditions they would prohibit by legislation pillar extraction of coal; the general answers of these witnesses were in the affirmative from the sound mining or safety point of view, but in the negative from the commercial or profit-making point of view.

Nothing can be more graphic than the committee's description of the coal-mining industry as a whole: "In short, to use a sporting metaphor, the coal trade in India has been rather like a race in which profit has always come in first, with safety a poor second, sound methods an 'also ran,' and national welfare a 'dead horse' entered perhaps, but never likely to start. Neither Government nor the landlords can escape responsibility for allowing this state of affairs to prevail for so long, but this does not alter the facts nor, still less, will it justify further inaction on the part of all concerned."

Several major disasters are mentioned in the report, some of which, at any rate, were of an avoidable kind. Apart from destruction of life, there is considerable waste in the methods now adopted in the Raniganj and Jherria fields, the average according to the committee being 35 per cent.

In regard to the plantations, it is difficult to be definite because of lack of first-hand knowledge. The plantations have been closely guarded preserves, and though with the new legislation in force, conferring on the worker the right of returning home after three years at the expense of his employer, and a Controller of Emigration supervising recruitment, it is difficult to say how far conditions have actually improved beyond the terrible description of the British Trades Union Congress delegation in 1928 that "in Assam tea the sweat, hunger, and despair of a million Indians enter year by year."

It is true that under the new Constitution a measure of representation has been accorded to tea plantation labour in Assam and Bengal, and there is some relaxation of the rigid inaccessibility of the tea estates for outsiders. But no resolutions may be moved in the Provincial Legislatures, no questions even asked, about "the backward areas" which are the recruiting centres for plantation labour, except with the sanction of the Governor of the province. This provision in the new Constitution is not likely to remove the suspicion with which the problems of plantation labour have so far been surrounded. Nor will the fact that for about half a million children in the Assam plantations there were only a hundred primary schools in 1936, attended by 6,200 children—most of them of lower middle-class Bengali clerks—help to create the impression that an educated new generation of workers will be able to safeguard its own interests.

Some reference to the general conditions of women in industry may not be out of place here. So long as housing conditions remain what they are, it is not surprising that few women enter industry. At Sholapur (in Bombay) it was ascertained by an enquiry into the economic status of the women workers that out of a total of 482 women employed in five cotton mills (446 of whom were married), 388 said that they worked only from necessity, and would gladly have remained at home if they had not been driven to the

These workers live on street pavements all their lives, seeking temporary shelter during the rains on a verandah

A dwelling of the better type in a *cheri*. The roof is of cocoanut leaves

Katrak Studio, Bombay

Workers inside a textile mill

Katrak Studio, Bombay

Workers at lunch

mills by economic pressure. There are some factories which place obstacles in the way of women being recruited, and the passage of maternity benefits legislation in some provinces will not be an inducement to employers to engage more women. In the textile industry a few women are employed in the reeling and bundling departments on, of course, lower wages than those paid to men. In the jute mills a larger number are employed, as also in the seasonal factories, because of their proximity to rural areas.

Very few women are members of trade unions. Their natural shyness to come forward and represent their difficulties is, undoubtedly, a great factor; moreover, they have not only the work in the factory to attend to, but domestic work besides, both before and after factory hours. The lady investigator of the Bombay Labour Office said that the health of a woman was more affected than that of the male worker by the present conditions of living. Conditions inside factories have no doubt been improved for women by the prohibition of night work, insistence on crèches for more than a minimum number of women workers, and, in some provinces, maternity benefits, the amount prescribed being eight annas a day for three or four weeks before and the same period after confinement. These schemes have only just been introduced and will, like other measures, take time to come into real operation. The practice in many mills has so far been for the *maistri* or jobber to give notice suddenly to a woman expecting a child when she is, in his opinion, incapable of normally hard work. If she should desire to return to work after childbirth (which she does three or four days after the event) there is the usual bribe to be paid before reinstatement.

Regarding the maternity conditions of mill workers, Dr. Balfour, in her statement before the Labour Commission, declared that the still-birth rate among working women was much more than that among non-working women, and that the weights of their infants at birth were also lower; she came to the conclusion that the effects of factory work were injurious, not so much to the mother as to the unborn child.

A special enquiry was held, in connection with this matter, in 1930 into the mortality rates among working and non-working mothers in Bombay, covering over two thousand cases. Thirty-nine per cent were working mothers (the great majority being engaged in the textile industry) and the rest non-working mothers. The enquiry showed that working-class mothers had more children but more still-births than non-working mothers. From the statistics the conclusion was drawn that working-class mothers, on account of their comparatively better economic conditions and consequently having more and better food, were more prolific; but the larger figure for still-births among them suggested that factory work, while not interfering with the conception of children, had an adverse effect on child-bearing itself.

PART 7

THE FUTURE

CHAPTER XX

THE FUTURE

It is difficult enough to describe the general conditions of the workers in any coherent and intelligible form, with all their bewildering variety; it is almost impossible to indicate with any certainty what may happen in the future. The last twenty years, since the war, have witnessed changes in India which are essentially revolutionary in character. With the advent of popular governments in the provinces under the new Government of India Act in 1937, the pace has been enormously quickened.

Rural indebtedness, which the economic depression pushed to the fore, is being tackled in every province, and, as has been pointed out, more than thirty measures have been placed on the statute book within the last few years, all dealing with different aspects of the problem. Cottage industries are receiving special attention, particularly the handlooms, which can support with a little direct assistance and sympathetic supervision some millions of workers in the villages and find supplementary work for them in their spare time. The rights of the tenants are being safeguarded in a variety of ways, and though the Left wing elements in India may scorn the measures proposed, the opposition of the landlords—carried in many instances to the point of threatening non-payment of taxes and civil disobedience—is perhaps a more reliable indication of their nature and scope. Rural development schemes of the most comprehensive kind have been undertaken in practically all the provinces to improve the earning capacity and the economic status of the villagers who constitute seven-eighths of India's total population. These schemes include the expansion of the co-operative movement, medical relief, sanitation, distribution of improved seed, cattle-breeding, consolidation of holdings—in fact, everything that would raise the standard of living in the villages. A drive against illiteracy (92 per cent of India's population cannot read or write) has commenced in several provinces, and the services of educated young men without employment are being utilized for the purpose. Schemes of education of all kinds—primary, girls', and adult education—are being planned, and there is no doubt that the next few years will witness a considerable diminution of illiteracy. But it is not the mere removal of illiteracy that Provincial Governments have placed before themselves as their objective. Under Mr. Gandhi's direction, a scheme has been evolved to alter the very basis of education so that it may hereafter centre round some basic craft. The new trend of educational policy and outlook in India is definitely in the direction of encouraging technical and vocational training to a very much greater extent than in the past.

All this work is sadly hampered by limited resources, as the financial conditions of the provinces are unenviable. It is common ground between the Congress and non-Congress administrations that social services, which, as the Simon Commission pointed out in its report, are practically non-existent in certain directions, cannot be developed with sources of revenue that are not only rigid but dwindling, and some of which, indeed, like excise, are likely to disappear in course of time. For instance, in the United Provinces the expenditure on education, medical relief, public health, agriculture, and industries for forty-eight million people is only about Rs.31 million per year of a total revenue of about Rs.125 million.

Expenditure is being cut down in every possible direction, but as the Premier of the United Provinces, who is also Finance Minister, observed publicly at the end of 1937: "I am oppressed by a sense of helplessness. On the one hand, we cannot abolish certain posts, though we see no need for their retention; we cannot touch the salaries and the allowances of the higher services. On the other hand, the possibilities of effecting savings or tapping fresh resources are really negligible. From inside the Government one realizes even more than from outside the terrible poverty and destitution of our people, and the fact that they are already overtaxed to an impossible extent."

Nevertheless, by a policy of vigilant scrutiny of expenditure and tapping new sources of taxation wherever they are available—Bihar is taxing this year agricultural incomes which the British Government would not touch for fear of losing landlord support—the Provincial Governments are courageously facing their problems. The Congress Party is committed to a policy of prohibition, and though excise is one of the main sources of revenue in the provinces and funds are badly wanted for the nation-building departments, practically every Provincial Government has initiated a prohibition campaign in selected areas.

India's political struggle is not over, and though provincial autonomy has functioned for a year with remarkable success, despite Congress declarations both before and after the elections of their intentions "to wreck the Constitution," similar threats are being uttered against the inauguration of Federation. Whether there will be a political crisis of a major character in India within the next year or two is a point of immense interest, but somewhat beyond the scope of this volume. But so long as fairly normal political conditions continue, and a policy of social advancement on a wide front remains the keynote of provincial administrations, a change must come over India's village life and her main industry, agriculture. The emancipation of the villager from the grip of the money-lender and of the landlord and the improvement in his standards of living—which must mean an increase in his purchasing power—are bound to produce reactions on the urban areas and the industrial worker in particular; for, after all, whatever legislation may be in force, the worker in the factory cannot hope to achieve for himself what is denied to the cultivator, beyond a certain point.

Provincial Governments have not confined their attention only to the villages and to the tenants. The outbreak of industrial unrest all over India, more acute and widespread than in any year subsequent to 1921, has compelled them to formulate their labour programme and make energetic efforts to implement it.

The statement of the Bombay Government on its labour policy, made in August 1937, was a more elaborate exposition of the principles to which all Congress Governments are committed than that of any other Provincial Government and is, therefore, summarized here:

The Government accepts special responsibility for the welfare of the worker since the process of industrialization has deprived him of his independence and placed him in a difficult environment, creating social and political problems of a peculiar and complicated character. The Congress Party is pledged in its election manifesto to reforms which constitute an undertaking to secure for the workers a decent standard of living, hours of work and conditions of labour in conformity (as far as economic conditions in the country will permit) with international standards, suitable machinery for the settlement of disputes between employers and workmen, protection from the economic consequence of old age, sickness and unemployment, the right to form unions and to strike for the protection of their interests.

With these objects in view the Government will examine the possibility of devising measures to set up minimum wage-fixing machinery to meet the special requirements, to promote better housing conditions, to control house rents in cities, to relieve and avoid working-class indebtedness. With regard to industries and industrial centres which fail to provide a living wage to workers, exhaustive inquiries will be undertaken by the Government with a view to determining how far wages in these cases fall short of the minimum budgetary needs of the workers, to discover what circumstances are responsible for the inadequacy and to ascertain the ways and means of improving wages to a satisfactory level.

The problem of developing a comprehensive system of social insurance is also before the Bombay Government. The machinery of the Labour Department has already been set in motion for the collection of material to enable the Government to evolve a sound and workable scheme in conformity with Indian conditions. The feasibility of legislation for leave with pay during periods of sickness is also under consideration, as a preliminary to a proper scheme of sickness insurance.

In regard to unemployment relief, the Bombay Government is exploring the possibility of alternative employment in home industries, and a scheme is under consideration for the extensive training of workers in secondary occupations. The establishment of employment exchanges in important industrial centres will follow the collection of statistics of unemployment and registration of both the employed as well as the unemployed. An immediate extension and improvement of the Factories Act is foreshadowed in several directions, such as provisions of the Act relating to a weekly holiday, the interval of rest and spread-over of the hours of work, satisfactory dining accommodation, adequate medical aid and regulation of night-shift work.

The Government will pursue an active policy with a view to maintaining industrial peace in the province, endeavouring at the same time to see that the workers obtain a fair deal. The basis of legislation, aiming at the prevention of strikes and lock-outs as far as possible, will be the requirement that no reduction in wages or other changes in conditions of employment that may be to the disadvantage of the workers will take effect until they have had sufficient time and opportunity to examine the facts and merits of the proposed change and all avenues of peaceful settlement of the dispute have been explored, either through voluntary negotiation, conciliation or arbitration or by the machinery of the law. A corresponding obligation will rest on the workers in respect of demands on their behalf. Collective agreements between workers' and employers' organizations will be encouraged, attention being paid to the question of their registration.

No Government action for the amelioration of the conditions of the workers, it is recognized, can be a satisfactory substitute for the organized strength of the working class. Efforts will, therefore, be made to remove real hindrances in the way of the growth of trade unions and to promote collective bargaining between employers and workers. This will imply measures being devised to discourage victimization of workers for connection with a labour organization or participation in legitimate trade union activity.

In the sphere of education, the Government realizes that the working class has its special needs and that illiteracy constitutes a very serious handicap to itself and a grave danger to society. The educational policy of the Government will therefore be designed to meet these special requirements. The Government's policy of prohibition has also a special bearing on the well-being of the industrial community, and it is the Government's intention to select important industrial towns for the early application of its policy.

Ambitious as this programme sounds, there is already a good deal accomplished in several provinces for which the worker must be grateful. The result of enquiries by committees in Bombay, Madras, the United Provinces, and the Central Provinces into the wages and conditions of work, particularly in the textile industry, has been an appreciable rise in wages and the grant of several amenities, the most important being the recognition of registered unions. The Bombay Government is introducing this year legislation for holidays with pay during sickness for two weeks in a year. A Bill is also before the legislature to safeguard the interests of shop assistants with particular reference to wages, hours, and conditions of work. Another measure, also in Bombay, foreshadows the establishment of an industrial court for the province. The Bill provides for the growth of a genuine trade union movement and at the same time seeks to check the existing arbitrary power of declaring strikes and lock-outs in industrial enterprises. Scope is given for conciliation proceedings, and the Commissioner of Labour will be the chief conciliator.

The application of the Factories Act has been extended to all establishments in the province of Bombay (whether using power or not) employing ten persons or more. The Bombay and the United Provinces Governments have made the establishment of crèches compulsory in all factories employing more than a certain number of women, and the latter has adopted a scheme of maternity benefits on a statutory basis, thus coming into line with Bombay, the Central Provinces, and Madras.

It is to the credit of the Congress Governments that they have, on the whole (though there has been criticism of one or two provincial administrations), refrained from taking sides in industrial disputes, even where their efforts to prevent them met with failure. A lock-out in Madura in South India lasted three months, from January to April 1938, and was notable for the fact that for the first time in India, section 144 of the Criminal Procedure Code was utilized, not against the workers but against the manager of the mills, restraining him from opening them except with the full complement of the workers—resulting in the employer's immediate acceptance of arbitration by the Labour Commissioner and the settlement including a rise in wages, thirteen days' leave in a year with pay, interest-free advances to the workers for house-building and unconditional recognition of the registered union. A general strike of 40,000 textile workers in Cawnpore, involving a loss of two million working days, was settled by the intervention of the Premier in July 1938, with the acceptance of a rise in wages as recommended by the Enquiry Committee, the establishment of a Wage Fixation Board, of a Labour Exchange and of a Labour Office, and the recognition of the workers' union on its reorganization in accordance with the proposals of the Committee. In general it may be observed that since the advent of the new Constitution the attitude of Provincial Governments (particularly of those under Congress control) towards labour has been clarified: industrial peace, not by suppression of the workers' organization and a denial of their demands, but on a basis of certain minimum standards of living and general rights of citizenship.

This new policy is in sharp contrast to that followed by the Governments which were in power from 1921 to 1937. Dominated and impelled by the fear of the workers' movement being utilized by political leaders for political purposes, they threw their entire weight on the side of the employers. Possibly their fears were not entirely groundless. Many of the Presidents of the earlier sessions of the All-India Trades Union Congress—Lala Lajpat Rai, C. R. Das, Jawaharlal Nehru, Subhas Chandra Bose—were all prominent politicians, though Nehru, since his contact with the workers' movement, has remained one of its sincerest and most powerful supporters. Though there has never been a general strike of a major character in India for a political objective, propaganda on certain occasions, like the visit of the Simon Commission, was undeniably in that direction. And throughout the period that the Communist elements were in power in the trade unions, they never missed an opportunity of emphasizing the identity between British Imperialism and the capitalist system in India.

The effect of this enforced alliance between the old Governments (not only in the provinces but also at the centre) and the employers was to impose on the workers severe control. In the provinces it was somewhat negative in character; but at the centre it assumed the form of conceding protection to various industries, without proper insistence on safeguarding the interests of the workers—to prove to the capitalist classes that the British Government was their friend, not the Congress. Generally speaking, the tariff policy of the Government of India has been moulded since the war from this standpoint. Summing up its effects, Sir James Grigg, the present Finance Member of the Government of India, observed in April 1938 that the customs and excise duties of the Central Government imposed a real burden on the people of India to the extent of 55 crores,* while the weight of protective taxation on the consumer he reckoned at another 50 crores per year. With the salt duty amounting to 7½ crores a year (which falls mainly on the masses of the people), and some other sources of revenue, the total annual burden of all indirect duties he estimated at very nearly 120 crores, as against which the yield from direct taxation by income-tax is 15 crores; in India indirect taxation being eight times as much as direct taxation. He added: "I will take another criterion; and that is, I will compare income-tax in relation to the national income in the United Kingdom and in India. I am speaking in round figures, but I know that the figures are sufficiently accurate for the purposes of a broad comparison. Income-tax and super-tax in the United Kingdom yield somewhere about £320,000,000 a year. The national income is somewhere about £4,000,000,000 a year; so that the income-tax and super-tax between them in England represent 8 per cent of the national income. If you add death duties, which yield something like 90 or 100 million in addition, the proportion of direct taxation to national income would certainly be of the order of 10 per cent. In India, taking 1,600 crores (£1,200,000,000 approximately) as the national income, 15 crores is the yield of income-tax on our national income."

Incomplete as is Sir James Grigg's picture—he failed to take into account the revenue systems of the provinces, some

* A crore of rupees is approximately equivalent to £750,000.

of whose sources of taxation are direct—in broad outline he was essentially right in pointing out the very heavy burden of indirect taxation weighing on the masses of the poor. A great deal of the gold which has gone out of India since 1931 (exceeding £260,000,000) is without doubt "distress gold," sold by the villagers to meet the demands of the money-lenders, the landlords, and the State. And even as regards income-tax, an authoritative report by two British experts in 1937 revealed a higher rate on incomes below Rs.5,000 a year, in comparison with the United Kingdom, and a lighter burden on incomes above that level. And, it would have been both relevant and correct if Sir James Grigg had added that for the entire system of taxation as developed in India, taxing the poor heavily and letting off the rich with far less than they could equitably bear, the executive must accept the entire responsibility.

It is pointless perhaps to discuss now what might have been the consequences if a more balanced policy had been pursued in India from the end of the war: if, for instance, trade unions had been given more encouragement in practice, and the administrations, both provincial and central, had not been dominated by capitalist considerations and interests. One thing, however, is certain. Even if India's industrial development had been less rapid, the foundations of industry would have been sounder, resulting in greater contentment among the workers.

The result of this one-sided policy, wholly unexpected perhaps, is seen to-day in the position which industry has achieved in India. In 1933 and the two subsequent years, safeguards to prevent commercial discrimination against British trade in India were inserted in the Government of India Bill which became an Act in 1935. The Central Government is still under an executive irresponsible to the legislature, and for its policy in commercial and financial matters, as in everything else, it is entirely under the control of the British Cabinet. But that has not prevented industry in India from rapidly pushing British manufactures out of the country: Lancashire, whose trade with India has dwindled to a tenth of its pre-war volume, is pleading at the present juncture for a guarantee of a fraction of her former trade in the Indian market.

So much for the past. But what of the future? In the provinces the workers are rapidly consolidating their position with the powerful assistance of the Provincial Governments. In this, they have the support, not only of the Governments but of the peasants' organizations which have grown rapidly in India within the last four or five years; while, inside the legislatures, groups of members representing the Harijans combine with them on most questions relating to the social and economic disabilities of workers, whether industrial or agricultural. It is certain that the trade unions will grow more rapidly in India than they have done during all these twenty years.

Left-wing elements have openly proclaimed their intention of capturing the Indian National Congress so as to wrest control from its "bourgeoisie" leaders and convert it into an organ of the workers and the peasants. The Socialist section inside the Congress, the "Congress Socialist Party," as it calls itself, is somewhat suspicious of the move of the Communists towards a united front of all the radical parties, and these internal difficulties (which are also to be found in the All-India Trades Union Congress) may prevent the overthrow of the present leaders of the Congress.

Whether federation will be inaugurated in the near future to replace the existing administration at the centre; what the attitude of the Congress Party will be towards the scheme if it is forced upon India—whether the answer will be civil disobedience or acceptance of office as in the provinces—on all these points no one is qualified to express a definite opinion. But even assuming that no serious clash takes place in India, it is unlikely that under the federal scheme the Congress Party will capture a sufficient number of seats to secure a majority. The Indian princes' representatives and those who will be returned by landlords, capitalists, British interests, and an appreciable number of Moslems will, in matters of labour and social legislation, take a conservative rather than a progressive line. The number of labour representatives in the Federal Assembly will be 10 in a House of 375, while in the Upper Chamber it will be open to the Governor-General to nominate one or two at the most on behalf of labour. In any event, even with the support of the Harijan representatives, the women and the large majority of Congress members, labour cannot hope to be in a position to compel the Federal Government of the future to be as progressive as the Congress Governments have been in the provinces.

One tendency to which reference has already been made, the drift of industry towards the Indian States, will probably gain impetus in the coming years. Indian capitalists, after vigorous protests, both in the Central Legislature at Delhi and from the platform of the International Labour Conference at Geneva, against the growing inequality in the labour codes of British India and the Indian States, are now negotiating with the latter for the transfer of industry to their territories. Some of the better administered States are copying British Indian legislation, but there are others which offer the capitalists immunity from strikes and the burdens imposed by fresh legislation as inducements for turning their attention to the States. If this should happen on an appreciable scale, the princes are only storing up trouble for the future; it is unthinkable that workers in the Indian States can tolerate for long conditions against which those in British India have fought with a considerable measure of success.

Mention may be made here of a very useful recommendation of the Royal Commission for the formation of an All-India Industrial Council "to meet, on the smaller stage of India, the needs which the International Labour Organization was created to supply in the international world." The necessity for such an institution is obvious for more reasons than one. In the first place, in India under a Federal Government, there may well be greater difficulty in adopting labour legislation in the Federal Legislature than under the existing Constitution. The Industrial Council contemplated by the Commission would consist of representatives of the Government (both Federal and Provincial), an equal number of representatives of workers and capitalists, a smaller number of representatives on behalf of the railways, and a small non-official nominated element. The Council would obviously have great authority in examining legislative proposals referred to it by the Government. In form and procedure, functioning on lines closely parallel to those of the International Labour Organization, it would serve as an expert body of experience and knowledge and do away with the present dilatory methods of referring proposals for legislative measures to the Provincial Governments in the first instance and then eliciting public opinion thereafter. Moreover, it does not need much arguing that an interval of three, four, or even five years between the first issue of a tentative proposal in a circular by the Government of India and the enactment of a measure in its final form in the Central Legislature is out of date, having regard to the quickness with which economic forces arise and shape themselves. In regard to such important subjects as holidays with pay, sickness insurance, invalidity, and old age pensions, workers will have to depend on all-India legislation, because it is practically impossible that one province can pass legislation imposing a substantial burden on industry ahead of any other province or State.

On the analogy of the Imperial Council of Agricultural Research, on whose governing body are representatives of the British Indian provinces and the Indian States, there is no reason why the constitution of the Industrial Council should not provide for representation of the Indian States.

Whether the present Government of India or the Federal Government of the future will bring into existence this Council it is impossible to say. But its creation has been urged both by leaders of labour and employers' representatives, and though the opportunity to give it a statutory basis was missed at the time of the inauguration of the new Constitution, one of its provisions accords sanction to such a body.

Whoever may come into power at the Federal Centre in the future, a Government, whether of the Right or the Left, is bound to adopt a policy of industrialization, on which all parties including the workers seem to be agreed. However unsatisfactory working conditions may be, new industries do provide employment for a portion of the superfluous population, especially in a country in which agriculture cannot possibly support its millions on standards compatible with human dignity.

At the same time, the radical elements in the country, which have gathered round Pandit Jawaharlal Nehru to preach the principles of Socialism, are determined to obtain for the workers a fair deal. Economic problems have come to the fore in India as never before, and this movement is bound to gain strength. Divisions on the basis of religion and caste, of which so much is made to-day, have no place in the India of the future.

The struggle, in fact, must sooner or later assume a new aspect. Landlords, millowners, industrial magnates, whether British or Indian, will all be drawn closer together to fight the growing power of the working classes in India. Whether the struggle will end in a peaceful readjustment of the social and economic order without serious dislocation or bloodshed will depend on the willingness of the "haves" to make the necessary sacrifices.

INDEX

www.ingramcontent.com/pod-product-compliance
Lightning Source LLC
LaVergne TN
LVHW010629300926
849162LV00001B/103
* 9 7 8 1 0 4 1 3 7 2 5 2 3 *